Angels at My Fingertips

Also by Lorna Byrne:

Angels in My Hair
Stairways to Heaven
A Message of Hope from the Angels
Love From Heaven
The Year With Angels

Lorna Byrne

Angels at My Fingertips

CORONET

First published in Great Britain in 2017 by Coronet
An Imprint of Hodder & Stoughton
An Hachette UK company

This paperback edition published in 2018

4

A CIP catalogue record for this title is available from the British Library

B format ISBN 9781473635906
eBook ISBN 9781473635883

Typeset in Sabon MT by Palimpsest Book Production Limited,
Falkirk, Stirlingshire

Printed and bound in Great Britain by Clays Ltd, Elcograf S.p.A.

Hodder & Stoughton policy is to use papers that are natural,
renewable and recyclable products and made from wood grown in
sustainable forests. The logging and manufacturing processes are expected
to conform to the environmental regulations of the country of origin.

Hodder & Stoughton Ltd
Carmelite House
50 Victoria Embankment
London EC4Y 0DZ

www.hodder.co.uk

I dedicate this book to all those who help spread love and peace throughout the world.

Introduction

AS I WRITE THIS, IT'S BEEN MANY YEARS SINCE THE ANGELS told me of my mission to remind people that they each have a guardian angel and to tell them about the spiritual reality of their lives.

I am learning more about angels all the time. I wasn't told everything all at once when I was a child, but I am told things as I become able to understand them – and I write about them when I am told the world is ready to understand them.

Sometimes I am told things that I am forbidden to pass on and at other times I am allowed to reveal things that previously I have been told to keep secret. For example, I have for a long time been forbidden to talk about my own guardian angel in any way.

This book contains many secrets of this kind that I have now been told that I can and must reveal.

This book is a sequel to *Angels in My Hair* and tells the story of my life subsequently, including stories of raising my children, encounters with Archangel Michael, Angel Elijah, my Bird of Love, episodes of great happiness and unhappiness and of loves lost and found.

In this book, I reveal ways in which you can grow closer to your guardian angel. My guardian angel taught me these things as a child so that I could pass them on to you so that you can become more spiritually connected with your own guardian angel.

When I look back on my life now, with the knowledge I have gained since *Angels in My Hair*, I understand much more clearly what was happening to me and why – just as I understand more clearly what is happening to us all and the world we live in. In my previous books and public speaking events I have focussed on the role of angels in our lives. In this new book I also focus on the role of our departed loved ones, souls from heaven who are allowed to visit us briefly, and I talk about how we should interact with them. I talk, too, about how we can pray to God with the angels and how these prayers transform the whole of our being.

Above all, I understand much better how the angels see us, how they love us and what they can do for us and what they want from us – what they see.

God and the angels are all around us and can help us in every moment – all we have to do is ask and of course, listen. That is why I call this book *Angels at My Fingertips*.

CHAPTER I

The Beginning

I WAS IN A WORLD OF MY OWN, COLOURING IN A PICTURE with crayons scattered across the floor. I was doing my best to keep within the lines but wasn't very good at it, and sometimes would get a little frustrated. I was about four years of age at the time.

On this day an enormous, golden hand, full of light, appeared over my little hand. The touch of this angel's hand filled me with love so I almost forgot about the picture I was colouring. I focussed instead on the angel's hand over mine, mesmerised by all of the light and details. Its long fingers were so perfect as they moved with mine, guiding the crayon in my hand, and as they did so the tips of the angel's fingers glowed. In fact the angel's whole hand radiated such brightness that it was like a torch, brightening up the floor where my picture was, with all the crayons strewn around me in a circle.

Then the angel said to me, 'Your mum is coming.'

Mum walked into the room and stood beside me for a

moment, saying, 'That's a lovely picture.' I smiled up at her and then my mum turned and went to the window, pulling back the curtains to let in more light. I spoke to the angel without words, as I often did. There was no need to say anything out loud.

'Mum doesn't see the light you have made for me. She doesn't know that I don't need her to pull back the curtains.'

The angel said, 'Lorna, remember, you must keep the secret, say nothing.'

I said, 'Okay.'

My mum left the room to go back to the kitchen.

Our little front room was dark most of the time. During the day, Mum wouldn't allow us to turn the light on. Looking back, my parents were very short of money. I had almost finished colouring my picture when Blackie, our cat, walked into the room and sat down beside us. The angel lifted its hand away from mine towards some of the crayons on the floor. Then, pointing one finger, the angel made the crayons move without touching them. I laughed as Blackie reacted by reaching out with her paw and starting to play. She caught a crayon between her paws and then rolled over on to her back with it. She would do this again and again, trying to hold the crayon between her paws as she rolled.

I asked, 'Can Blackie see the light that is coming from your hand?'

The angel said, 'No, Blackie can't see the light.' The angel's hand moved back towards my picture on the floor and the picture lit up with the radiant light shining from the angel's hand.

With delight I said, 'It's finished!'

As I picked it up and had a good look at it the angel whispered in my ear, 'You know, Lorna, you can colour a picture perfectly yourself without my help.' It said this, I'm sure, because as a young child I didn't think I was good enough at colouring without the angel's help.

'Thank you, angel, for teaching and helping me' are the words I would say every time when the angel would put its hand over mine to help me to colour my picture.

I have seen angels physically every day of my life since I was an infant. I couldn't imagine what life would be like not seeing the angels physically or conversing with them. This is normal for me but I know it is not for you.

All I can say to you is please put your doubts to one side and give yourself a chance to realise that you're not just a human being. You are a billion times more. You have a soul. You're a spiritual being as well as a physical person. Just think about that for a moment. If you are sceptical in any way, if you are cynical even, ask yourself: what do you have to lose by opening up to the possibility that you have a guardian angel?

One cold winter's day, I asked my mum if I could go out into the backyard to play. My mum said, 'Yes, but you have to dress up warm, okay?' I said I would and I ran out into the hall to get my coat. Mum came out into the hall. 'Here's a pair of old gloves. They will help to keep your fingers warm.' I ran across the hall and paused at the workshop door. It was so dark in there. I always had to allow my eyes to adjust so I could see in the darkness to make my way safely through the clutter and out the back door. (At this time, we were still living in our house in Old Kilmainham.)

Our house in Old Kilmainham was like a little doll's house. We lived there from the time I was born until the roof collapsed when I was about five years of age. I'm not very good with remembering exact ages so I'm never one hundred per cent sure. However, after the roof fell in we moved to Ballymun, into my cousin Netty's house. She lived alone. Her parents had died when she was young. We only lived with Nettie for a few years, and after Nettie's we moved to a council house in Edenmore, Raheny. All the houses there looked the same. Dad was injured during an accident at work. As far as I know they gave him a managerial position instead of money as compensation. The extra money that came with being a manager meant Dad and Mum could save up. They bought a house in Leixlip, a town outside of Dublin, after a few years. I was a teenager at the time. I lived there with my family until I married Joe and we bought a cottage in Maynooth with a council loan.

I walked down the path of our garden and then stepped up on to the bank at the bottom of it. I walked over to the little wall and started to play. I was building a house out of sticks and stones when I heard my name being called. I turned around and Archangel Michael was standing about three feet away from me at the door of a small shed, our outdoor toilet. I gave Michael a big smile and said hello as I continued to pick up some more little stones from the ground. I asked him if he had come to help me.

'No, Lorna,' he said, 'I have just come to talk to you.' I stopped picking up the stones. Just as I was about to put the few I had left in my hand on the wall for safe keeping an enormous, golden hand full of light appeared over mine. Archangel Michael asked me, 'Lorna, do you know whose hand that is?'

'Yes, I do. It's the angel that is with me all the time even when I'm asleep in bed. If I open my eyes for a few seconds I can see the angel's arms around me. It's my guardian angel.

Don't you know that, Michael? Everyone has a guardian angel, so I must have one too.' Archangel Michael's laugh was like thunder and it made me giggle. 'I was just waiting on you to tell me,' I continued. 'I was a little worried. I was afraid to ask you just in case you might say I didn't have a guardian angel like everyone else, but now I'm happy.' I could see everyone else's guardian angels standing behind him. Archangel Michael had talked to me about guardian angels before but he never explicitly mentioned mine. As a child I was always thinking 'What about mine?', waiting for Archangel Michael to tell me for sure I had a guardian angel of my own.

Just then the angel with the enormous golden hand, which was still over mine, holding my hand, appeared in front of me. I said to the angel, 'I have never seen you stand in front of me before.'

The angel said, 'I have done so many times, Lorna, but mostly when you were sleeping. Sometimes I stand in front of you when you are colouring and you don't need my help. You just don't notice.'

Guardian angels occasionally move from behind people to in front of them. At times, even though your guardian angel is behind you they are actually all around you at the same moment. It is difficult to explain. A guardian angel will move in front of someone, especially in times of crisis, to help that person to connect with them, to see a way through the crisis by sensing their guardian angel's presence and feeling that hope.

Archangel Michael then asked me, 'Can you recall what I told you about your guardian angel?'

'I think so!'

'Tell me what you remember then, Lorna.' I thought for a moment and then I remembered. I realised that until that moment I had forgotten all that Archangel Michael had previously told me about guardian angels.

I said to Archangel Michael, 'I was sitting on my bed, upstairs, when you walked into my bedroom. You had a book in your hand and it was open. You read from it, telling me about my guardian angel. You told me that my guardian angel would never leave me for one second, that I would never be alone and that it loved me. You know that big word, Archangel Michael? I can't pronounce it properly.'

Archangel Michael said, 'Unconditional love.'

'Yes, that's the word.'

'Say it out loud, Lorna.' I did about six times before I was able to pronounce it correctly. Because of my dyslexia it's taken me my whole life to learn to pronounce that phrase first time, let alone understand it!

Then I said, 'Unconditional love. I can always say that word when you say it, Archangel Michael. What else did you tell me about my guardian angel?'

He replied, 'You are the most important person in the world to your guardian angel.' I smiled up at Archangel Michael, thinking that I now remembered everything, but he said, 'Is there not something else?' I looked up at my guardian angel, who was standing in front of me, smiling down at me and holding my hand. I stood there for a moment, pondering. I was trying really hard to remember if there was anything else. I glanced up at Archangel Michael and it all came back to me. I shouted with excitement.

'Yes, I remember now, the gatekeeper of my soul!' I stood there, looking at my guardian angel. I could not take my eyes off him. To me he was more beautiful than any angel I had ever seen. The radiant light coming from him allowed me to see the human appearance he gave. I was trying to look at every part of him. I was looking at my guardian angel as if my eyes were a magnifying glass; not wanting to miss anything. I didn't want to miss one spot.

He was dressed in golden robes that flowed down to his toes. I couldn't make out how many robes he was wearing, but every fold of the material was perfect. His clothes seemed to be swaying as if there was a gentle breeze.

I went to step forward to embrace him but Archangel Michael said, 'You can't walk into your guardian angel, Lorna, even though it may look like that at times. Whenever that happens it is only your guardian angel putting one of the robes around you. It cannot happen otherwise. You could not do it yourself, Lorna. Only your guardian angel can.'

'I know,' I said sadly to Michael, 'I just wish I could.' My guardian angel smiled down at me, but did not say a word. He seemed like a giant to me. All of a sudden, my guardian angel's wings opened up and went around me. They were made of golden feathers of all different shapes and sizes. I could see every strand on every feather, every detail. They looked so soft. Some were shaped like feathers that you would see on birds, like the feathers we know and recognise every day; but others were shaped in circles, triangles, squares, crosses and so many more.

Archangel Michael called my name and at the same time my guardian angel started to draw back his wings, moving them very gently and opening them like a door. I looked up and as I did Archangel Michael touched some of my guardian angel's feathers with the tips of his fingers. They lit up! Some of the feathers shaped like symbols started to spin in a circle and almost touched me. I could *feel* a gentle breeze. Then Archangel Michael took his finger away and they stopped spinning. I asked if could I reach out and touch them.

It was my guardian angel who replied, saying, 'No.' But as he unfolded his wings he allowed just one of the feathers from the tip of his wing on the right to touch my hand. It felt so soft, like a wave of love going through my body. At the same time, my guardian angel let go of my left hand.

Archangel Michael then said he had to go and disappeared.

I turned to my guardian angel. 'I'm glad you don't have to go anywhere.'

He whispered in my ear, 'I'm always with you, Lorna.'

I put my hand to my mouth and jumped back, saying, 'Oh, I forgot to say to Archangel Michael that I'm not allowed tell anyone your name. It is to be kept secret.' My guardian angel gave me a big smile, saying that he knew, and pointed to the stones I was playing with. I picked up the stones off the garden wall and went back to playing, building a little house with sticks and stones.

Angels are neither male nor female. It is just that sometimes they give a male appearance or a female appearance, sometimes neither. My guardian angel has always given a male appearance. I have never spoken about my own guardian angel before because I wasn't allowed to. All through my life, my guardian angel would keep on reminding me that I was never to speak about him or give his name, but that one day I would be allowed to tell a little. I will never be allowed to give my guardian angel's name or tell you everything. When my first book, *Angels in My Hair*, was published, I was reminded constantly, not just by my guardian angel but by all the angels, that I was never to answer questions about my guardian angel.

When I did radio interviews, or appeared on television, or when I was onstage and the interviewer would ask me about my own guardian angel, it actually gave me a fright. I would talk to the angels there and then onstage: 'What should I say?'

My own guardian angel would whisper in my ear, 'Tell the truth.'

I would take a deep breath and just say, 'I cannot talk about my own guardian angel. I'm not allowed to.' Sometimes an interviewer would try to get an answer out of me, but I would have to say no, and at times this embarrassed me.

CHAPTER 2

My Guardian Angel

ONE WARM, SUMMER DAY WHEN I WAS ABOUT TWELVE, I
went fishing with my dad and his best friend, Arthur. They
were like brothers. I think my dad and Arthur went to every
fishing competition there was in the country.

I loved going fishing with my dad. On this particular
weekend, he asked me to get the campfire ready over at part
of the embankment where there were a lot of stones. My
dad had told me that he and Arthur were going to fish the
pool a little bit further up the river for a while and then we'd
all have lunch. I said, 'Okay!' and I happily walked towards
the embankment. It was like an inlet, full of stones of all
sizes. Some were big enough to sit on. I knew that when the
river was high this would become covered with water, like a
part of the river. There were lots of angels with me. I said
to them, 'Where should I start?'

One of them called me over, saying, 'I think this will be
the right spot, Lorna, to get the campfire ready.' My dad had
taught me how to make a campfire when I was about four

years old. I had helped him gather stones. I wasn't very good at it then because the stones I tended to gather were a bit on the small side. Nevertheless, my dad would put them on the outside of the circle of stones he had made for the fire and would tell me that I had done a good job.

From that day on, I always tried to pick up bigger stones for my dad. Sometimes the angels would still say, 'No, Lorna, that stone is too big.' I would listen and pick up a smaller one instead.

On this day I put my bag down on the ground and started to gather stones to make a circle. Then I gathered some sticks and other pieces of driftwood from trees that would have been washed into the river when it was high. I felt I had everything ready in no time at all. I opened up the bag that had all the sandwiches in it and took the billycan and walked to the river. One of the angels said, 'Lorna, don't walk into the river with your shoes on.'

I turned to the angel and said, 'Of course not! I'm taking my shoes off.' Then I walked into the water almost up to my knees. The angels were around me all of the time. I filled the billycan up with water and walked back out again. I left my shoes and socks off. The stones were warm and most of them were smooth and round, so it was nice to walk on them barefoot.

I sat on one of the rocks just looking out at the river, enjoying the sunshine, listening to the birds as well as watching the angels. One angel in particular was with me that day. Now he was mimicking fishing at the edge of the river and making me laugh by pretending he had a fish on an invisible fishing rod. Another angel was mimicking holding a fishing net as the first angel pretended he had brought the fish to the shore. When the other angel, the one pretending to have a fishing net, was just about to put the net under the fish the angel with the fishing rod seemed to fall backwards and almost drop the fishing rod. They were pretending that their invisible fish got away. It looked so funny. I laughed and laughed.

While I was watching the angels' antics with the fish a beautiful golden hand came over my left hand. My guardian angel was sitting beside me.

'Are you enjoying the day, Lorna?' my guardian angel asked.

'Yes, I am,' I said. 'I hope my dad and Arthur catch some fish!'

'I'm sure they will, Lorna,' said my guardian angel.

'Sometimes they don't catch any fish and I feel disappointed.'

'Does your dad act disappointed when he doesn't catch fish?'

I looked at my guardian angel, a little surprised with what he said. 'No. My dad never seems to be unhappy when he doesn't catch fish. He enjoys the fishing so much and simply being out in the countryside. I think that they will be back soon.'

'Not for another little while, Lorna. They have forgotten all about time and lunch.'

'I'm starting to feel hungry,' I said. '. . . Do we have a little time then to talk?'

My guardian angel gave me a big smile. 'Yes, Lorna.'

I said, 'There is something I have always wanted to know. You might not answer my question but I'm going to ask it anyway. I have always noticed since I was a little child – I know I'm still little now, I'm only twelve going on thirteen – I have never seen an angel touch a guardian angel or a guardian angel touch another guardian angel.'

'Look back towards the river, Lorna.' I did and there I saw two of the angels that had been making me laugh reach out to each other ever so gently. They just lightly touched each other's hand, with the tips of their fingers. As I watched, the angels suddenly allowed me to see their wings. I felt so privileged, as I always do. It was such a surprise when these two angels unfolded their wings just a little, and for a brief second as one angel passed the other it allowed the tip of its wing to touch the other angel's wings. I was allowed to see this in slow motion; I don't know what other way to describe it.

'You see, Lorna,' said my guardian angel, 'angels do touch each other but only when God allows it.'

'What about guardian angels?' I asked. My guardian angel smiled at me and said that my dad and Arthur were on their way back, so I got up off the rock I was sitting on and walked in the direction where I knew my dad would be coming from. A few seconds later I saw them and ran towards them, waving. When I reached them the first thing I said was, 'Did you catch any fish?' My dad took a big trout out of his fishing bag with a huge smile on his face.

'Great!' I said.

At the campfire Arthur told me that I'd done a brilliant job. It only took a minute to get the fire going and in no time at all the water was boiling in the billycan to make tea. I enjoyed sitting on the rocks, drinking hot tea and eating a sandwich with my dad and Arthur and all the angels that surrounded us. We fished all day and only headed home when it was starting to get dark. Sitting in the back of the car I spoke to my guardian angel without words. I wanted to know why I had never seen a guardian angel touch another guardian angel.

My guardian angel whispered in my ear, 'Close your eyes and sleep while your dad drives home.'

*

I wrote this sitting here in front of my computer in the old farmhouse, Angel Hosus with me. There were some other angels in the room too. It was a cold morning, but the sun was shining in the window.

Angel Hosus asked, 'What's on your mind, Lorna? Why have you stopped?'

'Hosus,' I said, 'I'm just thinking about when angels touch each other. It is something I have seldom seen and it is so rare. I remember asking Archangel Michael if he would explain a little bit more to me about why angels don't seem to touch each other the way we human beings do. You know what, Angel Hosus, I think I will take a break and go downstairs and make a cup of tea.'

I got up from the computer and went downstairs to make tea. While I was on my way back up the stairs, taking little sips of tea, I heard my name being called. I looked up and there was Archangel Michael standing at the top of the stairs.

'Good morning, Lorna!' he said.

'Good morning, Michael!' When I reached the top of the stairs I added, 'I'm glad you came. There is something I would love to talk to you about.'

Archangel Michael said, 'I heard and that is why I'm here.'

I walked to the room where I was working and sat down. I took another few sips of tea. The other angels that had been in the room were gone. Only Angel Hosus was still there.

I said to Archangel Michael, 'All those years ago when I was a child you had a book in your hand. You read from it, telling me about my guardian angel. My guardian angel never got around to telling me anything more about angels touching each other. How much am I allowed to tell people about angels?'

Archangel Michael gave me a big smile and reached out his hand. Automatically, because my grandparents had taught me it was the polite way to behave, I reached out to shake his hand. It filled me with so much love and happiness. Archangel Michael's hand embraced mine. My hand was lost in his.

He said, 'Angels don't shake hands, Lorna.'

I replied, 'I know but why not?'

'Because we are creatures created by God. We have no desire, no need, to touch each other. We are not like human beings. If an angel touches another angel it is only because God has allowed it. That occurs on special occasions.'

'Yes, Archangel Michael. I know it's very rare. I'm just thinking about it. I remember once, a long time ago, seeing a guardian angel actually touch another angel. Can I talk about it?' I asked.

Archangel Michael said, 'Yes, Lorna, and I will help you to remember it.'

It was the time when I was working for my dad in the Grosvenor service station in Rathmines. I asked my dad if I could get off work at two o'clock. I got the bus into Dublin city centre. One thing I always love doing is sitting on the bus and listening to all the people chatting and seeing all the angels around them, including the guardian angels of course. Seeing angels as physically as I see people is quite ordinary for me.

I got off the bus at the far side of O'Connell Bridge and walked up O'Connell Street. I was actually heading towards Penneys off Mary Street. I had saved up a few pounds so I could buy some new clothes. I was hoping to get a top and skirt. I turned down Henry Street and walked through the shoppers, heading towards my destination. I was coming up to Moore Street, which has a market, full of stalls selling fruit and vegetables. You can always hear the women calling out, 'Apples! Oranges! Bananas! For sale!'

I always loved glancing down that street because sometimes, the angels would allow all the energy coming from the fruit and vegetables in balls of light to bounce around the place.

On that day, just at the corner there was a young woman buying some fruit. I stopped because I saw her guardian angel reach out its hand. Its fingertips seemed to touch the hand of an angel standing beside it.

'Am I right, Archangel Michael?' I asked. 'When the young woman's guardian angel reached out to the other angel the tips of their fingers seemed to touch ever so lightly, almost not touching at all.'

'Yes, Lorna,' said Archangel Michael. 'You would almost say they did not touch at all, but they did. It is barely a touch at all. No angel needs to touch another angel. Angels don't need to embrace each other.'

'Archangel Michael, do archangels ever touch each other?'

'Only if God needs it to happen and only then. I don't need to touch another archangel or any angel. But God does allow us to touch human beings: men, women and children. It is not a full touch, as you know, Lorna.'

'Yes,' I said. 'As a child my guardian angel would put its hand over mine. It was the light of my guardian angel's hand that touched me. Not actually the hand.'

Archangel Michael said, 'Yes, that's right, Lorna.'

I said, 'Even when you shook my hand, even though my hand got lost in yours, they did not actually touch. It was only the light of your hand that was around mine. That warmth, that love, from you allowed me to feel the shape of your hand and the fingers, even though they were not actually touching my hand.'

Archangel Michael said, 'What else do you remember about the guardian angel at the corner of Moore Street when the tips of the guardian angel's fingers touched the angel standing beside it?'

I said, 'How can I explain? It was like at that moment when the tips of the guardian angel's fingers touched the other angel an infusion of light, like an explosion, came from the guardian angel's fingers. It was the left hand of the guardian angel of the young woman. The guardian angel's hand looked more radiant than any guardian angel I have ever seen but only his hand. It was as if it all happened in one brief moment of time. I remember the young woman's guardian angel looked over at me as I stood in the street. It was dressed in a gown of purple, green and gold. The angel was infused with delight from the guardian angel of the young woman.'

'What else do you remember, Lorna?' said Archangel Michael.

I thought for a moment and I said to Michael, 'I remember asking the guardian angel why did it touch the other angel but the guardian angel never answered me.'

I saw the young woman pay for her fruit and turn and walk away from the stall. It was only at that moment that I realised the other angel had disappeared.

I said to Archangel Michael, 'You angels definitely don't seem to need that embrace, that touch of love or companionship that men, women and children seek every day of their lives. Sometimes, Archangel Michael, I cannot understand the ways of the angels. You angels give so much love to every man, woman and child. Guardian angels love us unconditionally. I wish, Archangel Michael, that we could love each other as you angels love us.'

Archangel Michael said he had to go and disappeared.

I turned to Angel Hosus. 'Do you have to go as well?'

'No, Lorna, I can stay.'

As soon as Angel Hosus said that three other angels came into the room.

I smiled and said to them, 'I hope you are going to allow me to have a lunch break?'

The angels replied simultaneously, 'At three o'clock you can go for a walk.'

I smiled and said, 'Thank you.'

Pain in the Past

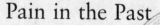

WE WERE LIVING IN BALLYMUN AT THE TIME. MUM ALWAYS brought me into Dublin to help do the shopping. I would be in charge of the cart that was like a shopping bag with two wheels and a handle. Almost everyone in Ireland used them at that time. They were so handy. You just pulled it behind you. On a Saturday morning, Mum and I would head down for the bus. Mum always went shopping in Henry Street and Mary Street and the cart would fill up with fruit and vegetables from the women's stalls on Moore Street. I always loved to walk down and watch all the hustle and bustle going on.

On big occasions Mum would go into the GPO, which was on O'Connell Street. It is a large post office and a historically famous building in Dublin because it is one of the main buildings where there was fighting for Ireland's freedom during the Easter Rising of 1916. I always felt nervous but excited about going into this post office and that is because every time I went into it, it was crowded with people. There were always queues for every tiller. The angels would show me things that had happened there in the past.

Most of the time, my mum would only want to use the telephones. When we went through the doors – the doors were very big and heavy – the telephone room was to the left. We would turn into a room with no door, full of cubicles with telephones.

I must've only been about ten or eleven years old on this particular day. Mum had to go up to one of the counters and the queues were very long. Mum stood in a queue and I stood beside her. I remember starting to count the people in the queues and sometimes I would smile because the angels would be standing in among all the people.

I would talk to them without words, saying, 'Can you move out of the way so I can count?'

They didn't.

Then my mum turned to me and said, 'Lorna, I think I'm going to be in this queue for some time. You go and stand over there by that counter near the back wall.'

I said, 'Okay!'

So off I went.

While I was standing there watching all the people and looking around, seeing all of the angels in among the crowd, I saw Angel Hosus walking towards me.

He said, 'Hello, Lorna.'

I smiled at him.

Angel Hosus spoke again, saying, 'I want you to pay attention, Lorna. You are going to be allowed to see some of the things of the past that happened here.'

I sighed and said, 'I don't like seeing the past, especially in here or outside.'

The angels had already shown me the fighting outside the

GPO that had happened in the past. I was afraid of seeing the people with guns, people being shot and wounded. The noise was always very loud and frightening – shouting, screaming and guns going off.

Angel Hosus said, 'You will be okay, Lorna, I'm right here with you.'

'Okay,' I sighed.

Within seconds the room changed. It was as if I was seeing the past and present together. Like watching a movie, but two movies at the same time, one over the other with the present being more dominant than the past.

Then the next moment it changed again. I was standing there in the GPO in the past. There was a lot of noise and the place seemed to be dusty. There was shouting. I could see Angel Hosus standing beside me.

I looked up at him and he said, 'Lorna, pay attention.'

I did. I saw a young woman holding on to a young man who seemed to be hurt. She was struggling, almost carrying him, as they walked across the room. I heard her call out for help and someone else hurried across to them from behind one of the counters. I could hear them talking but I could not make out what they were saying as they supported the young man. I felt very sad and hurt because I knew he was in pain.

All of the noise and the dust that seemed to surround them made me ask Angel Hosus, 'What is wrong, Angel Hosus? The young man has been wounded.'

All of a sudden I saw the present coming forward and I saw the past starting to fade away. The young woman and the young man seemed to disappear in the crowd and then everything went back to normal. My mum was still in the queue but she was a little closer to the till. I was very sad.

Angel Hosus stood in front of me and said, 'Lorna, it was war.'

I said to Angel Hosus, 'I don't understand.'

Angel Hosus said, 'I know you don't. Just pray. Your mum will be leaving soon.'

I looked up and there was only one person in front of my mum. A few minutes later we left. Angel Hosus walked out the door with us. I smiled, knowing my mum didn't know he was right there beside us. She knew nothing about the angels. She didn't even know I could see them as physically as I saw her. We walked on down to Henry Street and Mum did the shopping. Then later on we got the bus back home.

The angels show me things of the past so that I can tell the world in order for us to stop repeating war over and over again. If we continue to do that there will be nothing left, only bitterness and hate for the children of the future. We have to strive towards peace. I write in *Angels in My Hair* about how Angel Hosus described Northern Ireland as the cornerstone of peace for the world. Northern Ireland never experienced peace until the people from opposite sides came together because they realised they had to stop killing each other and give their children a chance to have a life, to have freedom and peace.

Joe's family was involved in the 1916 Easter Rising in Ireland. His Aunt Dolly was in the GPO at one stage. I remember sitting at the kitchen table with Joe while Dolly told us the story of how she brought food and guns in to the rebels. She prayed the whole time that she would not get caught as she slipped into the GPO under gunfire.

As she told me the story my guardian angel whispered, 'Lorna, do you remember seeing her there when we brought you back to that time?'

As soon as that was said I remembered seeing Dolly. She was only a young girl then and she was loading some guns with ammunition and handing them to the young men. I was about fourteen when the angels brought me back spiritually to experience that time.

It is horrible being put into the past, especially where there is war and so much pain. I always feel the emotions and spiritual suffering of all the men and women involved, on all sides. It tears me apart.

Because, as I've written about elsewhere, my family considered me what was then called retarded I was allowed to see many things that other members of my family were not privileged to see. I guess they thought I would never understand or be able to talk about these things, but of course, I did understand and am now able to talk about them. I have always had the best teachers in the world: the angels.

My dad and I both worked at the Grosvenor petrol station. Every morning, I would go to work with Dad, but on this morning he took a detour instead of going straight to work and as he did this, I heard my name being called. I turned around and looked into the back seat and there was Angel Hosus.

He said to me, 'Lorna, when you're with your dad we need you to pay attention so that you remember all you see.'

I spoke to Angel Hosus without words. 'Okay.'

My dad asked, 'Is there something you need off the back seat?'

I replied, 'No, I was just looking.'

A few minutes later, my dad found a parking spot by a row of shops. I would give you the area but I think it's best not to because what I saw with my dad is probably still there.

We got out of the car, crossed the road and walked up the street of old Georgian houses. As we got close to our destination I saw Angel Hosus standing beside two parked cars outside one of the houses.

Angel Hosus said, 'Lorna, the police officers sitting inside the cars are armed.' I took a deep breath. Angel Hosus said, 'Don't be nervous.'

Angel Hosus came and walked alongside me.

. My dad didn't notice the police officers sitting in the cars. Dad hesitated outside the gate for a moment and said, 'I think this is the right house.'

We went through the gate and up the steps to the door. It just looked like an ordinary Georgian house from the outside but when the door opened I saw that it was no ordinary house at all.

An armed guard opened the door. Dad gave his name and the guard welcomed us in. As we stepped in through the door we saw there were other armed guards standing in the hallway and that the hall door was not a normal door, it just looked like one from the outside. On the inside it had another door made of steel attached to it.

We walked down the hallway and straight into an office. It was my grandfather's office. I didn't know until I saw him there sitting in the chair behind his desk. It was not an ordinary office. Grandfather Cruthers had a big desk and chair but what was strange was that the office was full of guns.

My grandfather welcomed my dad with open arms. He said hello to me and gave me a smile. I smiled back at my grandfather.

He said to my dad, 'Jim, let me show you around.'

I followed behind them. Angel Hosus said to me that my

dad and my grandfather were talking one day about the past in Ireland, about the IRA and about the English occupation of Ireland. My grandfather listened to his guardian angel that day and shared a secret with my dad that led to my grandfather bringing Dad to his place of work.

I said to Angel Hosus, speaking without words of course, 'You didn't just do this for my dad. This was for me too?'

Angel Hosus said, 'Yes, Lorna, it is mainly for you so pay attention.'

We walked out of my grandfather's office. We were accompanied by two guards the entire time. I wasn't used to seeing guards armed because out on the streets in Dublin the police never carried guns. It was scary.

As we went from one room to another I noticed every door was reinforced with steel, and each room contained huge numbers of guns of all kinds. The rooms were dark. There were cabinets full of guns and all the walls were covered with guns as well. I have never seen so many guns in my life. As I walked around with my dad and my grandfather I felt overwhelmed. To me, it was very frightening because I knew guns killed people and animals. Sometimes, when I would be looking around at all of the guns Angel Hosus might be standing in the corner. He would give me a big smile and that would calm me down. I didn't want my dad or grandfather to notice I was nervous.

We went back to his office and sat down. My grandfather talked to my dad as if I was not there. All of the time there were guards with us. Some were in police uniform and others plain clothing. My grandfather told my dad that he had been a gunrunner for the IRA but when the Republic of Ireland gained its freedom and established its own government he became the supplier of weapons for our country. I guess that meant the Irish army and police.

I always remember when my grandfather died. He was buried with the Irish flag with many Irish army officers in attendance. Six Irish soldiers fired a gun salute over my grandfather's coffin.

CHAPTER 4

Making Room for God

THERE IS ONE THING I HAVE NEVER SHARED WITH YOU about my own guardian angel. I know I have told you all that your guardian angel never leaves you for one second. I've told you about times when God is with me and ruffles my hair. I've already told you in *Angels in My Hair* about the time when He walked through the fields with me and we sat by the River Shannon at the old chalet in Mountshannon, County Clare. My guardian angel doesn't leave me at these times, but stands to one side, and it's as if I am alone with God. I actually physically feel the presence of my guardian angel, his energy, his essence as he steps to one side of me. Explaining this to you is not going to be easy. It is as if part of me has stood to one side. Your guardian angel is connected to you by a very fine thread of light and I guess this is why I would feel this on different occasions. This only happens when I'm in the presence of God.

I have often turned my head to the right when God is there and I would see my guardian angel standing there just a few feet away from me, but yet it would feel as if my guardian angel was a million miles away from me. I know my guardian angel has to step to one side when God visits me and I do thank my guardian angel for doing it ever so gently. Feeling that powerful force of your guardian angel stepping to one side is really quite incredible. I know I'm not really explaining very well, but the other part is that when your guardian angel steps back the infusion of its power around you is so welcoming. You feel so relieved.

On occasion, when I have looked back at my guardian angel and seen him standing there, God has said to me, 'Don't worry, Lorna. Your guardian angel can never leave you.'

'What question do you want to ask, Lorna?' said Angel Hosus one day. He must have seen I had something on my mind.

'When do people experience this stepping aside?'

'Lorna, people only experience this when they have already died. When their soul has gone to heaven with their guardian angel. It is only at a certain point of time when they are in heaven that your guardian angel can step away from your soul, because when your soul is in heaven you don't need your guardian angel with you all of the time. Your guardian angel is always in constant prayer for those who have been left behind: your loved ones and their descendants. Your guardian angel can never be anyone else's guardian angel. It can only be the guardian angel of the soul that God had appointed it to and that guardian angel is with that soul in heaven for eternity, but they don't need to be with each other every second.'

I would often dilly-dally when walking home from school. We lived in Ballymun at the time and it was a fair walk. There was a school bus but I always preferred to walk. On this particular day, I wandered into one of the fields and was picking some wild flowers. I sat down on a clump of grass and spread my flowers out on the ground, putting them in bunches of white daisies, yellow cowslips, a wild flower that was purple in colour. I started to talk to my guardian angel.

I was actually giving out, saying, 'Well, I asked you for a feather. Three days now have passed and I have not found one feather anywhere, not even in this field.' I waited for a minute and then said to my guardian angel, 'Are you not talking to me?'

I got no reply and felt very guilty. I told my guardian angel that I was sorry for giving out about the feather.

Still sitting on the grass I said to my guardian angel, 'I would really love a feather to go with the flowers. A black and white one would be lovely but I don't think you are listening to me.'

I sorted out my flowers, got up and started to walk across the field to the far side. There were no angels around me. I knew my guardian angel was there though, but I was not very happy with my guardian angel because I hadn't got the feather I had asked for.

As I walked across the fields I picked the odd flower. I dropped some of them and as I bent down to pick them up my guardian angel's hand went over mine.

I said, 'You're here!'

My guardian angel replied with excitement, 'Yes, of course I'm here. Lorna, do you really want a feather?'

'Yes.'

'You do know I can't give you one of my own.'

I laughed and said, 'Of course not.'

'So I'll have to get a bird to leave the feather for you. Lorna, walk over towards the big tree over there.'

'Okay,' I said and just before I reached the tree I found a feather in among the grass.

I jumped for joy! It was black and white.

'How did you do that?' I said to my guardian angel. 'A black and white feather is not easy to find.'

'I know, Lorna, but I knew you would ask again today for a black and white feather. Yesterday there was a jackdaw that had a mixture of black and white in some of its feathers and it lost one, so it could be left for you.'

'Thank you!' I said to my guardian angel, but I hoped that didn't mean the bird would be feeling a bit cold if it lost its feather before it should.

'Don't worry, Lorna. Another feather is already growing in its place, you don't have to concern yourself about the bird feeling cold.'

'Thank you,' I said as I admired my feather, holding it up to the sunlight and blowing on it.

That was the way the angels taught me how to clean a feather and put it in among the wild flowers. I skipped almost all the way home. I gave the flowers to my mum and she put them in the window of the kitchen. They looked very pretty. I loved bringing home flowers to my mum.

I have seen angels give people feathers all of the time. It is one of the many signs that the angels give us when we need hope in our life; if, for example, we are asking for a sign of hope when a loved one has passed away. Sometimes, we ask for a further sign to know that they are at peace and are in heaven.

I often remember being at fishing competitions with my dad in different locations across the country and the angels telling me that one of the fishermen, called Pat, had been praying to God asking for a sign. It was to give him hope that everything would be all right for himself and his family, that things would work out.

On this particular outing, Dad was fishing with about ten other fishermen and they would move along the riverbank. The angels pointed out Pat every time he picked up his fishing bag to move along to fish at another spot. There would be a feather just under the bag or beside it every time, and I can tell you I had a good look around searching to see if there were any other feathers anywhere else but there were not. This kept happening over and over again. But Pat wasn't noticing.

It was starting to get dark and my dad said, 'I think we'll have to head home soon.'

One of the fishermen replied, 'Just a few more casts into the river and then we'll pack up.'

All the while I was just watching the angels working so hard that day to give this man a feather to provide him the hope he needed. I thought he would never notice it, but just as he was packing up his fishing gear and as he lifted the bag from the ground he hesitated for a moment. Then he bent down and picked up the feather. He looked at it but did not say a word to anyone and put it in his pocket. At the same moment, I saw his guardian angel embracing him. I asked what was wrong but I didn't get an answer. The angels didn't say anything to me. I often see angels giving people feathers but most of the time we don't notice them.

The angels really work hard, giving us signs, and it's not easy for them. They use the feathers of the birds of the air, so birds have to play their part too. They tend to use feathers because they are light. Angels find it easier to move minds than physical objects. I have described physical manifestations of angels in my books – knocking on doors or windows or causing winds to blow – but they are quite rare.

Most of the time when you ask for the sign of a feather you will find it in an unusual place, somewhere you are not expecting to find a feather. There were no feathers along the riverbank. Only one each time beside Pat's fishing bag. To me that is a miracle. I just don't know how the angels do it. We are just so slow, even myself at times, to recognise the signs the angels give us. We pass them by.

There was a friend of mine who said she would love to get a feather from an angel. She said she had been asking all her life but never received one. The angels around her that day told me she had already received lots of feathers but never saw them. Even when the angels put them directly in front of her she would dismiss them, thinking they were not really from the angels because they didn't appear in places where you really wouldn't expect to find a feather.

So I asked on her behalf and it was about six months later when I met her again and she said to me, 'Lorna, I received my feather.'

I said to her, 'I told you that you would. Where did you find it?'

She said, 'You won't believe this but I found it in my shoe.'

'That is incredible.' I asked her, 'Are you happy now?'

She said, 'Yes, I am.'

How did the angels manage to put a feather in her shoe? I really don't know but it is the way of the angels. Sometimes, there is no explanation for how the guardian angels do it. I know they have other angels to help them – and that they need our cooperation as well, so if your guardian angel puts a thought into your head respond to it. Someone may have asked for a sign and you're meant to help to give that person that sign. What you are asked to do might be very simple. It might be to make that phone call or write a letter. It could be to give someone a flower, a smile or your seat so they can sit down. It might even be to buy someone a cup of tea or to give someone a helping hand, even a stranger. One thing my guardian angel and all of the other angels have always taught me is something that my grandmother used to say as well.

They always repeat these words to me, 'Give with a pure heart and expect nothing in return.'

One of the occasions when my mum was in hospital, my sister and I were staying at my grandmother's. We had been living in Ballymun at the time but my grandmother didn't live very far from Old Kilmainham, so I knew the area. Sometimes my granny would send me down to the shops to run a few errands. I loved going to the shops because it gave me a little time to spend on my own and of course, I would never stop talking to my angel on the way down to the shops.

Sometimes, I would play a game. One of the games I played was trying to step into my guardian angel's enormous feet but I never succeeded. I knew it was impossible to do so because my guardian angel told me it wouldn't be allowed but we played the game anyway. When I would step forward with my right foot my guardian angel would put its right foot forward first. I was to try to step into my guardian angel's foot but it would always disappear no matter how fast I walked.

I would often say to my guardian angel, 'That's not fair! Let's start all over again and no cheating!'

My guardian angel would laugh. Its laughter was not like Archangel Michael's laughter. It was much softer.

My guardian angel would say, 'I don't cheat. I can't. That's impossible, Lorna.'

I would stop and say, 'Okay, let's go again. Right foot first, then left.'

I would be walking as fast as I could, almost running, trying to step into my guardian angel's feet. Sometimes, I would laugh so much that when I got to the shops I would have to stop and take a deep breath.

A woman carrying shopping bags one day stopped and asked me, 'What kind of game are you playing?'

I smiled at her because I didn't know what to say. At the same time I spoke silently to my guardian angel.

My guardian angel said, 'Say you're trying to play a game of catching up with your feet but you can't because your feet are always ahead of you.'

I did exactly as my guardian angel said and repeated the words to the lady.

She hesitated for a moment before she replied.

'You're right,' she said. 'You can't catch up with your feet. That's a funny one.'

Off she went, carrying her shopping bags.

My guardian angel said, 'Lorna, you cheered her up.'

During the school summer holiday, when we were living in Edenmore, I was out playing with some other children on the street. I may have been twelve years of age at the time. I had run down into the far cul-de-sac when a neighbour called me and asked me if I would like to take her baby for a wheel in the pram just up and down the road. She was trying to get the baby to go to sleep. The mother, Catherine, wheeled the pram out the front garden gate and then I took over, wheeling the baby up and down the road for at least an hour.

I often did this for mothers who lived on the street and I loved doing it. The baby was restless and cried every now and then.

I just said, 'Angels, can you help the baby?'

Its cheeks were all red, so I knew the baby was teething.

An angel came alongside the pram dressed in a golden flowing gown and said to me, 'Lorna, stop for a moment.'

I did and the angel bent over the pram looking at the baby. Then the angel put its hand over the baby for a second. I don't know exactly what the angel did but all I know is that the baby stopped crying and its little eyes started to close and it fell asleep. The angel turned and smiled at me. I said thank you to the angel and then it disappeared. A bit later some friends came over and had a look at the baby in the pram fast asleep.

Later I took the baby back, going through the gate just as its mother came out the door. I said to her that little Jack was fast asleep. The baby's mother gave a big smile as she looked at her little baby and at the same moment, loads of angels came around the pram. I said goodbye and walked up the road.

My guardian angel said, 'Why don't you go down to the green, Lorna, and sit by the river?'

I did exactly as my guardian angel said and sat down on the grass by the riverbank. It was only really a small stream. It was on the outside of the housing estate running along the main road. When you sat at the riverbank you couldn't be seen from the main road and I liked that because I felt I would be alone with the angels.

CHAPTER 5

The Depth of Angels

ON OCCASION AS A YOUNG CHILD, WHILE I WOULD BE sitting there watching the birds, watching the stream flowing and watching the insects, butterflies, dragonflies and all of nature around me, I would start to pray, automatically and rhythmically. Every now and then during this time an angel would stand in front of me, not saying a word. I would just look at the angel and after a few minutes it would disappear. I would stay sitting on the riverbank until my guardian angel told me to get up, that it was time to go home.

I'm going to describe one of these angels to you to help you to learn more about their appearance. I have never really spoken at great length about the depth of all angels. You can see into an angel but you cannot see through it. You cannot see all the way into an angel but when you look at an angel it is similar to looking into a room. It is as if you could walk into that room, walk into that part of the angel's body. I only call it a body because I don't know what other name to give it as the angels have never given me a name for their physical appearance, but hopefully they will soon.

Imagine there is another room behind the first as if the depth of an angel's body is never-ending. It is like you open another door and the depth of the angel continues. It still eludes me to this day. I always look at an angel in wonder and surprise. You could say the depth of an angel is like water that's crystal clear, so pure that you can see everything of the angel and it seems to continue on and on.

Every particle of an angel has this incredible depth even when an angel uses its fingertips. The depth within the fingertips is separate to the depth of the fingernail. Every part of an angel seems to be separate but yet one and radiating light.

I myself believe this has to do with the depth of an angel's body and yet I do not know if you can accurately say an angel has a body because the body is not like our human bodies. I have never seen an angel grow old or get sick like we do.

Angels have this incredible depth in every single part of them. This particular angel, on that day, stood at the far side of the little river. This angel was dressed in a unique emerald-mauve colour. It didn't have an appearance of being either male or female. It just stood there looking across at me and I at the angel. I was looking in wonder at every detail of the angel. Every line, every curve, every movement, especially when the angel raised its hand and waved to me and then disappeared.

Sometimes an angel may be wearing a cape or something like a tunic flowing over its body. I know you can all imagine that easily but I have never explained about the physical depth of an angel's body in every single part of it, and that even includes the clothing. I do believe this is why you cannot see through an angel, not even a shadow, and yes, you can see what I call the depth no matter what part of the angel you focus on.

It may be that the angel makes its face or wings or another part of its body stand out more than the rest of it. This usually happens when an angel is showing you something. Sometimes, an angel's face becomes more radiant, or its hands, or it could be the wings or it could be the clothing that it's dressed in. Every part of the angel's body is also alive in every way you could possibly imagine.

As I was sitting at my desk writing this I asked Angel Hosus, 'Am I explaining this right?'

Angel Hosus replied, 'Yes. Keep it simple, Lorna, so people can understand more. Remember, Lorna, God has allowed angels to give a human appearance so humankind can have a picture in their mind.'

'Okay,' I said, 'I know I could never describe the beauty of an angel or even any part of it but what I can say is that God has allowed every angel to give a human appearance. I'm so glad, Angel Hosus. Thank you for being with me, Angel Hosus, and for always giving that familiar human appearance within yourself. It is like seeing a reflection in still water. I could never describe you otherwise.'

'Turn around Lorna,' he said.

I swung my swivel chair around to have a good look at Hosus. He was standing at the door of the room I was working in. His appearance was the same as always: he looks like an old-fashioned schoolteacher wearing a funny-shaped hat and a robe that swirls at times, is blue it most of the time but changes colour on occasion.

I had to smile and I laughed at him because for a moment he changed the colour of his robe, to purple on the outside and that beautiful blue colour on the inside. Angels can change colour and, like here, even the type of dress they are wearing can change. I have never seen an angel put on clothing or take clothing off. It seems to be part of the human appearance the angel gives. It's not like you and me where our human body is separate from our clothing.

I said, 'Even looking at your robe, it has that incredible depth in appearance as if you are wearing a multitude of robes. As if I could walk into one of them and could continue to walk for miles and then step into the next one. The depth of the physical appearance of your robe is incredible. It is full of life. That's the part I don't know how to describe.'

He replied, 'Describe it as light.'

'Okay. Here goes. If one could see light physically, not just light reflecting or lighting up furniture in your room or the flowers and trees in your garden, but light itself. Hosus, I know I'm not doing this justice! I'm not a scientist. I don't know if science has discovered a way to see light and only light itself.'

'Lorna, use the sun because the sun gives light.'

'Okay,' I replied, 'I could say it's like looking at the sun under a microscope to see that light full of life, a light that is moving all the time in the depth of the physical appearance of the angel. This is one of the reasons why, Hosus, I would love to step into any angel because it would be stepping into that depth of an angel, into that light that is alive.'

'Lorna, you know God won't allow that. An angel can put its arms around you or even its wings or put its robe around you, Lorna, but no angel can allow any man, woman or child to step into that depth of the physical appearance of any angel.'

'Hosus, I understand.'

'Lorna, it is snowing. Look out the window,' he said.

I turned and looked out the window. Sure enough, it was snowing.

'Do you think the weather is going to get colder for 2016, Hosus?'

He didn't answer my question. Instead, he just told me to go downstairs and make myself another cup of tea. Then he disappeared. I did as he said, and an hour later I came back upstairs. The room was full of angels. I was a little disappointed as Angel Hosus was not there, but a few moments later he appeared and I started to work again.

The angels are always reminding me that they are creatures created by God, long ago, and that you and I are a billion times more radiant and important than any angel because we have a soul that is that speck of light of God. That tiny speck of God is so small and yet it shines in such a way that it fills every part of the human body. Our souls are perfect. We are children of God. Each and every one of us, no matter what you believe. That is the reason why you have a guardian angel.

I am going to tell you a little about that speck of light of God that is our soul. You must understand that everything I tell you I had to get permission from God first. It is usually through Archangel Michael, but sometimes it's another archangel. On other occasions it may be one of the other special angels that God has in my life who tell me I have permission to let you know more.

I was on holidays with my mum and dad and sisters and brothers. We went down to my granny and grandad's house in Mountshannon. I loved all the countryside around the area and over time, I got to know it very well. Every opportunity I had I would wander off across the fields in all directions. I knew I could never get lost or be in any danger. It was a great opportunity to be alone with God and the angels and to have nature around me. The angels would always play with me and my guardian angel so I was never alone. But one day in the woods the angels told me to sit down under one of the old trees and told me that I was to pray. I sat down with my knees up and my hands clasped around them. I don't know how long I was praying for. I was surrounded by angels that were in prayer with me when I heard my name being called. I looked up and I saw Archangel Michael coming towards me along the little path through the trees.

I went to stand up but he said, 'Lorna, remain sitting.'

He knelt down in front of me on one knee and his right hand looked like it was on the ground, but not one part of him can touch the earth. No angel can actually touch the ground. There was what I call the cushions of air between Archangel Michael and the earth.

He said, 'Lorna, I'm going to take your soul. God wants to talk to you. Don't be afraid.'

Angels surrounded me. They were like a blanket.

'Look into my eyes, Lorna,' said Archangel Michael.

I looked into Archangel Michael's eyes and at the same moment, with his left hand he reached into my body and for a split second it took my breath away. In the next moment, I seemed to be alone, just for one second, but I wasn't really. It was very bright. Everything was an incredible white and then I saw more angels.

They seemed to walk through this white light. The angels were dressed in white too. At the same time, I felt a hand ruffle my hair and I realised where I was. I was in heaven, and I knew who it was. I looked up and then He took my hand and we walked a little distance. I don't know how far we walked but God sat on something I could not see because everything was so bright. Then He lifted me up and put me on His knee. He seemed to be enormous but all I could feel was His love: that overpowering love. I just wanted to melt into Him.

He said to me, 'Lorna, I'm going to show you a soul being born.'

God was dressed in white light. A white light that is brighter and purer than any white you have ever seen. As God raised His hand light flowed from His fingers. Part of God's sleeves covered the palm of His hand as they have always done.

He spoke to me in a gentle voice as a father would to his child, saying, 'Lorna, watch carefully.'

As I sat on His knee, I watched His left hand go towards His chest. His chest area opened up. It almost blinded me. I found it hard to see and then I saw His heart. It moved forward. It was a radiant, deep red. Coming from His heart was light, shooting forward in every direction. God reached into His heart with the tips of His fingers and took the tiniest piece of His heart and put it into the palm of His left hand, into the dead centre on top of His sleeve that covered the palm of His hand, and He breathed upon it. It came to life and started to grow into a child, a child of God, and He held this soul, this tiny baby. Then an angel came and stood beside God.

A moment later, God said to the angel, 'Take this child of mine.'

The angel reached out ever so gently and lifted the child from God.

CHAPTER 6

A Surgeon Who Sent a Patient to Me

LAST SUMMER I GOT A SURPRISE VISIT FROM MY FRIEND Audrey. We always try to meet up every now and then. One thing I have always said to the angels is that I would love to have more time to spend with my friends. I don't see them often enough. I have known Audrey for many years. Sometimes a year could pass or more before we would get to see each other. On this particular summer's day I remember Audrey's car pulling into the drive. At the same time the yard became full of angels. It was wonderful to see her. On different occasions over the years I've seen her guardian angel and on this particular sunny day, as Audrey walked towards the door of the house with a big smile on her face I saw her guardian angel again. On this occasion, it gave a female and a beautiful appearance. It was dressed in the most incredible violet colour. It was as if there were one million different shades of violet streaming through the clothing. It just flowed over her guardian angel. It was extremely tall, towering over Audrey. I had to smile because the next thing her guardian angel did, and it is something guardian angels don't always do, was open its wings slowly. It is only on special occasions that guardian angels allow me to see their wings and those times I always feel privileged. This was even more special as it was the wings of my friend's guardian angel.

Its wings opened up slowly but not fully. They seemed to be moving ever so gently, almost not moving at all. I smiled because they seemed to be causing a little breeze around Audrey – I saw some of her hair move as if the wind was blowing it. This is something I rarely see happening. Audrey's guardian angel spoke to me and said it was allowing the gentle breeze from its wings to touch Audrey.

I asked her guardian angel, 'Does she know this?'

Her guardian angel said, 'No.'

Her guardian angel raised its left arm, bringing it gently around Audrey. The beautiful garment that it was wearing flowed gently around Audrey, concealing her from my sight. I could only see her toes. Her guardian angel raised its arm and the sleeve of the garment seemed to fold like a curtain. Her guardian angel put its beautiful, radiant hand upon her shoulder.

I spoke to her guardian angel at that moment without using words. 'Can I tell Audrey?'

But her guardian angel said, 'No.'

Today, I was talking to Audrey on the phone and when I hung up Angel Hosus was with me.

My guardian angel said, 'Lorna, you have permission from Audrey's guardian angel. You can write about seeing her guardian angel that day.'

So I'm speaking into the computer and doing so. I welcomed Audrey and we embraced each other as she stepped in through the barn doors. I was so delighted to see her. We had a lot of catching up to do so we never stopped talking. We had lunch out in the garden.

I was all the time telling the angels, 'Please do not let it rain and keep the sun shining.'

I have to say they did.

Audrey shared something with me that she had never told me before. She said that many years ago a friend of hers had come to see me. This was before I had even written the books. As well as seeing angels as physically as I would see you if you were here in the room, I can hear them too as clearly as I would hear you if you were talking to me. But the angels talk to me in many different ways. Sometimes they talk to me just like you and I would but they also can talk to me without words and I talk to them the same way. Some people call this telepathy. I call it simply talking without words. Many times it's three angels talking with me, sometimes even as many as five angels could be talking to me at the same time. Yet, I hear each of them individually and clearly. I can keep up a conversation when in the company of my friends or my family. This is because the angels have taught me how to do this my whole life so it is second nature.

Audrey said her friend, let's call her Hannah, had a bad back and unbeknownst to me her specialist in England told her that she needed surgery, but that it would be very dangerous. It was the only thing they could do for her. The surgery would be very tricky. If it went perfectly well all her pain would be gone and she would have no problems walking or doing the everyday things, but if it went wrong she would end up in a wheelchair and would continue to be in constant pain. For this reason she was very apprehensive about the surgery. The surgeon had wanted her to think about it. It would be her decision.

As Hannah was about to leave, the surgeon said to her,

'I'm going to say something to you that you may think strange but I would like you to go and see Lorna Byrne in Ireland. We must not tell any doctors I've sent you to see her because they would not agree. You must not tell her that your surgeon asked you to see her either. Just tell her that you have a bad back and you're considering surgery. If she says yes, go ahead and have the surgery and that it will be successful then I would do it without hesitation.'

Unbeknownst to me this lady did come to see me.

I said to Audrey, 'I don't even remember.'

Audrey said, 'I knew you wouldn't remember her. Hannah told me the only thing she said to you was that she had an awful lot of back pain and that her doctor said she needed surgery and that she was very afraid to go ahead with it. You had a look at her and you prayed over her. Then you told her to go ahead and have the surgery. You told her that it would be successful and that she would never look back. It was successful, Lorna. She *has* never looked back.'

I said to Audrey, 'I'm glad she didn't tell me beforehand. I wouldn't have wanted to know. I never want to be influenced. I just want to see what I see physically. I'm happy she did exactly as the surgeon had said, but that is incredible, a surgeon having the faith to send a patient to me.' I was so happy for the woman, Hannah, to have her life back.

Audrey said, 'Yes, Lorna. Hannah also told me that you told her to do exactly as the surgeon said after the surgery. She did exactly as he instructed. You gave her the Prayer of the Healing Angels as well.'

I replied, 'We all know how powerful prayer is. I pray and I thank God for allowing the surgeon to be successful in such a delicate operation on the spine. I thank God for all of His healing.'

I knew the surgeon must have prayed and asked for God to guide his hands through the surgery. The operating theatre must've been packed with healing angels. I know Hannah's guardian angel would have been looking down upon her, watching over her.

I had a great day with Audrey. I was feeling a little sad when she had to go. When she drove her car out the gate loads of angels went streaming after her car.

I said to them, 'Get her home safely.'

One of the angels turned around and said, 'Don't worry, Lorna. We will keep her safe.' Most of these angels were dressed in beautiful, pastel colours of blues and greens but mainly that incredible white.

My life is forever changing and I do try to share as much of my life with all of you as possible.

Sometimes, I say to Archangel Michael, 'People would not be interested in what happened to me.'

Just today he reminded me about a lady who had walked up to me one day in a shop and said, 'Hello, I'm so happy to meet you personally. I have been asking my guardian angel to allow this to happen one day. Thank you very much. You have made a huge difference in my life. You have made it worth living. It is as if I know you personally through your books.'

I'm always shocked when someone says something like that. I am feeling cold at the moment as I speak this. I have a woolly cardigan on me and a blanket over my knees, but I am still shivering a little.

Angel Hosus suggested I go downstairs and make myself a cup of soup. I did so. At the same time I let our little Yorkshire terrier, Holly, into the house.

I said to the angels, 'I'm feeling cold so I imagine Holly might be feeling cold too.'

I know some of you may have seen a photograph on Facebook or on my website of Holly. The other day around four o'clock my guardian angel whispered in my ear. It said just one word, 'Holly', so I went downstairs and brought Holly into the house.

As she walked in the door I noticed she was limping a little.

I said, 'Thank you,' to my guardian angel.

I got Holly to lie down on the mat and I started to massage her back leg. At the same time, I prayed that it would be healed. An angel knelt down beside me and Holly lifted her head from the mat. I knew she could see the kneeling angel. Sometimes animals can see angels, not all of the time but when it is necessary. It is an angel that keeps an animal calm when it is hurt.

The angel told her, 'It's okay. Be still. You are being helped.'

Holly put her head back down on the mat and completely relaxed as I continued to massage her back leg gently.

The angel said, 'She strained it running around the garden.'

I was to try to keep her quiet for the rest of the evening.

I said, 'Thank you,' to the angel but it had disappeared.

CHAPTER 7

John the Baptist

ONE THING I ALWAYS GAVE OUT TO GOD ABOUT, ESPE-
cially when I was a child, was when God on occasion would
have Archangel Michael or sometimes the Angels of Prayer
or another angel take my soul. I always found it hard and I
still do so even today. The body feels the breath being taken
from it, which is painful and frightening for a brief moment.

An angel only takes my soul when God wants to take it
to heaven to be in His presence or when He gives me a vision
and puts me in the past or in the future.

There was one time, when I was about nine years of age,
when this happened. We were living in Ballymun. We had a
huge garden and there was a big haystack three-quarters of
the way down the garden. It never seemed to get any smaller
because when the grass was cut, it was just piled on top of
it. Sometimes, I would go around the back of the haystack.
I would love to go and sit behind the haystack and just be
alone with the angels. I would be facing the garden wall,
which was six foot tall.

On this particular day, I went down the road to my friend Rosaline's. I climbed up the ladder and I walked along the wall down to Rosaline's house. As I did so the angels whispered in my ear and told me that I must not stay long down in Rosaline's house. I was only to stay a few minutes just to say hello and come straight back.

I said, 'Okay.'

I went up the wooden ladder that my dad had made so that us children could climb up on to the wall. I walked along the top of the wall and then climbed down into Rosaline's garden and ran into her house through the kitchen and into the dining room. She was sitting at the table, drawing a picture. I stopped because there were three angels around her drawing on the same piece of paper.

It made me happy seeing the angels helping her to draw the picture. 'Hello, Rosaline!' I said and she looked up and said, 'Great. You've come to play.'

I said, 'No, but I will be back later. I just wanted to see what you were doing for a few minutes. I'll be down later on to play. Bye!' I turned around and went back out the door and ran down her back garden to the corner, where I climbed up on to the wall and walked home carefully putting one foot in front of the other on the wall. Then I climbed back down the ladder into my own garden. The back door was open and I saw my mum in the kitchen. I didn't see any of my brothers and sisters around. When I heard my name called I saw Archangel Michael standing by the haystack.

He called me. 'Lorna, come here.'

I ran over. 'Hello,' I said. 'Why are you here?' I was worried because Archangel Michael always comes to tell me something momentous, something life-changing or important for the world. 'Is there something wrong?'

Archangel Michael replied, 'No, everything is okay. Lorna, you are a little worrier and you are so young.'

On occasion during our important discussions Michael makes himself so human in appearance that others can see him too and fail to realise he is an angel. Archangel Michael was dressed sombrely in dark trousers and a jacket. It was something like what my dad and my friends' dads would have worn at that time.

'God wants to show you something. He is going to give you a vision and He wants me to take your soul there.'

Archangel Michael reached out and my hand became lost in his. He knew I loved him to do that. Holding his hand filled me with his love and the knowing that I was safe.

He said, 'Sit down. I know you like sitting here by the haystack, Lorna.'

I guess I had a sad face on because I was a little frightened. Archangel Michael said, 'Don't worry, Lorna. You will be okay. I'll be right there with you.'

I sat down with my back against the haystack and snuggled in a little. I was facing the garden wall. Archangel Michael knelt down in front of me and with his left hand reached out towards my chest. For a brief second, I gasped for breath but in a flash, I was in the past.

I was a little girl of maybe about the same age as I was in my real life. I did not see Archangel Michael but I knew he was there close by with me. I was in a barren and dusty field, picking up stones and putting them into a basket, and a little boy was helping me and then taking the basket away when it was full. He looked about the same age as I was. He came back and started to help me to put the stones into the basket again. Every time the basket was full with stones he took it a small distance and emptied it out on to a rough, grass mat so we could drag it along. We were helping to clear the field. He was very quiet. He wasn't saying anything and neither was I. Then a woman in a dark shawl called us. She spoke in another language but I understood.

The boy said, 'Run!' and I ran as fast as I could but he ran faster.

When we reached where the woman was standing she gave out to him and said, 'John, you should have let your friend win.'

She was telling him that there was not another boy or girl as fast as him. We went into the house. It was small but it did have a walled garden. The wall was quite low and the garden was quite small. I was giggling at John because he was making faces. His mum told John to go and get his father. John went out the door and I went after him.

He stopped at the little garden wall and said to me, 'You wait here until I get back.' So I sat on the little wall for a while and then I got up and walked to the door of the house and opened it slowly. I could hear John's mum praying, and when I peeped in I saw she was praying to God. She was kneeling on the floor facing a small window. She had her hands clasped together and was praying with every fibre of her body and soul to God. She was praying to God about her son, John. I heard her call out his name to God many times. As she prayed she wasn't praying alone. Her guardian angel was praying with her. It gave a male appearance. He was dressed in white and sky-blue clothing. Her guardian angel was bent forward over her with its hands joined together in prayer. Every time John's mother said the word God her guardian angel looked straight up into heaven and raised its hands in prayer.

I stepped away quietly, praying God would answer her

prayer. I was standing with my back to the door looking out across at the field where I had been picking up the stones with John when I knew Archangel Michael was standing to the left of me. He was dressed like some other men who were standing around and talking.

One of them passed by and said, 'Hello.'

Archangel Michael said, 'Lorna, don't be sad. What God has written will come about. John, your friend, is John the Baptist.'

I said, 'I know.'

I looked up at Archangel Michael with tears in my eyes and said, 'How do I know this already?'

'Because, Lorna, you and God had a conversation in heaven before you were born. God is allowing those memories to flow back into your mind. We are just reminding you.'

I said to Archangel Michael, 'John's mum loves him so much.'

Archangel Michael reached out and took my hand.

I said, 'Thank you, Archangel Michael.'

'Go now,' he replied.

So I ran back to clearing stones in the field. It seemed as if hours had passed before I saw John and his father walking back towards the house. I called out and John ran over. He started to play chasing with me and some other children joined us.

All of a sudden, I was back in my own garden, sitting down at the haystack. Archangel Michael was still kneeling in front of me. He smiled at me.

I sat there looking at him for a moment and then in a quiet voice I said, 'The boy?'

Archangel Michael said, 'God gave you a vision of John the Baptist when he was a young boy, a long time ago.'

I asked, 'Did he do something very special for God?'

Archangel Michael said, 'Yes, but it was a long time ago.'

I said, 'He was a nice boy. I played with him and I was in his house. It was very small and we were gathering stones. His mum did give us something to eat. I remember that but I'm not sure if it was a biscuit or a piece of bread. It was shaped round and tasted nice.'

Archangel Michael smiled and said, 'Lorna, you stay sitting there now and rest.'

I did and I must've fallen asleep for a little while. That was the first time that God had given me a vision about John the Baptist. I will share others with you, but later on, in another book.

CHAPTER 8

God Takes My Mum

GOD TOOK MY MUM HOME TO HEAVEN WHEN SHE WAS eighty odd years of age. It was a year ago. I miss her and I know the rest of my family do as well. I knew her time was getting close and it was a very hard decision for my sister to put her into a nursing home close to where she lives but that was the best decision she ever made for my mum. Mum settled in over time and became very happy there. But the last few weeks of my mum's life I believe was hard for us all. I went into the nursing home as often as I possibly could. On two occasions, Father John came with me.

Father John is a priest. He used to be the chaplain of Limerick Prison. Many years earlier he'd sent me a letter that the angels had told me to keep and set aside, and over time we became firm friends.

On one of these visits to see my mum, Father John and I had lunch with her. We sat there talking with her about all the things she remembered in her life. She laughed many times, going back into the past, remembering all of us when we were children and remembering my dad. She talked about the times when she moved house. I never heard my mum talk so much as I did on that day. She seemed so happy.

There were two angels at each side of her. I smiled at them because they were constantly rubbing her back as her back and her hips often pained her. I enjoyed that day, having lunch with my mum.

Before we left, Father John gave my mum a blessing. I told her that I would be back in to see her again soon, but then my sister called and said Mum had had another stroke and it didn't look good.

I remember driving up and down from Kilkenny just to spend some time with my mum before God took her home to heaven. Every time I had walked in through the doors of the nursing home two angels would always meet me and walk ahead of me down the corridor to the little room. The angels would stand each side of the door. They were dressed in gold clothing and when they did this they were both holding one candle in the centre of the palms of their two hands. They glowed so brightly. Now I was entering the room and there was my mum lying on her bed, so frail with her guardian angel holding her soul that my heart cried inside of me. I wanted to pick my mum up and hold her in my arms and just cradle her, but I knew I could not do that for it would have only caused her pain.

For the first couple of days after her stroke she would come in and out of consciousness every now and then. Every time I saw this happen her guardian angel would whisper words in her ear. I do believe my mum's guardian angel was telling her who was in the room, naming my sisters and brothers and those who came to visit.

The last week or so of my mum's life was very hard for

us all because at that time her body was reacting badly to pain. The doctors had it under control. Most of the time. I know the only reason why she was in pain was because her body was so frail and it hurt her even just for somebody to touch her.

So many times I asked God to allow my mum's guardian angel to take her home to heaven but I guess it was not my mum's time. It is just hard when you see someone you love dying. On those last days of my mum's life, I saw the souls of my father and my two brothers visiting her. When my dad whispered in her ear I would see a little smile on her face. I knew she knew that he was there.

When our time comes our souls go back home to heaven and our human body dies. The souls of those we loved that went ahead of us visit us when we are dying. When I saw this happening at different times with my mum it filled my heart with joy. This happens for your loved ones as well. On my last visit to see my mum, she was lying in her bed like a newborn baby. Her guardian angel didn't just have a hold of my mum's soul with its hands but, on this day, its arms were completely around my mum's soul with its hands intertwined. My mum's guardian angel looked like it was lying in her bed with her but yet, Mum's guardian angel was not touching any part of her bed as it lay there with her.

Mum's guardian angel said to me, 'It won't be long now, Lorna. I will be taking your mum to heaven.'

This is something I don't see every day. I felt very privileged to see a guardian angel holding the soul of the person who is dying in that way. I stayed as long as I possibly could.

It was late that evening when my own guardian angel whispered in my ear, 'Lorna, you must go home.'

I didn't want to. I wanted to stay. I spoke to my guardian

angel without words, feeling broken-hearted because I knew that it would be the last time I would see my mum alive. Eventually, with hesitation, I gave in to my guardian angel's prompting words. I knew I had to leave. My guardian angel had told me that I wasn't allowed to be there when Mum's guardian angel took her soul to heaven. I so much wanted to be there but I knew it was not meant to be. I said goodbye to my mum and gave her a kiss. Then I said goodbye to my sisters. I left my two sisters there with my mum. Walking up the corridor, I said goodnight to one of the nurses who was in the hall. She opened the door and let me out.

I stood there for a moment, wanting to run back in and put my arms around my mum.

'No, Lorna,' whispered my guardian angel.

I stood there for another moment. The nursing home was on a hill and I was looking out across the night sky, praying for my mum. I could see the lights of part of Dublin city. It looked very beautiful but I was feeling so cold. I was only a little distance from the car. As I reached it I saw that Angel Hosus was standing by the driver's-side door of the car.

I walked over and said, 'Hello.'

I asked him if he was going to drive the car for me and Angel Hosus said, 'No, Lorna.'

I stood there looking up at him with tears rolling down my cheeks, overflowing from my eyes. Angel Hosus reached up to wipe my tears away with the tip of his finger. He did not touch my face but somehow he dried my tears.

'Lorna, don't cry,' he said. 'Your mum is only going home to heaven.'

I said, 'I know but that doesn't make it any easier.'

I got into the car and when I did Angel Hosus was sitting in the passenger seat.

'Drive home to Kilkenny, Lorna.'

I prayed and the angels prayed with me. In my prayer I asked that my mum's passing would be peaceful and that my sisters would experience something special for themselves at the moment when my mum's guardian angel took her soul home to heaven.

I miss my mum. I miss visiting her and bringing her out for lunch and doing some shopping. I know sometimes I didn't see her for ages but that is because God had me busy travelling around the world giving messages to the world of hope and love. Of course, my youngest daughter Megan would often visit her granny with me. Megan misses her granny.

All the times we went visiting her are filled with lots of happy memories. I remember one day visiting on my own. We were sitting at her kitchen table having tea and biscuits and she was telling me that at times she was lonely. She was too old now to go and visit her neighbours. It was something she loved to do and she missed it. I enjoyed that day with my mum. Her kitchen was always full of angels and at times, I was privileged to be allowed to see the soul of my dad walk into her kitchen and stand close to her with his pipe between his lips and his fishing hat on his head. He would just glance at me and smile.

On that particular day, the soul of my dad walked through the kitchen door and stood beside my mum and puffed smoke from his pipe just above her head. Then he walked around the table and out the back door.

My mum was looking uncomfortable. She said, 'Sometimes I smell the tobacco from your dad's pipe.'

'You do?'

She said, 'Yes.'

My mum's guardian angel told me to sniff. I did what it said and gave a little sniff in through my nose.

I said to Mum, 'I think I can smell the tobacco from Dad's pipe now.'

My mum just smiled at me and my mum's guardian angel said to me, 'Your mum was afraid to admit it openly in front of you.'

My sister told me that a few days before my mum had that bad stroke they had been on a day trip to Dublin. It was a beautiful sunny day so they went shopping. Shopping was one thing my mum loved doing, and going out for lunch. I don't remember where she said they had lunch but I know they sat out in the sun and that my mum had an absolutely great day.

It's always important for us all to do our best to remember all of the good times that we spent with our loved ones before they went home to heaven. Think of all the times they made us laugh. Remember the stories they shared with us about the different things that happened in their life. Bring back the memories of helping them paint the house or doing little bits of gardening with them. It is important to share all the little things that bring back all the memories of them. Memories are important to us all and we all need them. Always hold on to those happy memories, and if there are sad ones there too it is important for you to talk about them and share them with others so that in time, those bad memories become less sad. This will allow the good memories to come forward and overshadow them. You will find that what you thought of as sad or hurtful no longer is.

Always remember that your loved one loves you and is in heaven waiting for you to come when your time comes, but not before then. And no one dies alone, because the guardian angel is right there with your loved one holding on to their soul and at the moment of death they take their soul straight to heaven. There is no pain. There is only relief, joy and love at the moment of death. All the questions are answered. You meet those who have gone before you and you are joined together in love – that incredible love that I cannot explain in words because it is the love of God. When our soul returns to Our Father in heaven that love is so overpowering, so incredible, that when you go home to heaven you don't want to return, not even for those you love here on earth.

CHAPTER 9

Archangel Gabriel and Our Loved Ones

IT WAS SEPTEMBER 2014 WHEN I WAS DOWN IN THE orchard picking apples. I heard my name being called and I turned around. I didn't see anything except for the wildness of the orchard.

I just said, 'I thought that was you angels calling me but I must've made a mistake.' Just as I was about to turn around and go back to picking the apples a bright light appeared between the trees. Within that glowing light the outline of a doorway appeared. As the doorway opened slowly a brighter light beamed through it. Within moments, as I stood there watching, the doorway opened fully. I could see another light coming towards me as if it was a million miles away out in space and travelling towards the open doorway. As it got closer it got bigger and brighter. All the time it was like the moon spinning. Then the light stopped as it came closer to the entrance of the doorway and I could see an angel standing within the light. I knew, of course, who it was straight away.

Archangel Gabriel was standing almost at the entrance of

the doorway, but not quite. I recognised his extraordinary eyes and very youthful appearance – though he didn't look as young as Raphael. As he stood in the open doorway he was surrounded by beautiful, crimson light like round the moon but a million times more striking. Then as he came forward, slowly stepping through the doorway, the crimson light that had encircled him now streamed out from behind him. Finally he stepped completely away from the doorway into our world, and as he did so he took on a more human appearance. He was dressed all in black leather clothes like a motorcyclist.

'Hello, Archangel Gabriel. I wasn't expecting you. No one told me you were coming. What a surprise!'

'I have come to help you to pick apples and to tell you, Lorna, that one day soon you will see another one of God's glowing babies. I know you're missing your mum too. She's in heaven and very happy.'

'Thanks, Gabriel,' I said. 'Can I ask you a question?'

'Yes, of course you can, Lorna.'

'I don't know quite what way to put it,' I said.

Archangel Gabriel replied, 'Let me answer it for you without you asking the question.'

'Okay,' I said.

'Lorna, many times when someone is dying, whether it's a man, woman or child, God often gives extra time so that healing can happen between the person who is dying and their family and friends. I know you know of someone at the moment.'

'Yes,' I said, 'I'm just thinking about him. He fell out with his family thirty years ago and never spoke to them but now that he is dying he is reaching out to his family. He has asked them to forgive him for being so stupid over a row that happened so long ago. Archangel Gabriel, it is so wonderful to hear all his family are coming to see him. Just think about it. All he had to do was say he was sorry and that's what he did. They too have said they are sorry. I know he's just holding on and God is allowing it for them all to come and say their goodbyes.'

'Yes, Lorna, they all want to tell each other that they love each other and always have. God gives people these opportunities, even years beforehand, but sometimes families don't bother because of the hurt, the pain and the anger they may feel. Families need to get in contact with lost uncles and cousins when they hear from a family member about a falling-out long ago, Lorna.'

'His cousins didn't know about the falling-out until they heard by chance from family members. They didn't even know there *was* another part of the family. They wanted to know the story and went with open arms to see him. Then in doing so the rest of the family followed. I always feel that is very sad when some part of the family holds on to a grudge over something that happened thirty or fifty years ago and the family have been told not to bring that person's name up again.'

'Yes, Lorna, and then time can pass and the family have lost contact with a member of the family.'

'Archangel Gabriel, could you tell me some of the things people would have fallen out over?'

'Yes, Lorna. Sometimes, it was over land, a piece of property, over love or sometimes even someone criticising another member of the family, running them down or misjudging them. It can be lots of different things. Some are very simple and small like someone forgetting to include someone in an outing. Loads of little squabbles, I'm afraid, Lorna, separate family members with hatred and jealousy. Now I must go.'

Archangel Gabriel disappeared. I went back to picking the apples and then went into the house and made some apple tarts. I am thinking of apple tarts now, sitting in front of my computer. Apple tart and custard. It would really be nice but I must get back to writing. I want to continue talking to you about the loved ones in your family and friends.

Remember, your loved one can do more for you in heaven. They can intercede for you and ask your heavenly Father on your behalf. The connection between your loved one and yourself always remains even though we lose that loved one here on earth.

I have often talked about the importance of asking your guardian angel. Asking your loved ones is as important. A loved one can intercede for you in a very powerful way. I have seen the angels stand aside to allow a loved one to walk right up to the throne of God with a heartfelt plea.

I see angels all the time and I see the departed too. For example, at events I don't just see the guardian angel of everyone who is there. There are always lots of unemployed angels – the angels that God pours down in bucketfuls from heaven to help us in the everyday, trivial aspects of our lives – and other angels there but many times I also see the souls of loved ones. On occasion, there are so many souls of our loved ones fleeting by like a never-ending stream, moving so quickly. All the souls sometimes speak at the same time. This usually happens at the beginning of a speaking event, just as I walk into the room and get up on to the stage. It is just for the first few moments during the talk or sometimes during questions and answers. It is unknown to the audience. I have never spoken before about the stream of souls that show up.

The angels often tell me to pass on one of the simple

messages given by the souls of our loved ones. The most common message of all from the souls of our loved ones is, 'Tell them we're right there with them when they need us and we love them.' I know this message could be for many of those in the audience.

Sometimes, we find it very hard to move on, to get up and start to live life again, but your loved one wants you to start to live life again. A loved one does not want you crying all of the time. They do not want you giving up. They know you have that hole in your heart, that coldness, that empty space, that pain and hurt of missing them, but your loved one wants to help you to close it, to help to heal you. Your loved one loves you. It doesn't mean you should forget them. But you don't have to think of them all the time. They don't want you to because they know how it hurts you. It doesn't mean you don't love them any more. Your loved one knows you do, and they love you, but they want to see you happy. They want to see love and good things coming into your life.

Remember, your loved one wants you to live life to the fullest. God allows your loved one's soul to be with you for a brief moment when you think of them and also at times when you were not thinking of them. If you want to know what your loved one is trying to tell you, remember the last time you thought of them, and then try to remember, too, what you were thinking about immediately before the thought of your loved one came to you.

God allows the soul of your loved one in around you because God knows ahead of time that you will need them because of something that is happening in your life at that time. God knows you need them for the healing in your life and for so many other reasons. You may not feel their presence, but I can assure you they are there although they are in heaven as well. They are at peace. They are happy and one day you will see them again.

As I am talking into the computer here the angels are reminding me not to forget to tell you that if any of you have lost a husband, a wife or your partner that the soul of your loved one would like you to make a place in your heart for someone else so you can be loved by another man or woman and so that you can love again in return. It is up to you to make a place in your heart. That is what your loved one always wants for you. Don't leave it too late. I'm being told that many men and women pass up the opportunity for love to come into their lives again and again because they loved someone very special in the past but God took that person home to heaven. Your loved one wants you to fall in love once again, to make a place in your heart to allow someone else in, because your loved one in heaven knows it will be something you will yearn for. Your loved one does not want you to be lonely.

I asked the angels here with me, 'Did I say this correctly?' They said, 'Yes.'

Angel Hosus said, 'Lorna, that is what Joe wanted for you and we know you have found it very hard to open your heart to let someone else in. We know you have tried.'

I swung around in my chair and said to Angel Hosus, 'I did make a little place in my heart for someone else, but God took him home to heaven too. I definitely don't feel like making a little place in my heart for someone else. I don't think a man could cope with my life. I think I would drive him crazy.'

Angel Hosus just laughed at me and I said to him, 'Go away.'

He didn't though. I know the day I go home to heaven I

will see Joe holding our little son Michael's hand with my little brother Christopher, my mum, my dad and Garrett my brother, who have already gone home to heaven. I will see again all those I knew who died. I will embrace them and they will embrace me with love, with welcoming arms. The same will happen for you one day but in the meantime, please live life the best you can. Life is precious. Don't take it for granted. It is wonderful. Even with all our ups and downs remember, no matter what is happening in your life you will get through it. Later on you will be wondering why you were feeling so down, so learn to enjoy being alive. That is one thing the angels have taught me all my life. I know your guardian angel is always teaching you to enjoy being alive too, so keep on reminding yourself to enjoy the simple things that you are doing.

CHAPTER 10

My Life Day to Day

I SAID TO MARK, MY EDITOR, THAT I WANTED TO KEEP an autobiographical theme running throughout this book. He thought that would be a brilliant idea. My life has changed so much. I, myself, have not changed, but I know more and I learn more when people ask me questions I haven't been asked before. I am still me. One thing that I love in my life is when I have the chance to talk to children. They are so enthusiastic to learn more. They are intrigued that they have a guardian angel. They always have so many questions.

I was asked by a teacher in an Australian school to do a Skype session with her students. The teacher's name is Natasha.

I often get messages on Facebook asking when am I coming to Australia. I'm sorry to say that I don't know. I would love to go to Australia and do some talks and a book tour but that hasn't happened yet. You have to be known well enough in a country to be asked over by your publishers or an organisation there, otherwise you can't go, but I hope in the future I will be invited. I am really happy, though, that I was asked by the students and their teacher, Natasha, to talk over Skype. You are brilliant! I do thank God for technology because if we didn't have it and didn't have tools like Skype I would not be able to talk to children in Australia about their guardian angels.

There was a little mix-up with that Skype call. All of that week the angels kept saying to me, 'It is on Thursday, Lorna.'

But I said, 'No, it's Friday.'

When Thursday came the angels said, 'Lorna, you better leave your computer on.'

So I said, 'Okay.'

I didn't question it.

When I was downstairs around 10.30 p.m., relaxing with my feet up, my guardian angel whispered in my ear, 'Lorna, listen. What do you hear?'

I jumped up from the couch and I legged it up the stairs.

I said to my guardian angel, 'There is someone calling on Skype.'

My guardian angel said, 'Yes.'

When I reached the landing, Angel Hosus said, 'Hurry up!'

Just as I reached my computer it stopped ringing.

I sat there and said to Angel Hosus, 'It's the Australian school. I bet it's the teacher Natasha and her students.'

Angel Hosus said, 'Yes, and all the children are very excited. The classroom is full of angels.'

The next minute Skype rang again and I answered.

Natasha said, 'Hello, Lorna.'

All her class was delighted I had answered and were looking forward to asking questions.

I said to Natasha, 'I thought it was tomorrow night, Friday.'

She said to me, 'Today is Friday in Australia.'

I said to her, 'It's only Thursday here.'

The two of us laughed.

She said, 'Oh, I'm so sorry, Lorna. What a mix-up! Your Friday would be our Saturday.'

I said, 'Not to worry. It's all okay. If you and your students don't mind me sitting here in my dressing gown. I'm afraid I was ready for bed.'

Natasha turned to her class and told them I was in my dressing gown and was that okay and they said, 'Yes!'

They didn't mind. They were just so excited about asking about their guardian angels.

I don't know how many boys and girls were in the class-room but by just guessing I think their ages were between ten and twelve years old. They had a big screen on the wall, where the blackboard would have been in the past, at the front of the class. One by one, the children came up and sat in front of the computer. Each told me his or her name and then asked a question and the rest of the class could see me on the screen answering it for them. I love the questions children ask. They are always very simple and straight to the point. They all tried to ask different questions because their classmates were listening to the answer too. Now I'm trying to remember them so I can tell you them. I have asked Angel Hosus if he would help me.

He said, 'Yes, Lorna.'

A number of children asked what their guardian angel's name was. I said to them that I didn't know but they could ask for themselves. I told them to close their eyes with me and only think of their guardian angel.

'Just relax and don't try too hard. Your guardian angel will put the thought into your mind. It could be about something you see or do every day or your guardian angel could put a picture into your mind. It could even just be one word.

Whatever your guardian angel does, take hold of it. It is helping you to recognise its name.'

Most of the children, when they opened their eyes, had something that they related to their guardian angel's name. They talked about what thought or picture or what one word came into their mind.

When a young girl told me that she saw a daffodil I said to her, 'Then your guardian angel is telling you that you can call it Daffodil. It's only part of its name because a guardian angel's name has many, many letters. I don't think we could pronounce it or spell it.'

A young boy came up to ask a question and he did the exercise as well. He closed his eyes and asked his guardian angel what its name was. He said one word came into his mind and he named his guardian angel, Jack. He hoped that he was right with that name. I asked Angel Hosus what I should say. He told me to tell the little boy to ask the question to his guardian angel when he went back to his seat.

Another question was, 'What happens to my guardian angel when I die?'

I told them, 'Your guardian angel is yours and can never be anyone else's guardian angel. It goes back home to heaven with you.'

Another child asked a similar question so it gave me the opportunity to explain a little bit more.

I said, 'When your soul was in heaven, before you were in your mother's tummy, you met your guardian angel there. You and your guardian angel talked about many things and when the time came for you to be in your mother's tummy your guardian angel went with you.'

Many of the boys and girls asked what does a guardian angel look like? So for each one of them, I told them a little bit more about the appearance of a guardian angel. I would have loved to describe their guardian angels individually but I could not because we were not in the same room together. I said this to one of the boys.

He said, 'That's okay!'

I told him, 'Guardian angels are neither male nor female but sometimes they will give a male appearance or a female appearance. Sometimes they will give neither. They are about three steps behind you but yet, they are all around you. They are massive but yet, can look as if they are not much bigger than a human's physical body. A guardian angel looks different to all other angels. It is the light that comes from them. It's different from the light that comes from other angels. You know the way you would recognise a general in among hundreds of soldiers? It's the same with the guardian angels. They are just different. They have that special power of authority that other angels do not have because all other angels know that they are the gatekeeper of the soul of the person the guardian angel is with.

As the gatekeeper of a soul they guide it before birth, and help usher it through this life, but their most important job is to bring us back home to heaven.

When a child asked, 'Does my guardian angel always stay with me?' I said, 'Yes, your guardian angel never leaves you for one second, so you are never ever alone.'

They asked, 'Does everyone have a guardian angel?'

I explained, 'Yes. The reason why everyone has a guardian angel is because everyone has a soul, that speck of light of God, that fills every part of your body and being. Your guardian angel can never leave you for one second because they are the gatekeeper of your soul.'

The young students asked many more questions and it was

wonderful talking to them. The Skype broke down once or twice throughout but that didn't bother the students, or Natasha. She simply called me back and we connected again within a few minutes. I was talking with the children for about forty minutes or so. I hope they were happy with the answers. I look forward to talking to Natasha's students in Australia again. Please God, I will have that chance.

It's February and I have to travel to Maynooth for a meeting in two days.

My son, Christopher, gave me a call and he said, 'I heard, Mum, that you are going to be up in Maynooth on Tuesday.'

I said, 'Yes, I will be.' He asked if I was going to stay the night in his house.

I said to Christopher, 'What's up?'

He replied, 'There is a great picture on in the cinema. It's a comedy.'

He was just thinking would I like to go to it with him.

I said, 'I would love to. It's been a long time since we have gone to the pictures. What time do you finish work at, Christopher?'

He said, 'Not until seven o'clock. Could you pick me up after work and we go straight to the pictures, even though I will still be in my working clothes?'

I told him, 'That's great and I'm really looking forward to it.'

Christopher asked if I would not stay the night because it would be late. I told him no because I would prefer to head home. I don't mind the night-time driving. The roads are always quiet.

So two days later, I headed up to Maynooth for that meeting. I'd better explain. It would be about all the different things that are going on between publishers, interviews, talks, travel and so many other things. It would take hours and at the end of the day, my daughters, Ruth and Megan, and my son, Owen, myself and anyone else who needed to be there would be exhausted. Well, at least I would be. On that day, we got through an awful lot of work. I was looking forward to going to the pictures with Christopher. I love going to the pictures with Christopher. The films he picks are always action-packed and fast-moving, full of excitement. I guess I would never have really watched films too often in the past but now I definitely love action-packed movies, especially when they have a good story too. When we got to the new picture house at Liffey Valley, Christopher went to get the tickets. I went to get some popcorn, Maltesers and a drink to share.

While I was standing in the queue Christopher called me and said, 'Don't bother. We have to go to the next sitting. There are no two seats together.'

So we went into the restaurant next to the cinema and had something to eat. Then we went to the eight o'clock movie. It was very funny. Christopher had said to me earlier that it might be a little crude but he thought it'd be done in a nice way.

We came out of the pictures. I said to Christopher, 'That was brilliant. I really enjoyed it.' It was about superheroes. I said to him, 'It was done really stylishly. It was so funny.'

We drove home to Maynooth. Before Christopher got out of the car, he said, 'Mum, you look a bit uncomfortable when you're driving the car.'

I said to him, 'I've only had it a couple of weeks. It's a 2008 and a diesel. I have only driven it a few times but it's much better than my old car.'

He said, 'You seem to be holding the steering wheel a bit tight. Maybe it's not in the right position for you.'

He changed it and it made a big difference. He showed me how to change it back if I needed to and we said goodbye. He reminded me to make sure I sent a text when I got home safely.

I told him not to worry: 'I'll be fine.'

I got back to Kilkenny and drove in the gate. It was about twelve o'clock. The first thing I did was text Christopher saying I was home safe and putting the steering wheel in a different position made a huge difference.

I'm looking forward to going to the pictures again with Christopher but I know it might be months away because in a couple of days I am off to Africa. I have never been to Africa before and I'm really looking forward to it. Even though I'm excited I'm still a little scared but the angels tell me there is no need to worry. I am going with a group of other people and we are going to make a documentary. I don't know what this documentary is going to turn out like but hopefully it will move people's hearts to help to give any children suffering a better life, to put a smile on the children's faces. I have started my own charity to help these children and it's called the Lorna Byrne Children's Foundation. At the moment, I am helping three other charities – two abroad and one in Ireland. I hope that with the help of everyone out there we will be able to add another couple of charities to the list to help children because this is what God and the angels have asked me to do. Of course, I cannot do it on my own. I need your help. So I am hoping that you will look up the Lorna Byrne Children's Foundation and decide to donate. All donations make a difference no matter how small or big they are. Even the smallest donation is welcome. Hopefully, you might even donate every month to change a child's life.

Angel Hosus Sitting on my Bed With a Mysterious Book

I WAS AWAY IN ENGLAND DOING A TOUR IN 2016. I HAD one talk in Bournemouth, in Dorset and the other in Devon. I had only just come back from Ethiopia as well. I was quite exhausted on the morning of the twenty-second of March. I was snuggled under the blankets when I heard my name being called in a whisper. I peeped out from under the blankets, barely opening my eyes. What I saw was mostly just a bright light. Then I opened my eyes another little bit. There I saw Angel Hosus, 'sitting' at the top of my bed, where my pillows were, looking out the window.

I hadn't been sleeping on my pillows. I had moved myself down in the bed during the night and wrapped the blankets around me. I just wanted to stay where I was.

Angel Hosus turned his head and glanced at me with a smile on his face, saying, 'Good morning, Lorna.'

It was then that I noticed Angel Hosus had a book in his hand. There was no way that I could not notice the book he was reading. It looked big enough. He went back to reading it. Seeing Angel Hosus reading a book is really what woke me up because it made me curious. Even though Angel Hosus was sitting on my bed, no part of him was actually touching the mattress or the pillows. I know if you saw an angel sitting on your bed you would believe the angel was actually physically sitting on it as you would yourself, but God has always allowed me to see the space that is between these beautiful creatures, that God created, dividing our world from theirs. Many times, I have called this a cushion. It seems to come in all shapes and sizes. Again, that is why angels' feet don't actually touch the earth. I always like when angels do something like seem to sit on your bed or stand by it or sit on a chair in front of you.

Next time you are sitting at a table in your kitchen, having that little break, sipping a cup of tea, you can say to your guardian angel, 'It would be nice to have an angel to sit in the chair opposite me and you next to me, my guardian angel.'

Because maybe you could do with a teacher angel or an unemployed angel? Even though you won't be able to see the angels, trust that they will do this. The angels always did that with myself, many times around the table. From the time I was a child they would sit at the little table in front of the window in Old Kilmainham in Dublin.

This morning, as I threw the blankets off my head, I realised why the room was so bright. The first time I peeped out from under the blankets, I thought it was the sunlight coming in through the window and the radiant light from Angel Hosus. The blankets were shielding me from seeing more – what a surprise I got when I threw them off and saw that my bedroom was full of angels. There must've been about thirty in my room.

They all said in unison, 'Good morning, Lorna.'

I was now sitting up in my bed and I leaned forward, curious to see what book Angel Hosus had in his hand.

I turned to him and said, 'What are you reading?'

Angel Hosus continued to read the book. He just ignored me. I was sitting on the bed now with my knees up and my hands around my legs, hoping I could get Angel Hosus's attention by not getting out of the bed, but it didn't seem to work.

A few moments later he said, 'Get up, Lorna. It's time for you to start writing again. It has been a while since you did so. I know you have one more trip, to Taiwan and Hong Kong. But God would love you to write a little before you go.'

Angel Hosus had moved from the spot where he was sitting and moved right up to the headboard. I smiled because he had his legs crossed and he was holding the book he was reading in his left hand, and that made me smile even more. The book had a hard cover, that much I know. The colour was white with gold binding all around the edges but I couldn't see writing on the cover at all.

He looked up from the book and just as he was about to say to me 'Get up, Lorna' I said, 'I know. Okay, I will get up and get dressed but first of all, please tell me what you're reading.'

Angel Hosus turned to me as he closed the book and held it, in his left hand, close to his chest. He didn't turn his body around to me. He was sitting at an angle on the bed so now the book was completely out of sight, shielded by his hands.

He said to me, 'Lorna, I cannot tell you what I am reading. It is a book from God's library and it is very important for me to read it because God has me working with you, as do so many other angels.'

Then he lifted his cloak and tucked the book inside it on the left-hand side, about heart level in a human being.

I asked him, 'Do all the angels have to read that book?'

'Not this one, Lorna. This one *I* must read. God said that I had to take it from His library and from now on, I must carry it on my person.'

That is something I hadn't realised, or taken much notice of – that angels carry certain things with them.

Angel Hosus responded to me before I even thought to ask if angels carry things often.

He smiled at me and said, 'Not very often.'

I said to him, 'I know Archangel Michael carries the sword and shield always, even though it is only on rare occasions that I am allowed to see them.'

'No more questions. Up you get, Lorna.'

I thought for a moment, as I started to get out of the bed. Angel Hosus remained where he was.

I put on my dressing gown and I said to him, 'By the way, Angel Hosus, I hope you don't mind me asking you this question.'

I was ignoring what he said to me a few moments ago. I was taking the opportunity seeing as he had not moved from sitting on my bed.

Angel Hosus nodded his head and said, 'Okay, say what is on your mind, Lorna.'

'Archangel Michael. He's an archangel and stands on the throne of God. God has Michael in my life a lot as well as Archangel Gabriel and a few others, all archangels. Would they too have to read a particular book from God's library because God has put them in charge of my life? Am I saying that right, Angel Hosus?'

There was silence for a few minutes. Angel Hosus stood up and for a moment, the ceiling seemed to disappear. Then on my bedroom door there was a knock. I recognised the knock because, and this is something I have never told you, Archangel Michael often knocks. It sounds as if it is a million miles away but with each knock it gets closer. It is like a musical tune of deep notes like thunder. I turned and faced the door.

Archangel Michael walked in. He acknowledged with a bow the other angels that were in the room and they acknowledged him in return. Then they left but Angel Hosus remained standing by the bedroom window.

Archangel Michael came and stood in front of me and said, 'Good morning, Lorna.'

'I didn't call you, Archangel Michael, and yet, you are here. I'm glad to see you. It has been a while.'

'Yes, Lorna, it has for you, but not for me.'

Archangel Michael reached out and took my hand, filling me with that love and peace. 'Lorna, God sent me because of the question you asked. So say what is on your mind.'

'Archangel Michael, God has given Angel Hosus a book from His library.'

I looked over at Angel Hosus standing by the window. Angel Hosus walked towards us and said to Archangel Michael and myself that he had to go and then he disappeared. I was a little bit disappointed.

I said again, 'Archangel Michael, God has given Angel Hosus a book from His library.'

I know my voice must've sounded a little broken as then I lost my voice for a second. I gave a little cough and then said again about God giving Angel Hosus a book from God's library.

Archangel Michael replied, 'Yes, Lorna. God called Angel Hosus to the library to receive a particular book. Lorna, I'm not allowed to tell you very much, but you know yourself on many occasions you have been in God's presence and He has told you that no matter what has been written God can change his mind. That always depends on mankind and every decision that the leaders of the world make. Sometimes, if the world is not responding in the best way to what you do and say, God responds by changing His plans for you. The book Angel Hosus carries in his possession now has writing engraved on the pages by God about the changes that are happening within the journey of your life and the different paths that God sees that you may have to journey down, Lorna.'

'I wish you hadn't told me that, Archangel Michael. I'm not as strong as God thinks I am. I know He calls me His Bird of Love. With what has been happening in the world, at the moment it's very scary, and to know that things are changing and not knowing whether they are all for the better. I pray that most of these changes are for the good of the world.'

Archangel Michael held my two hands together and said, 'Lorna, look into my eyes. Why do you think God has you in the world at this time?'

I said to him, 'I don't know. I'm doing all that God has asked me to do. Even with all the changes in the world because of the choices and decisions mankind makes on behalf of the world. It doesn't matter. I will do it. I know He will never ask me to do anything wrong but to me, a lot of the time, it feels like it's a waste of time. It is as if I am talking to closed ears and people just don't want to hear how they can change this world into a beautiful place of love. A future full of peace. A magnificent future for the children of the future. Why didn't God pick someone else, Archangel Michael? If I was a man I believe and I know in my heart that I would be listened to. I would be called upon to help to guide the world in the right direction, but because

I am a woman I am looked down upon and not taken seriously. Why did God make me a woman? That I cannot understand, Archangel Michael.'

'Lorna, isn't it a woman, a mother, who nourishes and protects her children? Be quiet now, Lorna, and just listen. One thing that is in that book that Angel Hosus has, one message that God wants to give to you, is that you are to start to write a book that will not be published until after your death.'

I took a big deep breath and said, 'Archangel Michael, how can I possibly manage to do that when I find that there is not enough time in each day to do all of the things that God asks me to do every single day? Those things that people do not know about, and He wants me to write that as well as writing books for the world that are to be published now, especially the children's books?'

I had tears running down my cheeks. Archangel Michael reached up with his right hand and I saw he held a snow-white handkerchief. At least that is what it looked like. It was so bright, just like a light. As Archangel Michael touched my cheeks it felt so soft, like silk and velvet.

He said, 'Don't cry, Lorna. Remember, God has certain angels working with you and remember, I'm here too.'

That made me smile.

Archangel Michael spoke again, saying, 'Lorna, what's on your mind? Don't hesitate. Say it.'

'Okay,' I said, 'next time I'm in God's presence I know I need to ask Him about the Peacemaker.' The Peacemaker is an individual who will have a vital role to play in the course of world history, but I am not permitted to tell you about this individual yet. Soon, I hope.

I was waiting for Archangel Michael to say something but

he didn't say anything. He just held my two hands in his and we started to pray together. The touching of my soul and Archangel Michael's while praying creates a harmony, for a brief second, between myself and Archangel Michael, who has a place on the throne of God.

I don't know how much time passed, but when I stopped praying with Archangel Michael I noticed it was starting to get dark outside. Once you're in prayer, time can pass very quickly. Like the blinking of an eye.

I said to Archangel Michael, 'What about archangels like you? Does God get you to read a book to do with my life because you are in my life in such a way?'

Archangel Michael said, 'No, Lorna, but on occasion God will hand a scroll to me and yes, it will be about you and what is happening in the world at this time. The scroll contains instructions for me to pass on to you. You must keep on talking about peace, Lorna, and love. Continue talking about compassion, understanding, justice, freedom – and don't forget to add the birthrights of every child that is born to the world.'

I said to him, 'Maybe I should do that next? Every child is born defenceless and innocent.'

'Write in the morning when you get up, Lorna. Write it then. It's getting late now.'

Archangel Michael said he had to go and he let go of my hands, smiled at me and turned. It was as if he was walking down a path that was full of light. I knew the light was the light of heaven and the light coming from all the angels and from the souls of all our loved ones.

I was now standing in my bedroom. Archangel Michael was gone and I felt a little cold. It was getting dark. I thanked God for Michael's visit.

As I walked down the stairs I said, 'God, I don't actually quite understand everything. I don't believe that in my lifetime I will understand everything. I know when I go home to heaven to you it will all be very clear.'

Downstairs I opened the fridge and took out a container of mushroom soup. I poured it into a pot and put it upon the gas stove. I cut some nice bread that I had bought the day before. In no time at all, my meal was ready. I walked into the barn, which is what we call our living room as it used to be a barn before we renovated the house. I put my dinner on the little table and turned on the TV. The news was on. It was full of the horrors in the world that day. Hearing of the bombings at the airport and the metro station in Brussels was another blow to my heart. There are no words to console those families that were torn apart by the loss of a loved one and the injuries people suffered that day. I pray for all the families who are suffering from injuries and those who have lost their loved ones. We must not let terrorism become an everyday occurrence. All countries, all nationalities, all religions must stand together, become one, to conquer this evil and to bring back freedom to the people of the world so that people can travel in and out of countries to work in safety, so that children can go to school in safety. Think of all those men, women and children not getting to their destination, the terror and horror that terrorism has caused. The people of the world must pull together as one nation for freedom, peace and hope. Those things that all of mankind cherishes, that we hold in our hearts.

Yet as I watched I could see hope in among the bombing and terrorism. War anywhere in the world is wrong. We must always search for peaceful ways. We must never give up. We all must keep the light of hope burning for all of us. No matter how we may disagree about things. I know people, not just in Europe, but in other countries that have bombs going off, and where families have been killed. Lives are being shattered completely all of the time. It only breeds bitterness, hate and the want for revenge. This is where we must all, regardless of our religion or nationality, pull together to help the leaders of the world find the solutions. We must join together in prayer. Even as I write this now I know innocent lives have been taken. Innocent men, women and children are suffering. As Angel Hosus said, war is easy to make, peace is the hardest thing to keep. We all must pray for peace and join together as one nation, one unified people, who must not let hatred and anger grow in our children's hearts, children who are being affected by what is happening in the world today.

I know people are shocked but we must not turn a blind eye or say, 'Who cares?'

This happens every day. We must not allow ourselves to become accustomed to terrorism, war or any violence. We must always strive towards peace to give our children a future with love, justice and freedom. Your children have the right to a future, just as you have.

I started to cry sitting on the couch. I lost my appetite. Archangel Michael had only been with me a short while ago, upstairs, talking about love, peace and hope. We prayed together for all of the good things, for mankind to make this world a better place.

My guardian angel said, 'Change the channel on the TV.'

I did. It filled me with hope. There on the TV screen was a mother holding her child in her arms. The mother had a big smile on her face while she was talking to her child. Her child was laughing back at its mother and at that moment,

I could see all of the good that is in the world. The world is full of lots of hope and love. The image of the mother and child moved my heart. The programme was about family life in the country. One of the scenes was of a father walking across the yard with two young children running after him. They were full of joy and happiness at having the freedom to be children.

My guardian angel said to me, 'Now, Lorna, eat your food.'

I did and I enjoyed my mushroom soup and bread. I had planned that the first thing I would do the next morning would be to write about the birthrights of every child born in the world. I had promised Archangel Michael that I would do so but I had forgotten that my grandchildren were coming down for a few days. It was my guardian angel that reminded me and said that I better give the house a quick tidy before they arrived. I never got the chance that morning to write about the birthrights of every child that is born in the world. It was actually a few weeks later.

CHAPTER 12

Seeing Joe Again

I HAD ONLY ARRIVED BACK FROM LONDON ON THE twenty-fifth of March and my daughter, Ruth, was coming the next day to visit me with her children. After doing a quick tidy-up, I gave Ruth a call and asked around what time did she think she would get down to Kilkenny. She told me that Billy Bob, her son, didn't finish school until twelve. She would have everything already packed and they would leave straight away, so she guessed it would be around 2.30 p.m. I had to go into Kilkenny to get my hair done so I checked that she had a key for the house. When I was in the hairdressers I got a call from Ruth telling me that they hadn't arrived yet and to take my time. There was no hurry on either side. I told her I'd be another while yet. I asked if there was anything that was needed from the supermarket. She said no because they were only down for one night.

The next day, we headed up to Dublin as my daughter had an appointment for eleven o'clock. When we arrived in the town of Swords in County Dublin Ruth told the children to be good for their granny while she went to her appointment. We were beside a big shopping centre. We passed the time doing lots of walking and looking at the pretty things in the shops. It was cold but when the sun came out from behind the clouds it was lovely to feel the heat. On our walk around the shopping centre I was holding little Jessica's hand with Billy Bob walking beside me. He reminded me that this was an important day because I hadn't been to his home in a while.

'It is Grandad's anniversary,' he said. 'We can't forget to remind Mammy that we have to go to Woodies to get flowers and some bags of peat for Grandad's grave.'

I looked down at him and said, 'We won't forget. But we may have to go for something to eat first and I know Woodies is not far from here.' Woodies is a big hardware store and garden centre.

My heart was moved hearing my little grandson saying this to me. He never met his grandad but he knew all about him. We continued walking in the sunshine, but then it turned very cold so we headed back to the main entrance of the shopping centre.

Just as we were about to go in through the doors to get warm the children cried out, 'Mammy!' Ruth was back. They ran to her in excitement.

You would think she had been gone for hours. They reminded their mother about going to Woodies.

She said to them, 'Let's go for something to eat first.'

But the children insisted – Woodies first and then food after. So a few minutes later, we drove over there. The children helped to pick the flowers for planting at their grandad's grave. When that was done the children were very happy, so we went for food. Then we headed straight to Maynooth, through the town and up to the graveyard. The children got out of the car, full of excitement, and we carried all the stuff into the graveyard. Billy Bob was walking with me across the grass towards Joe's grave.

He said, 'Which one is Grandad's grave? It's hard to pick it out.'

I looked and said, 'There it is.'

As we got closer, I glanced around the graveyard. I saw around twenty angels. I knew they were waiting on people to come in and visit the graves of their loved ones. When we visit the grave of a loved one there are always angels around you, helping to comfort you and ease your pain. I've never passed a graveyard and not seen angels in it. The angels are not there for the dead, but for the living. It is only the human body that is buried in the ground. Their guardian angel has taken their soul lovingly to heaven.

When we were all at Joe's grave the children walked among the little white pebbles pulling the weeds out. With a small hand shovel I was taking the weeds out of the little sections where we were going to put the peat moss so the new plants would blossom later and have beautiful flowers. We need to take care like this, to grieve like this, showing signs of the love we have for the departed. Souls like to see us doing these things because they know it does us good.

I was working away when Billy Bob came over and stood beside me.

He said, 'Granny, do you want a helping hand?'

So I loosened the weeds and he pulled them out. I remember looking up and seeing my little granddaughter busy pulling weeds from among the white pebbles. She was so busy enjoying herself, helping and feeling the importance of what she was doing, even though she was so young.

I never shared this with my daughter or any of my family so I know this is the first time for them hearing the story. I just found it very hard that day. My heart was hurting. I felt very emotional. I was afraid if I told Ruth I would burst out crying. So now I will tell you what happened at the graveside. There was Jessica bent down, pulling weeds with her little fingers and feeling very proud whenever she pulled a weed out. She would hold it up and look at it with amazement. In her baby talk and touching the roots with her finger she asked what they were. She did not know exactly what the things dangling from the weed were but her mum explained to her that they were the roots of the weed. Jessica stood there for another moment looking at the weed she held up in her hand. Then she looked down at her feet and moved the stones. I didn't know what she was thinking or what she would do next. She walked over to the edge of her grandad's grave and threw the weed in her mum's direction. I watched her get back down on her hunkers as she found another weed to pull at. It was very tiny. It was then I heard my name called.

I looked up and saw the soul of Joe standing at the gravestone. My husband Joe died in March 2000. He was only forty-six. When I saw him at the gravestone he looked youthful and healthy again. He looked very handsome. He had one arm on the headstone, kneeling slightly over, looking down at her. Then he looked up and looked at all of us.

He gave a big smile and said, 'Hello.'

He stood there for a few moments, just watching his grandchildren. I was so moved because I had not asked or prayed that I would see Joe there at the grave but I knew he was letting me know that he was looking after them. I spoke to him silently, saying my other two little grandchildren could come but maybe it would be another day.

He said, 'They don't need to come. I'm there with them too.'

Ruth, busy sorting out the plants with Billy Bob, looked up in the direction of her little girl and called out to her that she was doing a great job. I can't express the way Joe looked at her with such love.

Joe turned to me and said, 'God just decided to give you a surprise, Lorna.'

When Joe was standing there for those few moments his grave was surrounded by angels. All I can say is a multitude of angels surrounded us all. Encircling us in a non-broken circle. The sun shone bright and warm.

I was distracted for a moment when my little grandson said, 'Gran, here's a nice flower to plant.'

He got down on his hunkers to make a hole in the peat to put the plant in. I helped him but when I looked back up Joe was gone. I was disappointed.

My granddaughter was now helping her mum take some plants out of the pots to be planted. We were all very busy. I was very moved. Every now and then, I would look up at Joe's headstone in the hopes that he would appear again but he didn't. I would be thinking of the way he stood at the headstone looking down at his granddaughter and then over at his grandson, how he was watching us all.

Later on, I know we'll have to explain more to the children that their grandad is not really there in the grave. His soul has gone to heaven. A grave is somewhere we can visit to remind us of our loved one. We feel we are still taking care of them by bringing them flowers, and looking after the grave helps with the grieving process. Even though my grandchildren didn't know Joe they are grieving in a different way the loss of the grandfather they have never met. I could see, on that day, how important it was for them to play their part, helping at their grandfather's grave. They were getting to know him in a spiritual way, knowing that their grandfather was in heaven with God.

There was one plant left and Billy Bob was about to give it to me when his mum said, 'No, we are going to bring that little plant up to baby Bridget's grave.'

I was very moved when I heard Ruth say this. I never expected her to think of baby Bridget's grave. I looked to my right to the wall of the graveyard where the car was parked and on the opposite side there was Archangel Michael. He was standing on the far side of the wall.

He spoke to me without words and said, 'Lorna, shortly you are going to meet an angel you have not seen in a long time.'

I didn't get a chance even to say hello or to ask questions because immediately after Archangel Michael spoke he disappeared. I didn't know what it was all about but I was happy that my daughter thought of baby Bridget's grave and of keeping one of the flowers to plant up at her grave.

Now I have something important to share with you of what happened next. Something that was completely unexpected for me. The angel that Archangel Michael spoke about was a complete surprise to me. Let me start with this part of the story first. It brings happiness and tears to my eyes. It really emotionally pulls at my heartstrings. I'm only going to tell you what happened on this particular day in Maynooth graveyard with my daughter and grandchildren. I know I have to give you a little bit of information that happened many years ago too but it's only going to be a sentence or two.

Many years ago baby Bridget's little body was found by a man walking his dog. I have written about this in *Angels in*

My Hair. It's the spiritual journey about baby Bridget and what happened before her little body was found. I know you will find it very moving but now I will go back to this particular day in question.

On that day at the graveyard, on March 2016, Ruth gathered up a couple of things from the ground and took Jessica's hand. Billy Bob carried the flower, holding it with his two hands, and they walked towards baby Bridget's grave. I watched them go and finished tidying up where I had been planting flowers at Joe's grave.

Ruth shouted back to me, 'Mam, hurry up!'

'Okay,' I said, 'I'm coming.'

I reached down, picked up my bag and started to follow them. Just before they reached baby Bridget's grave I stopped walking, and just stood there looking in the direction of the grave. I saw an angel standing by her grave who I have not seen since the day I met him on the bridge in Maynooth, years before Joe's death. It was Angel Arabic. He is the angel that as a teenager I went to meet every day on the bridge when I walked down to Maynooth village. He told me about baby Bridget before she was born. He was tall, slender, elegant and whiter than snow. Angel Arabic glowed like a radiant light. He stood to the right of baby Bridget's headstone.

'Hello, Lorna,' he said.

I said hello in return without using words. Ruth and the children were already at baby Bridget's grave.

Angel Arabic said, 'Come.'

I started to walk slowly and just when I was a few feet away the soul of baby Bridget, some people might say her spirit, peeped out from behind Angel Arabic. Baby Bridget gave a human appearance of a little girl who was about four years old with long wavy hair to her shoulders. She appeared to be wearing a little blue dress that just glowed and her feet were bare. She was giggling as she watched Jessica and Billy Bob playing. It was only for a few moments, yet standing there watching the soul of baby Bridget felt like an eternity.

Angel Arabic spoke to me without words. 'Lorna, we have to go now.'

At that moment baby Bridget looked at me with a big smile and at the same time changed her human appearance from that of a child to a teenager and then to a young woman. She was very beautiful.

I said to Angel Arabic, 'Will I see you again?'

He replied, 'Maybe.'

I asked if I would see baby Bridget again and Angel Arabic said, 'No. Only if God changes His mind.'

The two of them disappeared. Baby Bridget's little body was found in the canal in Maynooth. The angels brought her soul to my house in the early hours of the morning on the day her little body was found. For the few days before that the angels were lining the path from the canal, along the bridge and to my front door so that her soul could travel to me. I do believe that Angel Arabic appeared on that particular day with baby Bridget not only for me but for her mother and for her family to let them know that she is happy and that she loves them. Bridget is safe in heaven.

The little flower was planted on baby Bridget's grave. My grandchildren were happy they had done this. We all walked back to Joe's grave. I picked up all the weeds and put them in the bin that was provided at the graveyard. When we were finished we walked out of the graveyard hurriedly as it was starting to rain.

Later that evening I headed back home to Kilkenny. On the way home in the car I said a prayer for all of baby Bridget's family. One of the other things I thought about was the birthrights of every child. About half an hour after I arrived home, quite late, I made myself a cup of tea and then went to bed. I always keep a jotter on the little table beside my bed. I said my prayers. When I was finished I decided I would start to scribble things down in the jotter before going to sleep. Just a few little things mind you. You wouldn't be able to read it because it was more or less in my code that I understand. As you know, I'm not very good at spelling. It only took me a few minutes to write down a few notes and then I fell asleep.

Over the next few days I did very little writing of this book because I had a few visitors calling to the house. I had lots of other writing to do though: my newsletter, Facebook posts, tweets and Instagram posts and, of course, work with my charity, the Lorna Byrne Children's Foundation. There were a fair few meetings as well. Of course I am a mother like all the mothers out there with cleaning, washing and gardening to do. I also try to get out for a walk as often as possible. The angels are always at me to get out and go for a walk, to help to keep myself fit, but it rains an awful lot in Ireland so I don't get out very often.

CHAPTER 13

The Birthrights of Children

I THINK IT WAS ABOUT NINE O'CLOCK AT NIGHT WHEN Angel Hosus walked into the room and said, 'Lorna, I see you are thinking about writing what Archangel Michael reminded you of: the birthrights of children.'

I was delighted to see Angel Hosus. I said, 'Hi.'

He replied, 'Don't just think about it, Lorna. Go upstairs and get your jotter and pen. You should start to think out loud.'

Without hesitation I jumped up off the couch. I hurried past Angel Hosus before running upstairs into my bedroom and grabbing the jotter and pen that were on the little table beside my bed. The Bible is beside my bed as well.

My guardian angel said to me, 'Lorna, open the Bible.'

As I reached down to open it I said a little prayer as I always do, 'God guide me to where you want me to read and please let my guardian angel help me.'

I opened the Bible, flicking through the pages, stopping when I heard my guardian angel's voice saying, 'Stop there, Lorna.'

Another few pages slipped through my fingers, but that

was all right because on the particular page that opened was the Gospel of Luke about the birth of Jesus. My guardian angel helped me to read it. I will tell you about the part that sticks in my mind. It is not the exact words that are in the Bible. Joseph and Mary were in Bethlehem. Mary was pregnant and the time had come for her to give birth to her baby. She gave birth to a son, wrapped him in strips of cloth and placed him in a manger because there was no room for them to stay in the inn.

When I finished reading it I blessed myself and I said, 'Thank you, God.'

(I have been asked what a blessing is. When a priest asks for God to bless the people at the end of a service, he is asking God to touch them with His love and fill them with it, to give them strength and faith when they go out into the world again. A blessing can transform a person, all of that person, including the physical body. When I bless people at the end of my speaking events, something happens in addition to this, but I am not permitted to tell you. If I did, I would have a queue of millions! I know you will be allowed to know more and that someone I have chosen will share this information with the world after my death.)

I ran back down the stairs and as I walked into the barn there was Angel Hosus standing by the fire.

I said to him, 'I hope you're not cold.'

He laughed. 'No, Lorna, I don't feel the cold.'

I said, 'No, and I know you don't feel heat either from the fire but it just kind of looks funny seeing you standing by the fire and imagining maybe you feel cold.'

Angel Hosus made me laugh because he started to shake himself as if he was shivering and rubbed his hands together as he turned to face the fire as if to get himself warm. He had his back to me and then all of a sudden, without him saying a word, he swirled back around to face me. As he did this his cape moved in slow motion, spiralling like waves in the air. It changed colour. Instead of black on the outside as it was earlier, Angel Hosus's cape became this beautiful golden colour with purple lining on the inside.

I said to him, 'I love when you do that because when your cape moves like that and sometimes when you swirl it with your arm it is as if I am seeing a multitude of capes. It is sometimes dazzling. I can see a multitude of colours like a rainbow when you do that.'

I always feel privileged when Angel Hosus does that with his cape. He doesn't do it very often. It may be only ten times or so in my whole lifetime that he has done this. It is something very incredible to see. Now I'm giving you a little bit more information about what Angel Hosus does.

Angel Hosus moved away from the fire. It seemed to burn brighter. It was lashing rain outside and I could hear the wind howling. I sat on the couch with Angel Hosus standing a few feet away from me. I had the jotter and pen in my hand.

I looked to him and asked, 'Where should I start?'

He answered, 'Lorna, you have been thinking about the birthrights of every child that is born for quite some time now. Think out loud and as you do so, scribble down your thoughts on your jotter, but first of all, let's pray together for a moment.'

I said to Angel Hosus, 'Last time I did that with Archangel Michael an awful lot of time passed.'

Angel Hosus said, 'Today, it will only feel like a few seconds and that is all it will be for you, Lorna.'

Angel Hosus stepped closer. I put my jotter and pen on

the couch beside me. Angel Hosus knelt down on one knee. He reached out and took my two hands in his and we started to pray. When we stopped I realised Angel Hosus was correct. Only about sixty seconds had passed.

Being in prayer is like eternity. This is something else that I have never shared with you before. When I emerge from deep prayer I have little sense of how much time has passed, because I have been in a place where there is no time, and the soul continues to pray even when I emerge back into the world.

Prayer is extremely powerful, even if you only pray for one second. I have never told you that every time before I write I pray and the angels that are with me do so also. Of course every time someone prays the Angels of Prayer always pray with you, as well as your guardian angel, so you never pray alone. They are like a gigantic upside-down waterfall full of angels going up to heaven, enhancing our prayers.

When we finished praying Angel Hosus stood up. He just stood there as I spoke out loud my thoughts and wrote them down in the jotter. When I was finished Angel Hosus told me that he had to go and he disappeared. I looked at all the scribbles I had made in the jotter and went upstairs. I put them beside my computer but decided to do no more for the night.

It was the next morning when I sat down in front of the computer and started to read what I had scribbled in the jotter. I went over what I had written a few nights previously as well, and then started to speak into my computer. The words printed out on the screen in front of me. The room was full of angels but they never said a word. Angel Hosus wasn't there at that time.

The birthrights of every child born in the world.

Regardless of whether a family is rich or poor, everything

must be equal for every child born into the world. These children should have the following rights upheld.

1. Every child has the right to life.
2. Every child has the right to be a child.
3. Every child has the right to be treated equally.
4. Every child has the right to not be discriminated against because of religious beliefs or creed.
5. Every child has the right to be loved and cared for.
6. Every child has the right to be part of a family.
7. Every child has the right to have a home.
8. Every child has the right to have food and water.
9. Every child has the right to clothing and warmth.
10. Every child has the right to breathe clean air.
11. Every child has the right for nature to exist.
12. Every child has the right to be happy, to laugh and play in a safe environment.
13. Every child has the right to be born into a peaceful world.
14. Every child has the right to be free and not to be a slave.
15. Every child has the right not to live in fear or terror.
16. Every child has the right to a full education.
17. Every child has the right to reach their potential.
18. Every child has the right to full medical care.
19. Every child has the right to participate in all sports.
20. Every child has the right to see and touch trees, plants, animals, rivers and lakes and to see them free of pollution.
21. Every child has the right to have their rights as a child to be put first, before money and material things, because every child is the biggest and most precious asset of mankind.

I know the United Nations have written some documents on the birthrights of every child born in the world, but these birthrights are not acted upon in any way. We have children all over the world who are suffering today. Children don't seem to have any rights. They can be murdered. They are discriminated against in a multitude of ways because of their background, perhaps because of their family's religious beliefs or creed. Children are abducted and turned into sexual slaves or starved to death and allowed to die of thirst and cold. Children are denied the basic things of life. Governments and the leaders of the world are enslaving the children of the world today. They count how much it would cost to give these birthrights to every child born in the world today. We could start at any time, as all nations learn to act together, so that we all feel connected, one global people, and give the same birthrights to every child born across the world, but I don't see it happening in the near future. I wish I did. I know this is where the women of the world need to stand up and play our part and become the mothers of all the children of the world. Children are defenceless and innocent. They don't have a voice to speak for them, so this is why we must stand up for them. I take every opportunity I possibly can, through the books I write and through the media, to call for peace, justice and freedom. I call out to all the women of the world to save the children of the world, yours and mine. Be their voice.

On different occasions in my life when I have been in the presence of God He has always reminded me of the time Jesus was crucified. It is in the Gospel of Matthew. He shows me a very small scene, as if I'm looking out a window, of when Jesus is being rushed away and surrounded by soldiers.

He sees a group of women crying for him and Jesus says to them, 'Don't weep for me, but weep for yourselves and your children.'

That is all I see and these are the only words I hear. Children are innocent and defenceless. We are all mothers, whether we have children or not. I pray that one day all women will be the voice for the children of the world. I am going to stop now, just for a moment, and say a prayer for peace in the world as the angels surround me. I bow my head and go into a meditative state of prayer.

I heard my name being called: 'Lorna, can you hear me?'

I said, 'Yes.'

I lifted my head slowly as I came out of prayer. I made the sign of the cross and opened my eyes. It was my guardian angel.

'God told me to call, Lorna, and to tell you to remember that He always hears your prayers.'

I said to my guardian angel, 'Would you come downstairs and have a cup of tea with me?'

My guardian angel laughed at me. 'Of course I will go with you, Lorna. You know I cannot leave you for one second.'

'I know,' I said, 'but it's nice to invite you to have a cup of tea with me.'

So we went downstairs and made a cup of tea.

I went out into the sunshine and sat at the table in the garden. While I was out in the garden I couldn't even hear the sound of a bird. There was complete silence. If you dropped a pin, you would have heard it. I didn't even hear sound in the distance.

I said to my guardian angel, 'Have you done that? Have you blocked out all the sounds that are around me?'

My guardian angel said, 'Yes.'

I asked why and my guardian angel said, 'Because God said you need some stillness around you.'

I didn't say another word. I needed my guardian angel. I

just sat there, in the complete silence with the heat of the sun shining on me, sipping my tea and enjoying every moment. Half an hour later I went upstairs and sat at the computer. I was just about to start to speak when three angels walked into the room.

I said, 'Hello.'

One of the angels went over and sat on the pink exercise ball. This angel gave a female appearance. The other two gave neither male or female. They were all dressed in silver.

The angel that sat on the pink exercise ball said to me, 'Lorna, look out the window.'

I smiled because her clothing changed to a beautiful pink to match the exercise ball. I swivelled around in my chair and looked out the window from the upstairs room where I was working. Holly, our pet dog, started to bark as well as some other dogs that were passing with their owner. They always stop to say hello to Holly and she loves it. She flies around the garden with excitement and then at the little gate, she stops and says hello to the other dogs. They nearly always do the same, with their tails wagging while they make little soft grunting sounds, which I can hear through the open window. When the owner of the two dogs continued on their journey Holly ran around the garden again. I could see how happy Holly was. I had her at the groomers on Saturday and she had her coat cut tight. As she ran around the garden, I burst out laughing because I saw an unemployed angel running after her. I said to my guardian angel, 'That looks like Holly knows the unemployed angel is playing with her.'

My guardian angel said, 'Yes, Lorna. Holly is very aware of the angel.'

Holly stopped and sat flat down on the grass. The angel playing with her disappeared.

I'm always telling people that animals don't have individual guardian angels and that animals don't have souls, but if you love your pet so much God will have it in heaven for you. At times God may allow you to feel the presence of your pet. If you're going through a hard time in your life, God may use an animal as a sign to help to guide you to make the right decisions. Angels are always with animals when they are in trouble, helping to comfort them, taking away their fear. Angel Hosus told me many times that we, ourselves, are meant to be the guardian angels of all of nature and of all the animals. God has His angels reminding us time and time again to look after the animals and nature, to look after the planet. In recent times – the past few months – I have been seeing Angel Jimazen almost every day. This is because these days there is a greater danger of environmental catastrophe. I call him the gatekeeper of the earth. He is doing everything possible to keep Mother Earth alive but it's very hard when we keep on pouring pollution into the air, into the rivers and lakes, destroying all the life of our beautiful planet that was given to us as a gift. When you are given something that is free, you don't have any appreciation for it, and treat it as if it is replaceable, but the earth is not replaceable. Neither is nature or all of the animals and the birds of the sky. Next time you're out for a walk or looking out your window or maybe driving your car or sitting on a bus, just try to recognise the beautiful gift that you have been given and realise that you must take care of it. That would help Angel Jimazen. We all have to speak up and keep pressure on our governments and leaders about global warming. We are all feeling the effects of it right across the world.

It was the twelfth of April and that morning here in Ireland, the sun was shining. It was an absolutely fabulous day. I went out into the garden with a cup of tea in my hand and a slice of toast. It was about 12.30 p.m. I walked around the garden, and as I looked over the fence, I saw loads of dandelions blossoming. It is the beautiful yellow flower that my rabbit, Mimsy, loves so I decided that as soon as I finished my toast and tea I would go and pick her some. I have noticed that the dandelion plant is changing, even the blossom.

I just said to the angels that were around me, 'I hope this is not because of global warming or that something genetically has got into the dandelion and changed it.'

The angels didn't answer me so I gathered a handful. My rabbit is still eating them so that is a good sign.

CHAPTER 14

A Visit to Sainte-Chapelle

ANGEL HOSUS SAID TO ME THE OTHER DAY, WHILE I WAS kind of giving out to him because I didn't know exactly where to start, 'Lorna, we are always telling you but at times you will not listen. It is that stubborn streak of yours, Lorna, when it kicks in.'

Angel Hosus started to laugh. It seemed to rock the room and it made me laugh too.

Angel Hosus came over and stood beside my chair in front of my computer with a big smile on his face.

I said to him, 'You did enjoy laughing at me.'

He didn't respond and instead just said, 'Pay attention. Give Megan a call. She's just out of her lecture in college. You just missed her call to you. She will give you encouragement, especially when you won't listen to us.'

I turned to Angel Hosus and said, 'I do listen to you, all the time.'

'Lorna,' he replied with an even bigger smile on his face this time – I thought he was about to laugh again – 'I was telling you to write that story but the whole time you were looking for an excuse not to. You were putting it off.'

Every time Angel Hosus smiles at me it makes me smile back and feel happy. I could see the funny side to everything now.

He said, 'Lorna, how many times have you looked back at the piece you wrote a few weeks ago?'

I know I do that a lot and Angel Hosus is always telling me to stop doing that.

I picked up my mobile phone and saw the missed call from Megan. I gave her a call back. I was telling her about Angel Hosus and how he was laughing at me and telling me I was stubborn at times. I even told her how he said that I was to give her a call for her to give me encouragement.

My daughter laughed at me over the phone as well and said, 'That's funny because, Mam, Angel Hosus is right. You are very stubborn at times.'

Megan shared some of the things she was going to be doing that day. She had another lecture around four o'clock, and afterwards, she was going to meet a friend.

We talked for about ten minutes and then Megan said to me, 'Mam, I will say what Angel Hosus says to you. Get back to work. Start writing!'

The two of us laughed over the phone and said goodbye.

A number of years ago when I went to Paris with Christopher and Megan, one of the chapels we visited was called Sainte-Chapelle. When I walked into that church it was like walking into the past, hundreds of years ago. It was beautiful and full of angels – but also very cold. It was like walking into an ice cube.

The angels walked around the church in a line, one behind the other, carrying little lights like candles. The angels did not have all the candles burning at the same time. These tiny candles, which they held in their right hands, burned a beautiful glowing light that seemed to shimmer around this ancient church. It was a holy place where prayers were said and the angels were continuing to say the prayers of the past.

The angels seemed to be chanting in prayer. I didn't understand why I was feeling so cold. I was mesmerised though, watching these magnificent angels carrying the little candles as they walked around this tiny church praying. It was like a never-ending chorus; soothing and peaceful. I found that I too was going into a meditative state of prayer.

What may have only been a few minutes had passed when the angel walking a little behind me, just to the right of my vision, whispered in my ear, 'Lorna, you must not go into a fully meditative state of prayer.'

When you are in a meditative state of prayer you have allowed a connection between your soul and your human self. Your body becomes light, almost as if it doesn't exist. In this deep state of prayer no other thoughts can come to you, you can't hear a sound. Nothing from outside can penetrate it and you become aware that you are in a place you've already been to.

The angel touched my hand and at that moment I started to come out of the meditative state of prayer. When I heard the angel's voice whispering in my ear again it was standing behind me. As I came out of that meditative state of prayer, slowly but not fully, I turned to face the angel. I could not see this angel clearly. I want to say something but I found I couldn't.

I knew my soul was still in prayer and the angel spoke. 'Good things and bad things do happen in holy places, Lorna. Allow yourself to feel the love that is here too and not just the bad things that happened. That is why you feel a little cold and uneasy.'

It was when those words were said that I realised that it

was Archangel Michael walking beside me. I realised, too, that he was dressed in armour.

I wanted to ask lots of questions but I knew there was no need to. Not now anyway, because my soul was still in prayer. Later, perhaps. As I walked around slowly with Archangel Michael walking beside me I started to follow the angels that were carrying the lighted candles as they circled the nave, and I listened to their chant of prayer. I looked, too, at the carvings and symbols that were on the walls. I walked around the church a few times, downstairs and then upstairs. I would never have got bored. But then Archangel Michael whispered that it was time to go downstairs. At the same time Christopher and Megan called me to follow them back down. As I walked downstairs the angels walked ahead of me. Christopher and Megan had already gone down the ancient stairs. I walked slowly. I felt as if I was walking in the past again and I watched the angels walking around the walls of this part of the church, carrying lights as they did up above in the upper part of the church.

I was going to continue to follow the angels ahead of me but Archangel Michael said I was to follow him. I did so. He stopped at one point and showed me that there were steps underneath, covered over by stone slabs, leading down to a holy, a sacred place that had been forgotten about and been lost over time. But local people would still come in to pray at this spot, and so too would tourists like ourselves, sensing the holiness of the place. I knew my soul was in constant prayer – I could hear it – as I walked around with Archangel Michael.

When he said, 'Lorna, look to your right,' I turned around and I saw souls of the past coming into that part of the church. Some of them seemed to be soldiers by the way they were dressed. They seemed to genuflect and pray for a moment and then leave. There were men and women, civilians, the ordinary people of that town who would have come into this church to pray long ago. Most of them seemed to be dressed in dark clothing. I don't know why. Then they disappeared. Archangel Michael told me to walk a little further. I did as he said and then I stopped. As I did I looked around. I saw Christopher and Megan talking about things they were looking at, carvings of statues and symbols. Everybody was talking very quietly, respectfully, because it was a church. It was a place of prayer and you could feel that peace, calmness, security and safety that a place of prayer gives regardless of which religion is celebrated there.

I started to walk again and Archangel Michael walked beside me. The angels were still walking around the church, carrying those little candles and chanting in prayer, when I looked up because I heard a scraping sound. As I did the church seemed to darken as if it was dusk. The sound I heard was a soul of the past walking into the church. I could hardly see. Archangel Michael touched my hand and from that moment on the soul that had walked into the church became brighter. I'm not exactly sure what direction he came from but he was walking down to the front of the church slowly and heavily. It was as if his human body – when he lived – had been very tired, even exhausted on the day he walked into this church. The noise I heard was his sword. It seemed to scrape along the ground. He was dressed in armour, very heavy and with lots of straps. He seemed tall to me and he seemed to be blocky but that could have been because of the clothing he was wearing. It seemed very heavy and cumbersome. With every step he took it was as if he had a huge weight on his shoulders and was hardly able to carry it. It was a complete struggle. When the soul of this man passed me by I looked around and realised that now I could not see anyone else. I was actually standing in the past with Archangel Michael holding my hand.

I was in the past, watching the life of the soldier on the day he walked into this church. I started to feel his hurt and pain. His agony was ripping through him, his horrors and his guilt. He was now only about six feet in front of me, and suddenly he stopped and fell to his knees. He was crouched over as if he was in great pain. He was sobbing deeply within himself. His whole body seemed to shake. He started to cry out loud, begging God for forgiveness for what he had just done. This soldier prayed with all his being. He prayed from the depths of his soul. The anguish of the pain from knowing what he had just done was ripping through him and tearing him apart. I saw his soul come forward for a moment and then step back into his human body. I could see that on that day, in that church, he begged God for forgiveness.

Seeing the pain he had caused by the horrible things he had done, he was in a state of shock. I saw images appearing in his mind of Jerusalem, of war against Muslims, the faces of children looking up at him in terror before he mercilessly cut them down.

Some of the words I was allowed to hear were, 'Look at what I have done. Look at the blood upon my hands that can never be washed off.' He was looking for the good parts in his life, but they were hard for him to find. I knew then that his soul had come forward and I was being shown these things so that I could tell you and you could understand his anguish. He understood that during the Crusades he had killed many and that in every instance he had killed a spiritual being, one of God's children.

He was still on his knees in prayer when four angels came

up to him carrying what looked to me like a fine piece of silk. An angel was at each corner holding it up high as it shimmered. As they moved towards him, I could see through it. It was full of reflections. These reflections, these images, were of his life but they were the reflections of all the love that was in his life and of all the comfort. The angels allowed it to flow down upon him gently and wrapped the silk around him, comforting him. At that very moment, he seemed to take a deep breath as if life was poured back into him. But now he was feeling that the comfort God had granted him was giving him the strength that he needed to make right the wrongs he had done.

The soldier started to stand up. It seemed to be a great struggle for him to do so. He still seemed to be heavily burdened down and carrying a huge cross upon his shoulders.

I was told to stand still as he passed me by and I heard him mutter, 'Please forgive me.' I could see that he was having a spiritual awakening, that even though this soldier had done horrific things, God still forgave him, and the soldier went to heaven.

Then he seemed to walk slowly out into the darkness, and he disappeared. I knew it had been already starting to get dark when he went to the church to ask God for forgiveness. I also knew that when he left it was completely dark outside. By then, it was night for him.

I looked back to where he had fallen on his knees to ask God for forgiveness and I saw two angels standing there in prayer. They were dressed in gold.

I asked Archangel Michael, 'Why are they standing on the spot where the soldier was upon his knees?'

Archangel Michael said, 'The angels pray for peace. What happened to that soldier, Lorna, still happens today. It's important to pray for peace. God always wants you, Lorna, to keep on talking about peace. When that soldier died God took him to heaven.'

Just then, Megan and Christopher came over. They were wondering why I was standing there but I knew they knew in a way. One thing we all must remember about the great sacred and holy sites around the world, places we sometimes call spiritual places, such as Stonehenge or the great temples of Greece and Rome, is that in the past most of them were also used as places for trials and execution. They still are today. You only have to listen to the news to realise this. People in power always want to control the holy places.

I want you to remember that prayer is powerful so please pray for peace. Always add peace to your prayers regardless of what religion you belong to. Always strive towards peace no matter what is happening in your life or around the world.

We enjoyed walking around Paris. We visited a few places that Mark, my editor, had told us we should go to. We had a great few days in Paris. We visited many places and the people were very friendly. Christopher and Megan knew some French. I'm afraid I did not have a word of French, but I did try. I think it is a beautiful language. To me it sounds sweet like a soft melody. When I hear the French people speaking French it sounds to me like they are singing.

I said that to my daughter Megan, and she laughed, saying, 'The whole world thinks of French like that. It is known for being melodic and romantic. I love listening to it.'

I said to her, 'I love it too. All you have to do is just listen and let yourself hear the notes of the language.'

Hopefully, some day I will be able to visit Paris again. I would love to revisit Sainte-Chapelle. At the time we were there they were doing a lot of repairs, trying to save as much of the holy place as they could.

CHAPTER 15

Have Angels Been Made Trivial and Commercial?

I HAVE BEEN TALKING WITH THE ANGELS OVER THE LAST few years about what to put into this book – about my life and about them and about God. On different occasions I have talked to Archangel Michael about it. He's just reminded me about the time I met him when I had gone for a walk during my holidays. I was walking up along the canal I had visited many years ago. It was a place where Joe and I had sometimes been. As a young child and even as a teenager I had often fished along this stretch as well, with my dad and Arthur Mason.

I always remember the day I was there with Joe and my dad. We weren't married at the time.

The angels said to me, 'Lorna, go for a walk up along the canal and leave your dad and Joe to fish.'

I said to the angels, 'I can't just walk off. What excuse can I make?'

They didn't answer me. 'Okay,' I said. 'I'll just say I'm going to go up along the canal to see can I find some berries.'

So I went over to the boot of the car and I took a cup out

and said to Joe and my dad, 'I think I'll go up along the canal. I might find some berries to pick.'

They didn't take much notice of me.

They more or less nodded their heads as they prepared the fishing rods and muttered, 'Yes.'

So I walked off. After walking a short distance I stopped and looked back. I saw my dad talking to Joe and they both had fishing rods in their hands, ready to cast out. Then I heard my name being called. So I started to walk again. I don't know how far I had walked when I came across some small trees. The angels told me to wait there. While I was waiting I started to look for some berries. I didn't ask the angels. A few minutes later I heard my name being called again, from in among the trees, so I peered in. I smiled as Archangel Michael walked out of the trees and stepped up on to the bank.

I loved the way Archangel Michael would sometimes dress like a fisherman. I smiled at him and said, 'You know, Michael, you don't need those big wellies for today. None of the fishermen have to go into the water.'

Archangel Michael said, 'I know, Lorna.'

Suddenly, his welly boots disappeared and on his feet appeared an old pair of shoes looking quite tattered and faded.

I said to him, 'I wish I could change my clothes like that. It sure would be handy.'

Archangel Michael didn't answer me. He just said, 'Lorna,' as he walked towards the canal bank with the fishing rod in his hand, 'I'm here to remind you that one day you're going to write about God and us.'

I said to him, 'I hope you don't mean me.'

'Lorna, when I say you, God and us, I mean God and us

angels and yes, you and your life. But God wants me to give you another message. A time will come when God will allow you to see through His eyes. God may allow you to tell the world at some stage.'

I said to Archangel Michael, 'What do you mean?'

I was quite shocked by his words and in a whispered voice I said, 'Through God's eyes?'

'Yes,' Michael answered as he smiled at me and reached out and touched my hand and filled me with peace and love.

I was just about to ask a question when he said he had to go and just before he disappeared he reminded me to pray.

From that day on I have prayed about this message that Archangel Michael had given me. I guess I was quite terrified and afraid. Afraid of what God might allow me to see through His eyes.

I walked slowly back towards my dad and Joe. I did find a few berries on the way. Joe had caught a small pike and he was very proud of himself. I am allowed to tell you some of the things that God has allowed me to see through his eyes but I'm not going to tell you just yet. You have to wait.

About two years ago I was at home on my own. Megan was up in Dublin with her sister.

I was upstairs doing some ironing that I needed to catch up on when an angel peeped its head around the door and just said, 'Hello, Lorna' and disappeared.

It happened so quickly. I wasn't sure whether I recognised the angel or not and just continued ironing. About half an hour later when all the ironing was done I decided I deserved a cup of tea and went downstairs. As I walked into the barn with the cup of tea in my hand I got a surprise. Sitting at the table were Angel Hosus, Angel Elijah and Angel Bloema. (Angel

Bloema always gives a female appearance, dressed in a beautiful sky-blue silk. This angel has often accompanied the other angels that are always in my life. She often joins in the conversation but I've never asked her why she is here with me.)

'Hello, Lorna,' they said simultaneously.

I replied, 'This is a surprise. What are you doing here?'

'We've come to talk to you about us.'

'You mean you angels?'

'Yes,' said Angel Hosus, so I pulled out a chair and sat at the table with them and started to sip my cup of tea.

I realised I never offered the angels tea, so I said, 'Oh, sorry! Would you angels like a cup of tea? If I had known you were coming I would have put some cups out like I did years ago. I know you don't drink tea anyway.'

All the angels shook their heads and said, 'No, Lorna, we don't.'

They all gave me a big smile. Angel Hosus made me laugh when a cup appeared in front of him and he mimicked drinking from it.

'Lorna,' said Angel Hosus, 'you will be starting to write your book in a year or two.'

'I hope so,' I said.

'There is one thing that always concerns you, something that we know has particularly been on your mind lately.'

'Yes,' I said to Angel Hosus. 'Why you angels are not acknowledged or taken seriously.'

I laughed. 'I feel so embarrassed, saying all this, but you angels are considered trivial and it's hurting me to say this to you.'

The next moment I felt a hand on my shoulder. It was Archangel Michael.

He said, 'Hello, Lorna.'

'Hello, Michael,' I said, 'I'm glad you're here.'

'We want you to speak about this, Lorna, and we will help you to do so.'

'Oh, Michael. I really feel so ashamed knowing that millions of people around the world think this way of you angels and I know it is because they are ashamed that if they admit that they know they have a guardian angel or any angel that they would be ridiculed and laughed at themselves. I know I felt that way too. I think I was so afraid to talk about God and you angels.'

'Write what you have just said, Lorna.'

Archangel Michael said he had to go and disappeared.

I said to the other angels at the table, 'Do you have to leave as well?'

'No,' they said, 'we can stay for another little while to talk to you.'

Angel Elijah said, 'Write about angels becoming commercial, the good and the bad of it.'

Then Angel Hosus spoke to me about some of the different ways angels are being used as symbols, the way that symbols of angels have been commercialised even to the point of being big business – and the way that religion itself is becoming commercialised too. We talked together for another while and then they too said they had to go and disappeared.

So two years later, I'm up sitting at my computer, wondering how I can touch on the subject. I don't want to offend anybody. Again, I'm not in the room alone. The angels are with me and today is a wet, chilly day. As I look out the window, the mountains are misty. I have seen a few sheep in the fields with little lambs and they lifted my heart with joy. Just seeing them jumping around like little lambs jump with all four legs off the ground. When I need a break from writing

I do bits of housework, washing the dishes or putting on a clothes wash and, of course, have many cups of tea.

Maybe the question that should be asked is why angels became commercial and trivial. Archangel Michael is here again with me today and I asked him this question.

'Lorna, for many reasons humankind is less *connected* in modern times than in the past. Lorna, I would have to say that long ago people were more connected to nature and to the spiritual side of themselves. As society became more industrial, people rose up against injustice and looking for equality their minds became more open. Humankind wanted to learn more, to discover. However, they began to deny the spiritual side of themselves: their soul. You know, Lorna, even though all this has happened mankind is still hungry and thirsty to know more. Remember what God said to you, Lorna.'

'Yes, I remember that people are hungry and thirsty to know more, to know that there is more to life, that they have a soul, that they live for ever, that it is only the body that dies and turns to dust. They live because of their soul, Archangel Michael. Today we see for sale many statues of Jesus, Mary and statues of saints and statues of angels. I know lots of tourist destinations will sell statues of angels, for instance, and you have angel shops selling beautiful pictures of angels and statues and books.'

I said to Archangel Michael, 'I know some people look down on these things, but I don't have anything against them. I have seen many lovely cards and posters with beautiful pictures of angels. I know man can never paint a picture of the beauty of an angel because God has not allowed that to happen. I hope that will change in the future.'

As I said those words I looked at the angels in the room with me.

'Archangel Michael, a lot of modern stores in our shopping centres may on one level be cashing in on people wanting to buy statues or pictures of angels, but they are also comforting and give people hope. I see little angel brooches for sale. They are very pretty and I see many people wearing them because when wearing them they feel protected and safe. In some way they are acknowledging that they have a guardian angel and to me that is good, Michael.

'I believe the commercialism of angels is actually helping to bring mankind back to spirituality and to realising that we are much more than flesh and blood, that we have a soul. We are capable of incredible, wonderful things because of our soul if we allow our spirituality to grow. Archangel Michael, I wish mankind wasn't afraid of this side of themselves. It is part of the evolution of mankind. Why doesn't mankind wake up?'

Archangel Michael replied, 'You are helping mankind to wake up. You are doing exactly what God has said.'

I have seen businesspeople and those who have been or consider themselves well educated, people who have gone to the best universities, think of themselves as above spirituality. I have seen this idea of being above spirituality within small businesses, big multinational companies, governments and other forms of leadership across the world. Leaders, people in power, should be able to help direct the people of the world in the right direction, but are not listening enough to that inner voice of the spiritual side of themselves. That inner voice encouraging them to be moral and just and to strive towards making all the wrongs in the world right for the humanity of all the people of the world. To bring love and peace so that we all can have a future.

'Archangel Michael, I pray all the time for the leaders of the world and those in power that they will become conscious, even a little bit more, to ask God and their guardian angels for guidance because if they did the world would be so different.'

Humankind has taken a wrong turning many times in its history and it took a wrong turning when it began to deny that human beings have souls. If mankind was a little bit more spiritual and believed that there is something greater than ourselves, our planet would not be dying of pollution, we would not be having wars, or the huge displacement of men, women and children who are suffering every day. If mankind really believed in God, and that we have a soul and a guardian angel, we would not be causing such pain to each other. We would not be allowing the children of the world to be suffering, to be dying of hunger and thirst or of the cold. People in power in organised religions would not be using religion as a lethal weapon, giving permission to kill and destroy. If we had continued to allow ourselves to grow spiritually during the Industrial Revolution we would see the light of the soul in every child. We would be striving to make everything equal for everyone all the time. Life would not just be about economics or money but it would be about growing spiritually. It would be about the soul becoming intertwined with the human body.

As I said earlier in this book, the soul is inside of us and fills every part – but it is separate. Reading my books often helps people to recognise this, even if not always in a fully conscious way. Reading my books sometimes changes people because it encourages the soul to come forward, and when our soul does come forward that helps us to recognise that we really do have a soul and to accept it. When our soul comes forward our connections with God become stronger. We may go into a deep state of prayer and when we do that we are helping the process of the soul interweaving with the body, so that the body will be transformed, become lighter and more spiritualised, so that it will never become sick again. This is how humankind is meant to be evolving now.

I said to Archangel Michael, 'If we had only allowed this to happen. Maybe we would be at the stage where a lot of mothers and fathers would be able to see the guardian angel of their child.'

Archangel Michael said, 'Yes, Lorna, it would be so much closer, but now that is in the distance. The very far distance, I'm afraid.'

'So, Archangel Michael, you're saying man is only viewing angels as commercial because mankind is afraid and on some level deep down knows he is doing wrong? Another way I could put it would be that mankind is running away from himself.'

'Yes, Lorna, even though man at times is using God as an excuse to do wrong. Different religions are afraid of people getting in touch with God's angels. They are afraid of losing control over the people of that religion, but God's angels are working very hard to bring people back to God.

'Lorna, you must remember many are interested in the supernatural and go in search of ghosts.'

'Yes, I know, Michael. They are obsessed with the supernatural, attracted to the idea of ghost-hunting and haunted houses. This is to do with their hope of finding another side to life, beyond materialism, but these pursuits are often dangerous. Ouija boards are really dangerous, as is using drugs to achieve spiritual experiences. It's too easy to become fascinated by the other side, by the devil.'

Archangel Michael said, 'Yes.'

Then he had to go and he disappeared.

Many people take drugs in order to have spiritual experiences but they must remember those experiences are not truly real. They are contaminated by the other side and by the other side I mean the evil side, what many people call the devil. Using drugs for spiritual experiences can lead to the warping of your mind. It may be great fun at the time but I would advise you not to do so. I have met people over the years who have done this, where it led to mental breakdown and difficulty in their life. You don't need to take drugs to have real spiritual experiences. Meditate without taking drugs. Go to a deep state of prayer. Ask your guardian angel to help you to open up more spiritually and to allow you to recognise the spiritual things that happen in your life every day. You will be able to say you have had a real spiritual experience, uncontaminated by that evil force that loves to play tricks and fool the world.

It's getting dark outside. Now there are two angels in the room with me. All the others have left, even Angel Hosus. One of the angels is standing in the doorway. This angel is giving neither a male or female appearance but is dressed in a beautiful, green flowing gown and is quite masculine-looking. I have to smile at the other angel as it is sitting, would you believe it, on top of the printer but yet not touching it. I know if the angel was actually sitting on the printer it would break. It would be crushed. The angel is just smiling at me as I say this. I have a microphone that picks up every word I say and prints it out on the screen. This angel is dressed in many colours.

They are telling me now that I should finish up soon so I say, 'Okay, I would just like to write a little bit more.'

I'm now going to write about the time my first child, Christopher, was born. One sunny day my mum came to visit us. The pram was out in the garden and baby Christopher was asleep. I was delighted to see my mum. I made a cup of tea and we sat on the doorstep and chatted for a little while. Mum told me she had a present for Christopher and out of her pocket, she took a badge with a pin on it. It was a picture of Archangel Michael.

Mum said, 'This is to protect Christopher and keep him safe.'

I smiled at my mum and said, 'Thank you.'

It was very pretty. As I got up to walk over to the pram to pin it on to the inside of the hood Christopher's guardian angel was looking down upon him with such love. I turned around and looked back at my mum as she sat on the doorstep, sipping her tea and having a biscuit. My dad wasn't with her. He had dropped her off at the gate as he had to go and visit someone who didn't live too far away.

I said to myself that I would love to tell my mum that I can see her guardian angel as physically as I see her sitting on the doorstep, but my guardian angel whispered in my ear and said, 'No, Lorna, you know you must keep it a secret.'

That day my mum's guardian angel gave a female appearance and was dressed all in gold with its arms curved around her. In the hands of my mum's guardian angel there was a radiant light of white. The angel looked so beautiful surrounding my mum with a beautiful light.

As I walked over to sit down beside my mum I said, 'Thank you.'

When we were finished tea my mum asked if she could take Christopher for a little walk down the road for a few minutes before my dad got back.

'Of course,' I said and Mum wheeled the pram out the gate.

When she had gone I went and took some vegetables from the garden and put them in a bag to give to her. I was watching anxiously for her to come back. Then I heard the wheels of the pram on the road so I went and opened the gate. My mum looked so happy.

She was only back a few minutes when Dad pulled up at the gate. I took Christopher out of the pram and carried him over to the car. My dad said, 'Did your mum give you the little present for Christopher?'

I said 'Yes, it's already pinned on to his pram.'

Dad reached out and touched Christopher's cheek with his finger and said that he was sorry he couldn't stay. Mum said goodbye and got into the car, showing Dad the bag of vegetables. A moment later, they drove away.

I guess that if it hadn't been for the commercialism of images of angels, my mum would not have been able to give me that little brooch of Archangel Michael. I don't know exactly where she bought it. It could have been in a Catholic shop. Lots of grandparents, friends, aunts and uncles, even children buy a present to do with angels to give to those they love. Some of them are like mine, a little brooch of an angel. I see many people of all ages wearing these on their jackets or coats. Sometimes someone would say to me they got a present of an angel and they would show me their brooch. Sometimes it would be an angel on a chain around their neck.

When we give someone a present of the image of an angel we are helping to remind them of their own guardian angel and of all of the angels that God has in the world. They are helping us and reminding us that we are not alone.

Early in its history, even before the time Sainte-Chapelle was built, the Catholic Church started to make money by selling religious images, for instance selling medals of Our

Lady, Jesus and Archangel Michael, so it has been going on for a long time. If angels were not seen as commercial these days, as well, we would not have these little gifts to give to those we love and to friends. I have often carried an angel in my bag that was given to me by a stranger. It is round and smooth like a clear bead with an angel inside. It is something that feels comforting to hold in your hand. I know many people around the world carry symbols of angels, either on their person or in their belongings. So to whoever started to make angels commercial: *I do thank you*. Because of this we are being reminded of the spiritual side of ourselves and how much more we are than just flesh and blood.

I met a young man about four years ago while walking in a small park in London. He was pushing a pram with his small child in it. His wife was walking beside him.

They came up to me and the young man said, 'You're Lorna Byrne, aren't you?'

I smiled and said, 'Yes.'

He said his name was Stephen. He introduced his wife Joan and said their little girl's name was Lisa. Stephen told me that five years ago he would never have believed in angels or in God or in anything like that. He said if anyone had told him he'd seen an angel, he would have only laughed and said 'You're drunk or high on drugs'. He explained that he had been going through a hard time and nothing seemed to be working out for him. Then a friend of his called Paul gave him a tiny statue of a little angel.

He said that he told his friend, 'I don't want that!'

But his friend insisted, saying, 'Your angel can help you.'

He laughed at his friend, who slipped the little angel into his pocket anyway. A few days later as he got into his car to head home, he was rooting in his pocket for some money when in among the loose change he found this little angel. He said he looked at it and he found himself thinking about angels and what if he had an angel?

He just said, 'Help.'

Then, he threw the angel into the dash of the car and thought nothing else about it, but a few days later he started to notice the same thought coming into his mind. What if he had an angel? He kept on asking for help and he noticed things starting to change for the better in his life. He met his beautiful wife and two years later they had their daughter.

We talked for a little while and just before they left I said, 'You should pin an angel on to your daughter's pram. Somewhere she can't reach it, of course, but have it there to remind you how blessed you are. You have such a beautiful little daughter.'

Then we said our goodbyes.

That is an example of how the commercialising of the symbol of an angel – a small statue or a pin or an angel on a chain – helps to make us aware again of the angels around us. They remind us that we have a spiritual side, that side we seem to be afraid of yet are hungry and thirsty to know more about. We are always in search of the supernatural force that is guiding us back to who we really are: God's children.

Angels are a link that God has given us and they are a link between God and us, a link between Him and us as human beings: our souls. We sometimes find it easier to believe in angels than we do God because we blame God for everything that is bad in the world. I know if God hadn't allowed angels to be made commercial no publisher would ever have said yes to the books I have written. I would not have been able to do what God had asked of me. I definitely would have been turned away. Angels being made commercial opened the door that God had wanted me to go through to allow you to know the link between the angels and you. That connection is through your soul, that connector between you and God.

If angels weren't made commercial by the Catholic Church and other faiths long ago I would not have had the money to do all I do because in today's world, everything costs money. I am so glad that God allowed angels to become commercial so I can do the job he has given me to do. Whether people believe me or not doesn't matter once I'm doing what God wants me to do. It's up to you to decide for yourself.

CHAPTER 16

Angels Every Day

PEOPLE SOMETIMES SAY THEY ARE CURIOUS ABOUT HOW I interact with angels day to day, including on relatively unimportant matters, so that is what I am going to describe now.

A lot happened to me today, this Friday, so I'm going to tell you some of the things that made up this day. I planned to write all day and not leave the house but I'm afraid God and the angels had other plans.

The morning was cold and it rained the whole afternoon. When Angel Hosus said to me, 'Lorna, don't you think we should stop and take a break?' I said, 'No, let's just finish this. It's still early morning.'

Angel Hosus said, 'Lorna, all of us angels know you very well. You won't take a break unless we do something about it.'

I just shrugged my shoulders and took no notice of Angel Hosus and continued working.

When my daughter Ruth rang me on Skype I had to turn

off the Dragon Net – my dictation program – so I could talk to her.

I said to Angel Hosus, 'So you have worked out a way for me to have a break.'

To my amazement Skype wasn't working properly. My daughter could hear me clearly but I could not hear her.

No matter what I did I could not get it to work so I said to her, 'I will have to ring my friend who fixes my computer when anything goes wrong.'

Ruth said to me, 'Mam, you can't be calling him for the least little thing.'

She tried to help me to sort out Skype but it still didn't work so she had to give up. We said goodbye using my mobile. I looked at the time. It was after twelve o'clock.

I turned to Angel Hosus and said, 'You could have helped. You know I have to do an interview with the school in Australia. There are a lot of children looking forward to talking to me.'

Angel Hosus said, 'Give Gavin a call.'

I did and my friend said that he would do his best to get to the house and fix Skype for me.

Angel Hosus then reminded me that I had to go into Kilkenny as I didn't have a charger for my phone. I had left it behind in Cork. By this stage I was definitely getting stressed. I gave out, saying, 'This is not fair. I wanted to get an awful lot done today.'

Angel Hosus laughed at me quietly. I have to say not loudly. While talking on the phone with my friend Gavin I told him I had to go into Kilkenny. He said to give him a call when I got back and hopefully he would be able to call in to fix the problem.

Off I went to Kilkenny. The car was full of angels and

Angel Hosus was sitting in the front seat. I didn't say a word to him. I just prayed as I drove. Just on the outskirts of Kilkenny I drove into the petrol station deciding it was a good idea to fill the tank as I had to head off to Dublin at seven thirty in the morning. I had changed cars recently. My son-in-law and my daughter, Ruth, had given me their old car. It was a decent car and they had warned me not to make a mistake by putting petrol into it because it was diesel and different to my old car. I was very conscious of this so when I got out of the car I looked at the pump. I thought I was making it out correctly but seemingly I wasn't.

Angel Hosus said, 'Lorna, that's the wrong one.'

I said to him, 'No, it's not. I want to do this myself. I have to learn not to put the wrong fuel into this car, so leave me alone and let me work it out for myself.' So I took my hand away again from the petrol pump and I looked, but Angel Hosus was still shaking his head no.

Then all of a sudden I said out loud, 'I know I'm doing it right.' Of course the angels have never given me wrong information, but I'm very stubborn and get upset and want to learn to do things by myself without their help sometimes.

I picked one of the pumps and put it into the fuel tank.

Angel Hosus was shouting at me, 'No! Stop, Lorna! That's the wrong one.'

But I didn't stop straight away so some petrol got into the diesel car.

I said to Angel Hosus, 'How did I make that mistake?'

He reassured me, saying, 'Don't worry. It will be okay. Not too much petrol went into the diesel tank of your car.'

'I hate being dyslexic,' I said to Angel Hosus, 'and seeing things the opposite way around. Even though one petrol pump was black and the other was green somehow when I picked up the pump, I picked up the wrong one. I know I meant to pick up the black one.'

Hosus said, 'Ring the man who looks after your car for you.'

So I did and he answered. I was so relieved. He too said not to worry. It should be okay, he told me after he asked me a lot of questions.

He said, 'Now fill the tank with diesel and be sure to use the right hose.'

I said, 'Goodbye and thank you.'

Then I asked Angel Hosus, 'Would you please put your hand on the pump? The one I am to use.'

Angel Hosus said, 'Yes, of course, Lorna.'

So I filled the car with diesel.

When I went to pay, the man behind the counter said, 'I guess you made a mistake. I hope you didn't put too much of the wrong fuel into your car.'

I told him how much I put in and he too said that would be okay and laughed at me but with great sympathy. I walked back out to my car praying. Angel Hosus was already sitting in the front seat. I didn't say a word to him. I just turned on the engine. It started with no trouble. I headed to Kilkenny city and I got a charger for my phone.

I was walking back to the car – Angel Hosus was still with me – when he said, 'Do you not want to go into your little favourite restaurant and have a cup of tea and something to eat? You have not eaten all day and it is now two o'clock.'

I took a deep breath and said, 'Yes, okay.'

I had something to eat and relaxed in the restaurant for a little while and then headed home. Just as I drove in the gate I gave Gavin a call and told him I was home now. He told me he was just leaving Kilkenny and would come straight to me. He did, and got Skype working.

When he left, I said to Angel Hosus, 'I don't know why I plan anything because you angels and God are always changing it. You'd think I would have learned by now.'

About half an hour later Angel Hosus put his hand across the screen.

I said to him, 'I can see your hand. It is in the way.'

He just said, 'Lorna, look at the other monitor, the security camera.'

I did and there I saw a white van pull up to my gate. I recognised the man as he got out. He opened the gate.

I got up and I gave out to Angel Hosus saying, 'What are you angels up to?'

Angel Hosus said, 'You need a break.'

I went downstairs. The man was around the back of the house. I don't know his name, but I have met him on and off over the years. He was taking electricity meter readings. It was drizzling rain and the breeze was very strong. I said hello to him and we walked back round to shelter at the gable end of the house. We stood there talking for about ten minutes. I did have to smile at one stage when I saw a group of angels walk towards the white van and then in through the gate. They came over and stood right in front of us. I knew the man couldn't see them but they were busy writing down everything he was saying. I walked over to the gate with them and we said goodbye. Some of the angels went with him. Others stayed behind and followed me into the house. I said a prayer and asked God to keep the man as healthy as possible. I knew he had lots of ailments.

I went back upstairs. There was Angel Hosus sitting in the chair where I would normally sit.

I said to Angel Hosus, 'That gave me a break and some fresh air. Even though it was cold and raining, it was good.

Now how about, Angel Hosus, you give me my chair back?'

He swung around in the chair and I smiled. 'You are always good, Angel Hosus, at cheering me up.'

'That's part of my job,' he said.

A lot of other things happened that day and all I can say is I don't know how I actually managed to write almost six thousand words. Since I have to write a hundred thousand or more altogether I still have a long way to go.

Eventually Angel Hosus said, 'Lorna, turn off your computer. You have done enough.'

So now I'm going to say goodnight to you all.

Hello there. I'm talking to you whether you're sitting in a chair or in your bed or on a bench in the park. Maybe you are on holidays and you are reading this book. Yes, I'm talking to *you*. Many of you ask me this particular question and you may have it at the back of your mind now. You want to know how you can feel the presence of your guardian angel. Many times I've answered this in different ways because all of you experience this communication differently. Everyone's guardian angel communicates on different levels with the person. It is your beautiful soul that God has appointed your guardian angel to look after you. Your soul draws your guardian angel to you.

Many of you may already know that some people will say that if they pray for help, for instance if they're worrying about a job interview, they feel a tingle or a cool breeze, maybe on their face or on their hand. It might just be a sensation of peace in themselves for a brief moment. They could get an itchy spot on their little finger. That is the sensation of their guardian angel. Your guardian angel could be giving you these sensations to help you or to teach you to recognise them so that you can feel their presence. But one thing you may not have known, and that may be contrary to the norm or to everyone's expectations, is that there is not one human being in the world, no man, woman or child, who feels the presence of their guardian angel through the exact same sensation. On different occasions, when I would watch someone's guardian angel giving a person that feeling of being with them, the guardian angel would always tell me, even if they were doing something as simple as blowing gently on a particular spot on a person's face, that no guardian angel's gentle blowing feels the same as another's blowing. I think that is incredible.

Since I was a child my guardian angel and I have always played a game. I play this even as an adult and I know you can do this too with your guardian angel. We all can. So as you read from this book I want you to take in everything. I am saying this because your guardian angel wants to help you to feel its presence with you. I've been reminded to remind you that ninety-nine point nine per cent of the time you feel the presence of the soul of a loved one that may be around you more than you would ever feel the presence of your guardian angel. But your guardian angel can help you to feel its presence in many different ways. So many of you already know that it can be a sensation of tingling or a cold breeze. There are many other sensations your guardian angel can give you to help you feel its presence so that you know that it is right there with you. You can play this game with your guardian angel at any time.

Only the other day when I went for a walk down the lane I said to my guardian angel, 'Let's play the fingertip game.'

These are the words I've always used since I was a child because they are like the words my guardian angel said to me then, which were, 'Lorna, let's play a game.'

(In a sense I didn't need to learn to play games like these, but I would come to realise that the angels had taught me these games so that I could teach everyone else.)

'What game?' I asked my guardian angel.

My guardian angel answered, as it raised its golden hand and moved its fingers in slow motion, 'The fingertip game.'

I repeated my guardian angel's words, 'The fingertip game,' while giggling. I said, 'That name is funny.'

This is the same game I played with my guardian angel the other day as I walked down the lane.

I asked my guardian angel, 'How can I explain this lesson to the readers?'

My guardian angel said, 'Get them to stand in front of the mirror. Let them say hello to their guardian angel.'

I replied, 'That's a good idea – for them to use the mirror.'

That is what I want you to do. Stand in front of a mirror ready to move your left hand or right hand, whichever one you write with. As you stand there look at your reflection in the mirror. Now, raise your hand. Have your hand stretched out and your fingers spread out a little so that your fingers are not touching each other. Look at the reflection of yourself in the mirror and imagine your reflection is actually your guardian angel looking back at you and that your guardian angel has its hand at the same level as yours.

The first thing that your guardian angel needs you to do is move your hand slowly towards the mirror, coming close enough that you can touch the reflection of the tip of your finger and feel that gentle touch on the mirror itself. Move each finger, one at a time, just tapping and holding for a moment, or as long as you want, the tips of your fingers on the mirror. Make sure you are tapping the reflection of your own fingertips but imagining, at the same time, that they are the fingertips of your guardian angel. You may have to do this many times. In between times, when you're playing this game with your guardian angel, you may start to feel whatever sensation your guardian angel gives you to help you to feel its presence.

When you are ready, you can stop playing this game in front of the mirror. The next step is to ask your guardian angel to stand in front of you and they will do so. Imagine your guardian angel standing there, just as you imagined your own reflection in the mirror was your guardian angel. Keep the same distance between yourself and your guardian angel as you did with the mirror. Your guardian angel will be standing right in front of you. As soon as you raise your hand your guardian angel will have their hand right in front of yours. So start feeling your guardian angel's fingers. You may feel nothing at first but I promise you that over time you will feel a sensation of some kind, maybe even more than one sensation, when you tap the tip of your guardian angel's finger with the tip of your own finger. Hold it for a moment. Allow yourself to make that contact. Then take that finger away and tap your next finger. Don't forget the thumb. You can start with your little finger or your middle finger or your thumb. Your guardian angel doesn't mind which finger you use first. It is a wonderful game. You may find that you smile, laugh or that a funny thought comes to your mind – these responses are all because, by you and your guardian angel tapping fingertips, your guardian angel is helping you to become aware of your senses so you can feel its presence.

Some of the sensations your guardian angel may give you so you can feel its presence could be a tingle or an electric shock, ever so gently or very strong. It might even make you jump.

If this happens say, 'Thank you' to your guardian angel.

Talk to your guardian angel by saying, 'Let's play again.'

You can ask your guardian angel to be a little bit gentler or maybe a bit clearer. Remember, the way your guardian angel communicates with you may sound the same to you as what you hear in an account someone else gives of his or her experience but, as I said, they are not. I always laugh when my guardian angel gives me a really strong electric shock, going through my fingertip from theirs. It doesn't hurt. As you move along, doing this with your fingertips, you may feel as if you are touching something so soft you cannot explain it. It might be like something hot that feels like a burn, as if you'd put your fingertip over the flame of a candle or as if you were touching an ice cube.

There are many different sensations your guardian angel could give you but then again, it may only give you one. No other man, woman or child can feel that sensation in the same way you feel it. You must get to know this sensation really well, become connected to it, so you can really feel the presence of your guardian angel. It's not a one-off game. Your guardian angel is helping you to work on that sensation, to make it stronger for you, to feel its presence. To feel the presence of your own guardian angel, not of any other angel.

As I moved the mouse attached to my computer my guardian angel put its beautiful hand above mine and whispered in my ear, 'Don't forget, Lorna, that they must do this continuously through their life. Everyone's guardian angel can teach them many things to help them through life.'

I said to my guardian angel, 'Do you think the readers can do this?'

'Yes, Lorna. I know that you know all of your readers can do this and that you have no doubt whatsoever. You know that their guardian angel is real, just as they are, and that is why they can do it.'

'Yes, they can,' I said, as my guardian angel lifted its hand slowly away from mine.

My guardian angel said, 'Lorna, say the thought that has crossed your mind. Personally to the readers.'

'Okay, this is to the readers then. I know all of you can do this. I have no doubt whatsoever. Your guardian angel is real, just as you are, and that is why you can do it. Your own guardian angel will keep on reminding you. You can learn how to feel the presence of your own guardian angel. Remember, your guardian angel can be no one else's guardian angel. Only yours. Your guardian angel belongs to you.'

CHAPTER 17

A Listening Prayer

I WAS DOWN IN THE ORCHARD THE OTHER DAY LOOKING at the growth of flowers starting to burst through the soil. It was cold but the sun was shining. I sat on a piece of tree trunk and prayed for a little while, then I heard my name being called. I opened my eyes and looked up. There I saw Archangel Michael coming towards me. I smiled because he was dressed very ordinarily in jeans and an anorak but he looked as handsome as ever. You could not mistake him for anything other than an angel.

I said, 'Hello, I'm glad to see you.'

Archangel Michael said to me, 'Continue praying, Lorna, and I will pray with you.'

Archangel Michael stood next to me and I closed my eyes and started to pray.

Angels join us all the time when we pray. Your guardian angel always prays with you and so do the Angels of Prayer, but I always love these special occasions when Archangel Michael prays with me. I have asked if I can tell you more about what happens when Archangel Michael prays with me but I have been told I cannot. Maybe another time but God has not allowed it yet. I don't know how long Archangel Michael prayed with me that day, but when he touched me I knew it was time to stop. When I opened my eyes the sun had gone in and I felt cold.

Archangel Michael walked back towards the house with me and as we walked we talked a little. Archangel Michael spoke about people giving up too easily. He said people don't try hard enough when they are trying to make contact with their guardian angel. They forget their guardian angel can hear all their thoughts and knows, before they even say, what is on their mind.

I replied to Archangel Michael, 'Sometimes that annoys me about all of you angels. When you ask me what is the matter and I tell you even though you already know.'

Archangel Michael smiled at me and said, 'Lorna, it's because it is good for you to share. Just as it is good for every human being to share with their guardian angel and God. It helps people, men and women and even children, to share with each other. Sharing with each other is very important, Lorna, and people who are more open, people who listen to others and are more empathetic find it easier to become aware of angels. In a way, sharing with other people is more important than communicating with your guardian angel because if you cannot communicate with your fellow man how do you expect to be able to communicate with your guardian angel?'

'Archangel Michael,' I said, 'I think that's a huge problem in the world today. People are shy and afraid to sit down and talk to each other. They prefer to do it at a long distance. Then, when they meet, they cannot say two words to each other.'

As Archangel Michael and I walked back towards my house I said to him, 'One thing I know – I cannot keep any secrets from you, or any thought that crosses my mind.'

Archangel Michael replied, 'You might as well say it out loud to us, Lorna, because you know no matter what you think or say it never offends an angel.'

As I opened the little gate I said, 'That is something that I sometimes find hard to understand. No matter what I have been taught about God and you, Archangel Michael, and all the archangels and all the angels of heaven. It is still beyond my understanding and I believe it will always be beyond man's understanding until the day comes when our souls start to intertwine with the human body and become one. When we grow spiritually. I know we all give out to the angels when we feel things are not going our way, and we do so to God all the time. I know I do. I'm always giving out to God but now as I think about it I don't often give out to you angels. Again, we don't understand why our guardian angel won't miraculously allow something to happen for us, when we want it.'

God has many different plans for all of us all the time, some great turning points in our lives and also smaller plans, but the problem is that we often don't recognise these plans, sometimes believing that what is on offer is not good enough for us. We should try to listen as well as ask. Prayer is a two-way process.

Try to listen. I have written the prayer below to help you listen, to discover the plans, the blessings that God has prepared for you if only you will recognise them.

The more we pray, the more our soul comes forward and begins to intertwine with our body. We become aware of angels and loved ones. The more we live in harmony with them, the more we will become aware of God's loving intentions for the world.

When we ask for things in our prayers we sometimes believe we know what we need, and then if we don't receive what we ask for, we get angry. Some time later, when we look back, we may also be glad we didn't get what we asked for! Only God knows what we really need.

And God is always giving us a great abundance, more than we need, more even than we want – though we don't necessarily recognise the blessings we are being given.

God always has this abundance of blessings prepared for us, small blessings and great blessings. He wants to give every individual great life-changing blessings, beginning when that individual is born. These might include, for example, to meet and marry a particular partner, move to a great city, to have children, to move back to your country of birth and set up a successful business. There might be a connection of blessings between two individuals, so that if they don't immediately recognise they are meant to be together, God will keep pushing them together in different ways and at different times. God might really want us to have a very special blessing like this, and then He will do everything to make it happen, and they nearly always do happen, but He will never infringe on an individual's free will.

Before we are born we all know of all the blessings that there will be for us in our lives: our parents, the choices we will have to make, the good and the bad. When the soul comes from heaven, God doesn't want the spark of Himself inside us, the soul, to interfere with our free will, but he has given each of us a guardian angel to help us to be more spiritual, to recognise our blessings, to help us to bear heavy loads and to make the right choices.

All of us suffer bad things in our lives and bad things are also happening around the world all the time. In a sense we all agree to these things happening and we are all a part of every trial that happens to every individual. God sees the choices the whole world makes, and, of course, people don't always make the right ones, leading to war, poverty, disease and environmental catastrophe.

That is why it is important for us all to pray for our leaders, pray that they make the right decisions.

Sometimes people are surprised by all the trials I've suffered in my life, but I wouldn't be who I am if I hadn't suffered all my ups and downs. Bad events in our lives can help us to grow and learn to be a better person, to grow more confident of the good that is in us. For example, if you see a fight in the street and take the risk of stepping in to save someone taking a beating, that is a God-given opportunity to become a hero and a peacemaker that you have grasped with both hands.

Sometimes bad things happening to us can help us become more compassionate and caring. They can also prompt us to cry out for help in prayer, and help us realise, too, that we have a soul and that we are being given messages all the time, by our guardian angels and by our loves ones too. Something wonderful about all prayer – whether a single word of prayer or a deep prayer – is that it helps bring about an entwining of our souls and bodies so that we become more aware of the spiritual part of ourselves that is pure love and more aware too of the loving spiritual beings that are trying to communicate with us and help us.

We find it easier to ask than to listen, so sometimes our prayers are so focussed on asking for things, we forget to listen out for what God, the angels and our loved ones are trying to tell us. Here is a short prayer to help us to listen.

My dear guardian angel
I thank God for all the blessings in my life
but I am lost at the moment and do not
know what to do.
I find it hard to listen, so please help me to be
quiet and to listen to you and my loved ones
while you tell me what God's plans are
for me now . . .

(Leave time here to be silent and listen.)

. . . Thank you for helping me to listen,
Amen.

CHAPTER 18

A Glowing Baby

ARCHANGEL MICHAEL CAME INTO THE HOUSE WITH ME and we went upstairs. Archangel Michael went ahead of me. When he does something like this I think it is very beautiful. As he took the stairs, each step turned into a bright light then changed back into the normal wooden step. As I said earlier, his feet never touched the steps – I know that light is what I call the cushion that is between every angel and the earth. When we reached the room where I work, Archangel Michael stood beside me and I sat in the chair in front of my computer.

He said, 'Write now about all that we have spoken about.'

So I started to do so and about half an hour into it my phone rang and I saw it was Father John. In that moment Archangel Michael disappeared. He never even said he had to go, he just left.

I was telling Father John this on the phone and he said, 'I'm so sorry, Lorna. I will pray that when we are finished talking Archangel Michael will come back and continue to work with you.'

I said to him, 'Don't worry. Archangel Michael will only come when God sends him.'

I had to smile to myself as I spoke to Father John on the phone. It had been years since Archangel Michael disappeared like that, without saying he had to go.

Father John asked me to pray for a family who had just lost their twenty-three year-old daughter. She had died after a long illness. I said I would but reminded him not to forget to tell the family that the guardian angel of their beautiful daughter took her soul straight to heaven and that she was at peace and happy now. I said that I would pray for her family to get through this hard time but that it was important for them to remember all the happy times they had with her, not just the sad ones. A few minutes later I said goodbye to Father John.

I don't know how I am going to tell you this next story because for me it is very emotional. It is full of love and joy.

It was about a year ago. From the time I woke up that morning and got out of bed the angels were telling me there was a child that I would see that day, a little child. I remembered, too, that Archangel Michael had spoken to me in the orchard the previous year, telling me I would see another glowing baby.

A glowing baby is a baby that is evolved spiritually. God doesn't allow them to stay in the world for long because we are not ready. They stay here for a short while so that we can experience their unlimited love. God sends them now and then to help to us evolve more rapidly. I first wrote about glowing babies in *Angels in My Hair* and then in *Stairways to Heaven*.

I was up in Dublin with my daughter Megan. We had lots of things to do. Late that afternoon, I said to her, 'We'd better go and do some grocery shopping and get something in for dinner.'

So a few minutes later we left in the car. As we were driving Megan was talking to me about different things that a young woman would normally talk to her mother about, and we discussed as well some of the topics that came on the radio. When we were about five minutes away from the supermarket my guardian angel whispered in my ear that I would see the little child soon. Megan was talking to me at the same time.

She said to me, 'Mam, you are not listening to me properly.'

I said to her that I was very sorry but I was being distracted.

Megan knows exactly what that means and she said, 'I wish the angels wouldn't do that, especially when I am talking to you.'

As we pulled into the supermarket car park, I was very conscious of meeting this little child, but I had no idea what to expect. I have to say I was a bit apprehensive because the angels would usually tell me a bit more beforehand. As I walked through the supermarket door, a group of six angels walked ahead of me into the supermarket. I saw Angel Hosus standing by the vegetable stands.

'Hello, Lorna,' he said.

I walked over to where Angel Hosus was and started to put some vegetables into the trolley.

'I'm glad to see you,' I said.

Angel Hosus replied, 'Lorna, there is a little boy walking among the aisles. Watch out for him.' I said to Angel Hosus, 'Am I to stop and look at him?' He said, 'Yes.'

My daughter took the trolley from me and said she would go off and do the shopping. I said to her, 'That's a great idea.'

I smiled because I knew she had listened to her guardian

angel and had asked no questions. She just did what she was asked to by her guardian angel; help Mum do the shopping. I picked up a packet of carrots and a head of lettuce for my pet rabbit Mimsy.

As I moved along I saw the little boy. There were three beautiful angels around him. He was about two and a half years of age. He looked so beautiful. He was so full of life with a big smile on his face as he toddled along, enjoying himself and his independence. This little boy glowed. He shined. He was just a toddler. He was one of the special children born into the world every now and then. Love just radiated from him. It shone, and I knew he saw the angels as clearly as I did. He was playing with them. That and talking back to them. When someone passed by they looked at him and they seemed to be confused. They were attracted to him and wanted to lift him up and hold him in their arms but God wasn't allowing that. The angels were playing with him, making him giggle, putting an incredible smile on his beautiful face. All of the time, I was only seeing this little boy from the side so I didn't see his full face. It was only half of that smile, that beautiful smile, that I could see.

Angel Hosus was walking beside me. He said to me, 'Lorna, as you are passing the little boy you are to say "Hi there, gorgeous."'

I said, 'Okay.'

I didn't notice anything wrong.

I said to Angel Hosus, 'He is so cute. I wonder where his parents are.'

Angel Hosus said, 'Turn around. You will see his mum.'

She was some distance away and then I saw the father on the far side of the aisle. He was a little closer. I didn't understand why they were not beside their little boy but I knew there must have been a reason. I thought to myself maybe they know the little boy loves having the freedom of being inquisitive in the supermarket. I could see they were keeping a close eye on him all the same. The angels that were around the little boy called me to hurry up and do what Angel Hosus said as I walked by the little boy.

I said, 'Hi there, gorgeous.'

The little boy stopped and looked up at me, giving me a big smile. He kind of jumped in the air, with his feet dancing a little, and started to run towards me.

The angels around him said, 'Lorna, move quickly.'

I walked as fast as I could up along the aisle. I could hear the little boy's laughter and knew the angels were playing with him and keeping him happy.

How can I explain this part to you? This little boy had special needs and it was so clear to see when I saw his full face. His little body was crooked and his face looked all out of proportion. But I could only see his beauty. This was a glowing baby and it had been many years since I had seen one. To think that this little child is in our country to me is very special. I know seeing this little child means hope for the world. I understood as I walked along the aisle that the world needs hope now. Glowing babies are very special children. They are one million times more evolved spiritually than any of us. God does not usually allow them to grow up. He takes them back home to heaven because we, as mankind, are not ready to accept them. We, ourselves, have not evolved enough spiritually.

Megan called me and said, 'Mam, come here. Do you think it would be a good idea to get some soup and maybe garlic bread?'

I said that would be great and I picked some soup off the

shelf. Megan got the garlic bread. When I looked up, Angel Hosus was waiting for me at the far end of the aisle.

I said to Megan, 'I think I will go and see if they have the cheese I like.'

She said she was going to get some shampoo. I went in the direction Angel Hosus was standing.

He said, 'Go up along the aisle and pretend you are looking for some stuff. Then turn left and go down the aisle you've just come up. Take your time, Lorna. There is no hurry.'

So I took my time and when I got to the top of the aisle I turned left.

The little boy was on the same aisle as myself. He was toddling towards me, just watching the angels around him.

I said to Angel Hosus, 'I have noticed that no matter where this little boy is, there are very few people around him.'

The aisle was almost empty, except for his parents and two ladies walking up along the aisle with their trolleys. I pretended I was looking at stuff on the shelves and the two ladies got close to the little boy. He gave them a big smile but they seemed to shrug their shoulders in disgust.

I heard one of them mutter under their breath, 'What an ugly child.'

But to me I could only see the beauty of this child.

I said again, 'Hi there, gorgeous.'

The little boy gave a big smile. His mum and dad were very close to him at the time I said these words and they heard them. It filled them with joy that someone would say that their little boy was gorgeous.

The father hurried over to his little son and reached down and picked up his little boy and gave him a big hug.

The father looked at me with tears in his eyes and said, 'Thank you.'

The mother, at the same moment, went over to her husband and her little boy. The three of them hugged each other with love.

The angels said, as they surrounded the family, 'Move quickly now, Lorna.'

I gave them a big smile and walked back the way I came around the aisle. My daughter called me to give her a helping hand.

As I finished the shopping with Megan she said to me, 'What's wrong?'

I said, 'I'm okay.'

I spoke to Angel Hosus without words and said, 'Was that the first time the parents of that little boy ever heard anyone say their little boy was gorgeous?'

Angel Hosus said, 'Yes, no one has ever said that before, only horrible things.'

I pray for that mum and dad and their little boy because that little boy is a glowing baby. I know he's only here for a short while. It is so sad to think that when we look at a child we only see their physical appearance. We should always try to see the beauty and the good in every child no matter what their appearance is on the outside. I think the words the angels gave for me to say to the little boy were really for his parents to hear.

When I held a talk abroad just before Christmas I told a little part of that story, and I know it moved people and please God, helped them think twice.

During the blessing, when I was blessing some young men they said to me, 'Hi there, gorgeous.'

All I could do was just smile and continue on blessing everyone that was standing in front of me.

CHAPTER 19

My Last Year in School and Meeting St Francis

THE MOTHER OF JESUS HAS APPEARED ALL OVER THE world. She's the Queen of Heaven, the Queen of Angels, the Queen of Souls, Our Lady. She is the mother of us all. I'm a Catholic and when I was at school I was told to call her Our Lady Mary.

When a teacher talked about Our Lady Mary in heaven to us children, I could see the room fill with angels. There's a class of angels, the Angels of Prayer, which appear in situations like these because when we talk about God, Our Lady or even angels we are actually in prayer. Seeing these angels appear made me smile and feel happy as I sat at my desk, which was usually at the back of the classroom. I wasn't always so happy though.

The local school in Edenmore was just a stone's throw from the house where I lived for many years, a five-minute walk really, but it always took me much longer because I took little baby steps. I wanted to delay arriving as long as possible. Sometimes, I turned around and headed back in the direction of home but the angels would only allow me to go so far. Three or four angels would stand in a line across the path blocking my way.

I would give out to them, saying, 'The teacher doesn't even know I'm in the class!' I would stamp my feet.

They would say, 'No, Lorna, you have to turn back around and head to school.' But I never hurried. I always took my time.

On occasion, when I was late for school, all the children would already be in the classroom. As soon as I went through the school gate the angels would start telling me to hurry up, so I would run and push open the big, heavy doors of the school.

I loved going up the stairs. I would say to the angels, 'Watch how quick I can be!' and take two steps at a time, holding on to the banisters the whole way. My classroom was on the top floor.

Nothing was ever said to me for being late for school. As I walked into the classroom and towards my desk, the teacher would be standing over the desk of another boy or girl. The teacher would look up at me but wouldn't say a word. Other times as I walked into the classroom and sat down at my desk, it was as if I was invisible. Sometimes the angels actually hid me so the teacher wouldn't realise I was late. That always made me smile.

On this particular day – it was in my last year at school, when I was twelve – my teacher, who was a nun, gave us a spelling test. I knew my answers were all wrong, even though I had done my best, so I was giving out to my guardian angel and to the angels around me, saying, 'Why couldn't you have helped me a little more? I was trying so hard.' They told me I was doing fine and I felt a little tickle between my shoulder blades. I shrugged them off, but really I knew the angels were just trying to cheer me up. Now Sister wrote the words on the blackboard that she had called out. She gave us all a few minutes to check if our spelling was correct. I couldn't really make out what was on the blackboard. The letters just kept moving. So I asked my guardian angel.

My guardian angel said, 'The fourth one down is correct, Lorna.' I was happy to get at least one of my spellings right.

Sister then closed the book she had on her desk and stood up. She told us all to put our exercise books and pens away and then she picked up from her desk another book, a black one with a cross on the front of it. I knew what the book was. It was the Bible. She asked if any girl or boy in the class could tell her what the book she was holding up was. I looked around the class and saw that the other children had blank expressions on their faces. One of the girls in the front row shouted, 'No, Sister.'

Shyly, I put my hand up and she looked at me, surprised, but then she turned around, ignoring me, and walked back around her desk. She laid the book on the table and picked up some chalk. She started to write on the board.

My guardian angel whispered to me what she had written: 'Holy Bible: the word of God.'

I said to my guardian angel, 'I know. I recognise the word Bible.' Sister hadn't asked me to give the answer. She went ahead herself and read the words from the board. I was disappointed and said to the angels, 'Does the nun think I know nothing?'

My guardian angel whispered in my ear, 'Remember, Lorna, she knows no better.'

Sister started to ask if anyone's parents had the Bible in their house but no one put their hand up. Just then Angel

Hosus walked into the classroom – through the closed door. I felt happy when I saw him. As he moved across the classroom to the nun's desk his cape moved as if there was a strong breeze. The inside of the cape was a golden colour, radiant with a flickering light, but it was black on the outside, as Angel Hosus was dressed like an old-fashioned schoolteacher.

Without using words I said to Angel Hosus, 'Should I tell Sister that my grandfather has the Bible? I have often seen him reading it.'

Angel Hosus spoke back to me: 'No, Lorna, that's not a good idea. Sister Ann would only get very cross with you.' I felt disappointed. Now Angel Hosus walked among the desks. Sometimes he stopped and smiled down at the children sitting at them. There were two children to each desk, I forgot to tell you that.

When Angel Hosus reached my desk he put his hand on my shoulder and said, 'Lorna, don't be sad. Haven't you always enjoyed when Archangel Michael reads from the Bible to you?'

I looked up at Angel Hosus and said, 'Yes.' And I asked him, 'Is Archangel Michael going to come today to read something out of the Bible to me?'

'No, not today, Lorna, but in a few days' time.'

Suddenly Sister called out, 'You down there! At the back. Are you not paying attention?' I was startled – she usually ignored me – and jumped.

Angel Hosus said to me, 'Lorna, stand up and answer whatever questions she asks you.'

I stood nervously and said, 'I am.'

She asked me, 'Well, what did I just say?'

I said, 'You were speaking about Our Lady, the mother of baby Jesus, Sister.' She seemed to get very cross with me. An angry look came across her face and she was about to march towards my desk at the back of the classroom.

But suddenly, Angel Hosus was no longer standing at my desk. He was now standing in front of Sister Ann. He reached out and touched her hand for a brief moment. At the same time, Sister's guardian angel was whispering in her ear.

She just stopped and said, 'Sit down. Don't make me have to speak to you again.'

I said, 'Thank you' to Sister's guardian angel and I said, 'Thank you' to Sister for listening to her guardian angel and for doing what her guardian angel had said. Of course, I said all that silently. Sister did not hear me but her guardian angel gave me a big smile.

Now as Angel Hosus walked in and out between the desks, his cape was swooshing as if there was a very strong breeze, although of course there was no breeze in the room. What was lovely to see was his cape seeming to touch some of the desks. I knew his cape didn't *actually* touch any of the desks as it is only on extremely rare occasions that angels physically touch something in our world, but it looked that way.

As I have mentioned before, there is a space between the angels and physical things, even when it's all very crowded. Now the classroom was packed with angels and of course every child had a guardian angel as well, yet somehow there was enough room.

When Angel Hosus reached my desk again, he told me he had to go.

I said, 'Goodbye.' Angel Hosus walked towards the nun's desk. When he was only a few feet away from it he disappeared. Sister continued to tell us about Our Lady, about Joseph – her husband – and the baby Jesus.

When school was over, I decided not to go straight home.

I cut through the estate and set out along one of the country roads. I climbed up on to the bank that ran along the hedging. I loved walking along the bank because it made me feel so tall. A robin landed just in front of me. I almost stepped on it but it just hopped safely along in front of me. I was laughing and the little robin stopped suddenly and flew on to some wild flowers, picking greenflies from around the stalks, just under the leaves and the blossoms. I watched for a minute. Then as I said goodbye to the little robin it flew into the hedgerow. I heard my name being called and when I looked up there was Angel Elijah walking towards me. He looked as if he was quite a distance away but I knew he wasn't.

The first time I met Angel Elijah, when I was ten years old, he walked across water. Even to this day, that memory fascinates me.

Angel Elijah showed me Joe, my future husband, who I would love and who would die at a young age. Angel Elijah is the Prophet Elijah – an angel dwells in his soul. That is why he was human on earth. His soul and the angel are still intertwined. God has never separated them.

Within a few seconds he was standing in front of me. I was thinking of the time when I had last seen him and he had walked on water again, across the river.

In the intervening two years Angel Elijah had not changed one bit. As I stood still, watching him coming towards me on the bank, I was just imagining it was water beneath his feet. Everything about Angel Elijah is enormous and everything about him is the colour of amber, all the shades of amber you could possibly visualise. The material of his clothing. Even his face and hands. I'm sure that is why I love the colour amber.

I stood there looking up at him and said, 'Hello, Elijah.' I could never say his name right. It always sounded very funny because I just could not pronounce the word Elijah, but he didn't seem to mind.

He said, 'Lorna, follow me.' He turned around and headed back down along the bank the way he had come. He came to a gate and said, 'Let's go in here.' I had to climb over the gate but of course, Angel Elijah didn't have to do that. He just appeared at the far side of it.

I said to him, 'That's not fair.' It was a field I had been in many times before, sometimes by myself, except of course that the angels were always with me. Other times, I might have my neighbour's dog with me, an Alsatian called Shane.

As we walked, Angel Elijah said, 'Lorna, don't be worried. I have not come to tell you something that is bittersweet like I did before.' I stopped and stood in front of Angel Elijah. He really was like a giant.

'I was a little scared in case you did. I was only ten then,' I said to Angel Elijah. 'I remember everything you told me. I am twelve now, going on thirteen.'

'Archangel Michael has asked me to give you a message. That is the only reason I'm here, Lorna. The message is: You are going to meet a saint.'

I replied, 'I have heard about saints like St Bridget in school. Every year we make a St Bridget's Cross out of straw.'

'Lorna, it is St Francis who you will meet and there will be another angel with you.' It started to drizzle and Angel Elijah said, 'You need to get home before it rains too heavily.'

I asked Angel Elijah, 'Can you not tell me anything about St Francis now?'

He said, 'No.' I climbed back over the gate. Angel Elijah was already standing on the bank telling me to hurry up. As I climbed up on the bank Angel Elijah reached out his hand to me, helping me to climb on to the bank.

'Thank you, Angel Elijah.' I smiled at him and he smiled back. I said to him, 'Your legs are much longer than mine. You definitely can move much faster.' Angel Elijah just smiled again and turned. He started to walk. His feet were not touching the ground though. I followed him. When he stopped, I got down off the bank and crossed the road back into the estate. As I did, Angel Elijah said he had to go and he disappeared. That was in February and next month I was going to be thirteen years old.

In the course of the summer holidays that year, I forgot what Angel Elijah had said about meeting St Francis. But one day my dad took me fishing with his best friend, Arthur. They had gone fishing up along the riverbank but I stayed put because there were loads of daisies and buttercups growing along the bank. I wanted to make a daisy chain. I thought to myself buttercups would look lovely mixed in with the daisies.

Dad called out, 'Don't be too long.' I kind of half answered as I was already engrossed in picking the daisies and buttercups. I was in a world of my own. A few minutes later, I looked up along the riverbank but I could not see my dad or Arthur. I decided to stay sitting on the bank for another little while to finish off the flower chain. An angel came and stood in front of me. She was like a silver spiral – so smooth, elegant and tall. I hadn't realised that she was standing there at first. It was only when I heard Archangel Michael call my name that I looked up. I noticed that the light around me, and the daisies and buttercups, looked much brighter but I wasn't really taking any notice until Archangel Michael called me.

I looked up, saw him and said, 'Hello.' I put my hand over my eyes because his light seemed to be very strong too.

Archangel Michael said, 'Lorna, you are going to meet St Francis. We're going to go back into the past.' I went to get up but Archangel Michael said, 'No, Lorna, remain sitting.' He knelt down in front of me and then he reached forward with his right hand and said, 'Don't be afraid.'

No sooner had he said this than everything changed. I was still sitting by a river. It was only like a little stream though. The countryside was completely different. It was hilly. I saw a young man walking towards me. I smiled at him. I knew it was St Francis. He came along and sat down beside me. I knew it was him because he had a bunch of buttercups in his hand. He put them down on top of some of the daisies I had and he started to sort them out: one buttercup, then one daisy. I looked at him. He had a young face.

He gave me a big smile and said, 'Hello, Lorna.'

Shyly I said, 'Hello.' I smiled back at him. This close he looked very rough-skinned as if he had been living out in the open. His clothes looked old and ragged, but yet clean. He was small in height and looked very skinny. He was quite bony, I thought as he sat down beside me. His hands were chafed and red. He spoke to me about making the daisy and buttercup chain. It wasn't always in English but yet, I understood him. He put a big buttercup and daisy chain around my neck and another one on my wrist. Then he stood up and started to walk. I followed him. I had to run a little to catch up with him. He was a fast walker even though he was small. That beautiful, spiral angel came with us as well. I was no longer beside a river. It was as we were walking I noticed St Francis had a stick. Well, what we might call a walking stick but one made from the branch of a tree. I saw that he was heading towards a village. Some people might call it a small town.

When we reached the town, I was walking next to him on his right-hand side. The beautiful silver spiral angel was giving a female appearance and was walking behind us. It wasn't St Francis's guardian angel. It was an angel whose role it was to accompany me on another journey.

During the time I spent with St Francis he played with the children of the town. They seemed to like him. When he saw a woman stacking bundles of straw up against bushes he went to help her, without hesitation, and when the job was finished he walked away and never said a word to her. As we walked through the little town, some people seemed to welcome St Francis but others didn't. A few people threw stones at him or shouted at him. One of the stones hit him on the foot and made his toe bleed as he was barefoot, but he took no notice. He didn't say a word to me as we walked through the town.

Just as we reached the end of the town he walked over to a very small building, like a shed. It had a flat roof. He sat down on a piece of wood a few feet away from the little house.

I turned to the silver spiral angel and I said, 'I don't think St Francis knows I'm still here with him.'

The angel said, 'Yes, Lorna, you're right. He thinks you are still at the riverbank, making the daisy chains and buttercups. No one can see you.'

'He didn't notice I was running after him?'

'No, Lorna,' said the silver spiral angel. I felt a little sad that St Francis didn't know I was beside him. When the door of the little house opened a woman came out and invited St Francis in. I was now walking behind him. The little house was full of people and children. There was some bread on the table and a small fire was lit. The flickering flames of light seemed to be the only light in the room for it was quite dark. I could see the faces of men and women when the light of the fire danced across them. Some children sat on the floor over in one corner. They were playing quietly. No one was saying very much. I thought to myself that maybe they were all very tired after a hard day's work. St Francis spoke some words. I could not hear him very well but it sounded kind of funny. He walked across the room, muttering. It was then that I realised he was singing as his voice became stronger and everyone seemed to perk up. After a few minutes, I could hear laughter. St Francis was laughing too.

I said to the silver spiral angel, 'I can see why he's a saint. He makes people feel happy.' The angel didn't answer me. The next moment I was back sitting at the riverbank. I looked at the daisy and buttercup necklace and bangle that St Francis had helped me to make.

I got up and started to walk along the riverbank to find my dad, and then Archangel Michael came out from behind one of the trees and said, 'Hello.'

I said to him, 'I met St Francis.'

Archangel Michael said, 'Yes, I know you did, Lorna. I was there with you as well.'

I said to him, 'But I did not see you.'

'Lorna, you weren't meant to see me.'

'Why not?' I asked.

Archangel Michael said, 'No questions.'

'Just one more, please, Archangel Michael,' I begged as I admired the buttercups and daisies around my neck. 'Will I ever meet St Francis again?'

Archangel Michael said, 'Yes, you will.' Then he said he had to go.

I was about fifteen at the time. We were living in Leixlip. I was working for my dad in the petrol station in Rathmines. I usually worked from Monday to Friday, but sometimes my dad would ask me to work on a Saturday and then he would give me a day off during the week. I decided to take a Wednesday off on this particular occasion. I gave my mum a hand around the house hoovering and polishing the furniture in the front room and I cleaned the bathroom, but about two o'clock I went out for a walk.

I walked down to the church in Leixlip. I walked in through the main door. The church was empty, no one there except for the angels praying to God on our behalf. I walked down the aisle about halfway and sat on one of the seats to the left-hand side. A few minutes later, I heard my name called. I turned around and saw Archangel Michael walking down the aisle towards me.

'Hello, Michael,' I said. 'Have you come to join me in prayer?'

'No, Lorna, you are going to be brought back to the past to meet St Francis again. Sit back up in the seat.' I did as Archangel Michael said and I started to pray. At the same moment, Archangel Michael reached out with his right hand and took my soul. I always feel at that instant as if my breath has been taken away but the next moment, I was walking uphill along a road. I stopped and turned around. There was the beautiful silver spiral angel walking right behind me. I said hello to her and she just nodded her head. Then I started to walk again. I had only walked a short distance when I stopped to look around. I was at the top of the hill. It was then that I saw St Francis in the distance.

The silver spiral angel said, 'Lorna, watch carefully.' I stood there without moving. I was afraid I might disturb him. St Francis sat on one of the rocks alongside the road. It wasn't a road like we have today. It was a dusty road, a road made of clay and stones. He was having a rest. I was standing there, just watching him, when two little sparrows flew on to his shoulder. I was astonished. Butterflies started to fly around him too. They seemed to appear from nowhere. He rooted in his pocket as if he was looking for crumbs for the birds but he didn't have any. So he pulled the seeds from the grass that was growing beside him. As he sat on the rock St Francis held the seeds in the palm of his hand with his fist closed. They were in his right hand. He drew it towards his chest and clasped his left hand over his right. At the same moment, I saw the Angels of Prayer ascending to heaven as he prayed over the seeds that were held in his hand. When St Francis opened his hands there were no longer just little seeds in the palm of his hands but something that looked to me like cake.

The silver spiral angel said, 'No, Lorna. It's not cake. It is bread.' Francis broke the bread in half and put one piece in his pocket. Then he started to break the other half of the bread into small pieces like crumbs. He stretched out the palms of both of his hands and the two little birds flew on to them and started to eat the bread.

Within a few seconds, many more birds were around him. I smiled because St Francis started to sing and the birds were chirping as if they were singing with him as he held his hands out. The birds were still feeding on those little crumbs that just didn't seem to disappear, no matter how fast the little birds ate them. Then, St Francis stopped singing and he stood up. He reached into his pocket and took the other piece of bread out. He broke it up into crumbs and sprinkled it on the ground. He was surrounded by creatures of nature: rabbits, mice, hedgehogs, rats, a fox and some other kinds of very little creatures I did not recognise. Sometimes, a butterfly would land on his head and then take off. Then another one would do the same. The birds never went after the butterflies or the bees that were flying around either. All of nature was in harmony with each other, and all living creatures could feel the compassion for them, the gentle care and love for them that was in this man. God has put him in my life to help me tell everyone how important it is that we wake up and take care of the beautiful planet we have been given.

St Francis looked in my direction for a moment and he smiled.

I said to the silver spiral angel, 'Does he know I'm here? Can he see me?'

The angel said, 'No, he does not know you're here but he's thinking of you. He's remembering you at the riverbank when he was sitting with you, enjoying himself.'

All of a sudden the birds flew away and all the little creatures ran in all directions. It was then that I could hear the sound of the wind. I only realised then how silent it had been before and that God was only allowing me to hear the sounds of all the creatures that were around St Francis.

Now he stood up, brushed his clothes down and seemed to be trying to make himself look respectable.

The silver spiral angel said, 'Lorna, walk closer now.' I started to walk slowly towards him. He was looking the other way. In the distance a group of young boys were waving and they were calling to St Francis. Francis hurried, walking fast towards them. They stood all around him. I could hear them talking. What I could make out was that St Francis had to go and visit someone in another town. St Francis seemed to be nervous. He looked back to where I was standing. I knew he couldn't see me. I didn't have to ask the angels because I knew he was thinking of me for some reason, so I said a prayer that whoever he was going to meet would be kind to him. When Archangel Michael appeared beside me, the silver spiral angel disappeared.

Archangel Michael said, 'He does need your prayer, Lorna, for it is St Francis's father who has sent for him. Francis knows his father is not pleased with him because of the kind of life he lives. His father does not understand how close St Francis is to God.' Archangel Michael reached out and took my hand.

The next moment, I was sitting in the church. The church was still empty. Nobody had come in to say a prayer but there were angels in the church still and they were in prayer. Archangel Michael was standing in the aisle where I was sitting when he said, 'Lorna, a gift from St Francis.' For a brief moment, the daisy and buttercup necklace and bangle appeared around my neck and my wrist. It was such a surprise. I didn't know what to say. I touched the daisies and buttercups with my fingertips gently so the yellow flowers and the little daisies would not break. You would have thought that I had only just picked them. Archangel Michael touched my shoulder, saying, 'They are a gift from St Francis but they are going to disappear, Lorna.'

I smiled and said, 'Thank you, Francis.'

I asked Archangel Michael if St Francis could hear me and Archangel Michael said, 'Yes, for he is in heaven with God.' The next moment the daisies and buttercups glowed brightly. They shone like a bright light and then with a spark they disappeared. 'I have to go now, Lorna,' Archangel Michael said and he disappeared. I didn't get a chance to ask another question.

I remained in the church for a few minutes praying for everyone in the world. Just as I was leaving the church a man came through the doors. He knelt down to pray. As I passed him I asked God to send the man all the help he needed in his life and for him not to turn that help away. That was my prayer for him as I went out the church gate. A woman passed me heading up to go into the church to pray as well.

The angels are asking me to share one more time with you when I met St Francis. It was about a year ago, in 2015. I was down in the orchard at my house doing some tidying up. Angel Hosus was sitting on one of the tree stumps.

I said to him, 'It would be great if you could give me a helping hand.'

Angel Hosus answered, 'Yes, I will, by just sitting here with you.'

That really made me laugh.

When I stopped laughing Angel Hosus said, 'We have company.'

I turned around and saw Archangel Michael walking towards us from the old hay barn.

'Good afternoon, Lorna,' said Archangel Michael.

'Hello,' I replied. 'Have you come to help?'

'No,' said Archangel Michael, 'but I have come for another reason. I'm going to take you, Lorna, to visit St Francis again. It will be just for a moment.'

I sat down on one of the stones at the bank with rows of trees behind me. At the same time I was being surrounded by the angels. They were putting that spiritual blanket around me. Archangel Michael knelt down in front of me, reached out and touched my soul.

Instantaneously, it was night-time and Archangel Michael and I were walking towards a group of small houses. I saw the silver spiral angel radiating light as it stood by a window in one of the houses. It was so dark outside that if it weren't for the silver spiral angel, there would have been no light at all.

The angel acknowledged me and I said, 'Hello.'

When we were a few feet away from the window, a man in the house opened the little shutter on it. When Archangel Michael and I reached the house we peeped through the little window. There I saw St Francis lying on a bed. He was very sick and others were attending to him: two men, one young and the other older. Archangel Michael said that they were followers of St Francis. The younger one was skinny like the saint himself. He was repeatedly putting a damp cloth on St Francis's head, then rinsing it out in a small bowl of water and replacing it. The other, much older man seemed a lot heavier and more well-built. I was not sure exactly what he was doing as the room was dark except for the candle and its flickering light beside St Francis's bed. Every now and then the older one left and brought back blankets and would take the old ones off the bed and put fresh ones on.

In a whispering voice I said to Archangel Michael, 'If they are St Francis's followers are they then monks too?'

I was forgetting that no one else could hear me, only Archangel Michael.

'Yes, Lorna. They are some of his first followers.'

'I would love to be able to help him.'

'Lorna, he will be okay. He is stronger than you think but yes, he is very sick. He has a fever.'

St Francis's guardian angel was looking down upon him lovingly. He gave a male appearance and, at times, bent completely over him and seemed to cover Francis completely. His guardian angel was dressed in beautiful purple and gold clothing. He looked in the direction of the little window and gave us a big smile but I felt sad to see St Francis so sick.

Archangel Michael said, 'We have to go now, Lorna.'

The next moment I was back in the orchard sitting on the rock. Archangel Michael was standing in front of me. He stretched out his hand. As I looked up at him I reached out and took his hand. Archangel Michael seemed very big, like a giant standing in front of me. His hand seemed enormous – when your hand goes into an angel's hand your hand seems to become lost within theirs. I could feel the love coming from Archangel Michael as he helped me to stand up.

'I think you should go into the house now, Lorna, to make tea,' said Archangel Michael. 'Angel Hosus will accompany you for a little while.'

I replied, 'I think I will do that, Archangel Michael.'

He said he had to go and he walked towards the trees on my right and disappeared.

Angel Hosus walked back through the orchard with me and into the house. As I made some tea I automatically set a place for him at the big wooden table in the barn.

I said to Angel Hosus, 'Would you like to join me?'

'Yes, Lorna, but I can only stay for a short while.'

Angel Hosus sat at the table. In the same way that angels' feet never touch the ground, neither do they actually touch physical things. He himself never really touched the table or the chair that he was sitting on. It didn't look like he was sitting on the chair because, as I say, I can always see what I call that cushion between the angels and the physical world. They are only allowed to touch something physically if God allows it.

We talked about St Francis as I sipped my tea. Angel Hosus at times was imitating me drinking tea and sometimes he would make funny faces, pretending he did not like it. A few minutes later, Angel Hosus said that he had to go and he went back out the door that was wide open and walked across the garden before disappearing.

After Angel Hosus left I received a text message from my

daughter, Ruth, asking if I had got some pages printed out. I sent back a message saying no. My printer had run out of ink.

I had to go into Kilkenny to get ink for it. I had to do a few other little errands there too. I parked in Dunnes Stores' car park down along the river. I walked through the streets of Kilkenny. It is a beautiful, mediaeval city, very small but I love it. I can walk from one end to the other in forty minutes. I saw the guardian angels with everyone and of course, all those incredible unemployed angels cut through one of the lanes and came out on the main street.

There was a lady walking in front of me. She was walking very strangely and I know a young child might have laughed or smiled, wondering why she was walking the way she was. What was so beautiful to me was seeing the two unemployed angels either side of her, helping her to keep her balance as each foot touched the ground. She did not seem to be able to bend her knees and that's what made her walk look funny.

The unemployed angel that was on her left spoke to me without words, saying, 'Her hips don't work very well either but she is so happy and full of life because she can walk.'

She turned into one of the shops as I walked along the street. I thought to myself as I watched the men, women and children passing me by how lucky we all were that we could all walk, and what freedom it gave us.

I got home a few hours later. When I went into the house and turned off the alarm it seemed quite empty. I didn't see any angels, so I decided to go upstairs and to continue writing a little bit more about St Francis, but when I opened the door to the room where I work it was crowded with angels.

I said, 'Hello. Have you come to help me?'

All the angels spoke simultaneously but yet I could hear

each one individually. I don't know how I can do that. No matter how many angels are speaking at the same time I hear each one separately, and yet altogether.

I said, 'Hello,' and walked over to my desk. I pulled out my chair and turned on the computer and the Dragon Net. Before I started writing I looked out the little window to my right. Along the wall in the garden there are rosebushes. I watched three angels there. Two of them were holding baskets and one had what looked like scissors in its hand and was snipping a rose ever so gently and then putting them into the basket. When they did this the rose would appear in the angel's hand. Yet, at the same time, it would still be on the rosebush. All the roses on the bushes seemed to glow brightly. The angels turned and looked up at the window. They waved to me but never said a word. Things like this happen to me every day of my life.

I said out loud to the angels that were in the room with me, 'When I'm finished here I will go outside and pick some roses myself.'

I have met St Francis on different occasions and all I can say to you is that he is a saint and he was extremely close to God. That made him close to nature. He was full of love and no matter how badly people treated him at times, he only had love for them. He had a very hard life, but yet a life that was full of happiness and joy because he walked in the footsteps of Jesus. Since that day in the church in Leixlip when Archangel Michael told me the daisy and buttercup chain was a gift from St Francis, since that day in the springtime and all through the summer, watching the daisies and buttercups peeping through the grass reminds me of St Francis and his love.

As you know, I travel around the world a lot and I give talks, sometimes in community centres, hotels, churches and other places of worship of different faiths. On occasion I do get the opportunity where someone brings me to visit a place that is special because it is a holy place where Our Lady has appeared, the Queen of Angels, mother of Jesus, our mother.

I don't know whether you know or not but Archangel Michael has appeared in many places around the world as well. Anywhere Archangel Michael has appeared there is a place of worship built in that place and it becomes a holy place, a place of prayer. I never knew Archangel Michael had appeared in so many places around the world. I have asked on a few occasions why he hadn't told me but he never answers the question. I guess it was something I had to find out for myself. At times when I was in one of those places where Archangel Michael had appeared, and sometimes Our Lady, I felt a little overwhelmed that Archangel Michael had never shared this with me. Maybe he will talk to me about it some day. I don't know. You can never tell God or the angels what to do. You can only ask. When I ask a question about something that concerns me in the world, many a time that question is not answered there and then. It can be many years later. So I'm still in hope that Archangel Michael will tell me why he never shared with me about him appearing in different places around the world.

CHAPTER 20

Holy Places and Driving Tests

ONE TIME I WAS IN HEEDE, A TOWN IN GERMANY, AND I went to a holy place where Our Lady had appeared to two children. People were coming and going all the time, praying. Of course, the Angels of Prayer would be there as well. I remember entering the cave where people walk through and they would put little slips of paper with their petition to Our Lady between the rocks. I stood at the entrance for a moment because Angel Hosus was standing there.

He just said, 'Look, Lorna.'

I looked into the cave. Running through it was a small pathway twisting and turning.

As the people disappeared out of sight I saw souls as well as angels, and when Angel Hosus said, 'You can walk through now,' I saw souls followed by angels removing all of the little notes from between the rocks. Sometimes the angel's hand would disappear in among the rocks and other times, the soul's hand would disappear as well, but when their hands came out from between the rocks I could see they had retrieved a piece of paper that glowed brightly in the soul's hand. Sometimes the piece of paper was very tiny. Some were all crumpled or rolled like tubes. One time as one of the souls retrieved a petition from between the rocks the petition seemed to fall and float slowly downwards, but it never touched the ground as the soul put its hand beneath it and it floated into the palm of the soul's hand like a feather. Then the soul looked at me but never said a word. It just continued retrieving petitions. A man and woman were putting their petitions in between the rocks of the cave and at the same time, I saw the Angels of Prayer ascending in that incredible upside-down waterfall full of the light of angels.

I had to stop for a moment so the couple could move on, then I turned and asked Angel Hosus, 'Who are those souls I see that are taking those petitions from between the rocks?'

Angel Hosus replied, 'They are saints of Germany.'

Angel Hosus called out a few names in German, but I did not understand, so I cannot give you those names. One of those souls, one of those saints, turned and looked at me and then walked towards me. I hesitated and stopped for a moment as the soul held out both hands full of petitions and asked me to touch them.

Angel Hosus said, 'Touch them, Lorna.' As I did they all disappeared and the soul spoke in German.

I did not understand what he said but Angel Hosus said to me, 'Lorna, those petitions went straight away to heaven with the Angels of Prayer. Now, they are at the feet of God.'

I spoke to Angel Hosus silently and I said, 'I hope God will answer and bring love and hope into the lives of the people who wrote them. I hope that their prayers will be answered.'

'Lorna, all prayers are put at the feet of God. He knows the prayer before it is even on the paper or a thought in someone's mind. All angels and souls petition on behalf of the human race. No matter what religion they are or whether they believe in God or not. God loves them all and wants their guardian angel to bring their soul back home to heaven, but only when it is the time for their human body to die. God is the father of every man, woman and child. He wants you all to enjoy the gift of life.'

I said to Angel Hosus, 'I enjoy the gift of life.'

Angel Hosus said to me, 'Lorna, you do not always enjoy it. Sometimes you forget to do so through all the different ups and downs in life. It is important to enjoy the gift of life, to be able to love, to have emotions, to have compassion, to allow yourself to feel peace within your heart and to recognise all the gifts that are around you. It is important to realise how much you are loved unconditionally. Mankind are all God's children. That is why angels are here helping mankind to grow spiritually, to awaken them to feel peace and love in holy places.'

These places exert their influence and pull people towards them even if they are not always recognised. I remember seeing a lay-by in Germany where the veil between the material world and the spiritual world was unusually thin. It looked nothing special but I could see that many people were being drawn to stop there and absorb its special atmosphere.

'Angel Hosus, do you mean holy places, places of prayer, are for us all no matter what religion or faith we are, even if we don't believe in God, or that there is life after death?'

'Lorna, you know there is life after death because God has allowed you to see all of his angels and the souls of the living and the dead. You yourself know God is real because you have seen God.'

'Angel Hosus, I am giving that message. The message that

God has asked me to give, telling people all around the world, of all different religions and those that don't believe in God, that God is real.'

As I walked slowly through the cave and out into the sunshine I spoke to Angel Hosus silently, without words. Angel Hosus said that he had to go and he walked past me.

Today, he is in the room. He is beside me at the computer helping me to write the exact words.

I said to Angel Hosus, 'Holy places are so important. It doesn't matter if it is a Catholic church, a Presbyterian church, a mosque, a synagogue, an open field, under a tree, in a cave or on top of a mountain. It doesn't need a building. It only needs people to come together and pray in that place over and over again for generations. A place becomes a holy place, a place of prayer, full of peace and love and unity.'

I stopped talking into the computer and I looked out the window.

Angel Hosus said, 'Lorna, don't be looking out the window. It is not time for you to rest just yet. In another few minutes you can go down and make yourself a cup of tea. God has thoughts flowing through your mind. Keep speaking into the computer, for you are saying the right things.'

I swivelled my chair back around to face the computer and started to talk again. I didn't even look up at Angel Hosus. I just did as he said and started to talk again. Every single place of prayer is sacred and the human race should feel safe within these places of prayer. They should all be protected. We should all strive towards having respect for holy places because they are sacred. It doesn't matter what religion they belong to. They belong to us all because we are all God's children, regardless of faith or nationality or the colour of our skin, or whether we are richer or poorer. The more you pray in your home, the more your home becomes peaceful and full of love, but at certain times in our lives we should go to a place of prayer. We should go to one of those sacred places that may be nearby or close to us to pray. All religions have certain times of the year that are sacred and they ask people to come to the place of prayer to pray at that time. When a place becomes a holy place, a place of prayer, there are always angels there even if the human race or any religion turns around and says this place is no longer a holy place. It is, because the angels will always be there, continuously praying.

Again, in my travels, places have been pointed out to me where I was told people prayed for generations in a particular area but they are no longer a place of prayer because that religious group deconsecrated them, but I have to say I've always still seen angels there in prayer. I don't think you can take away the sacredness of a holy place, especially when God has allowed it to happen. A holy place is always a holy place, even if it is forgotten about for generations or hundreds of years. God has shown me that one day we all, as a people of the world, as one nation, will come under the one umbrella. We will all pray together as one. I cannot wait for that day, but today in 2016, in today's world, it seems so far away. Mankind is still using God as a weapon to justify the evil in the world. To justify war, terrorism and hatred. We have to stop hate and stop hating each other. We must stop looking for revenge and instead have love and compassion. We have to start to forgive, to love, to care, to strive towards justice and peace, for freedom and the right to love, to live life, to raise a family. We have to see the light of hope. God has the light of hope burning brightly in the world today, but mankind seems to have become blind to it.

When I stopped writing I said to Angel Hosus, 'I think I will make myself some tea and maybe a sandwich and go for a walk.'

Angel Hosus told me that he must go then and he disappeared.

I went downstairs and made a tomato and onion sandwich with a little cheese and toasted it under the grill. It was yummy. I hadn't realised how hungry I was. It was actually five past seven in the evening.

I enjoyed a walk up through the lane. I didn't meet anyone except for the swallows that flew around me. At times when I'm out walking and enjoying the fresh air and nature around me I meet people and stop and talk. Even then, though, I am in prayer. My soul is always in prayer and for the last five years, it has really become intense. It never stops, not even for one second. When I got to the end of the lane, instead of walking back through the town, I turned around and headed home the same way.

Just as I got in the door my daughter Ruth called me on my mobile. My two grandchildren wanted to say goodnight and talk with their gran. We had a little chat. I told them I was really looking forward to their visit on Friday. They were going to be staying the whole weekend. I love when my grandchildren come to visit, especially when the weather is fine and they can be outside on the trampoline. I love their inquisitiveness about everything around them, especially when they help me to do a little gardening. We often go on an adventure through the fields to see what interesting little creatures we can find.

I often ask the angels could they not allow my daughter Ruth to see the angels with her children on the trampoline as they jump up and down. I know if every mother could see what I can see they would just break their hearts laughing. Billy Bob and Jessica have great fun, trying to do all kinds of acrobatics, but if you saw the angels imitating the children and pretending they are bumping into each other you would burst out laughing. I have often counted twenty angels on the trampoline with my grandchildren and my daughter.

This weekend I'm hoping that the sun will be shining so I can watch the antics of the angels with my grandchildren. Angels are always playing with children. Whenever I see children having fun the angels join in the fun as well, or if a child is sad or feeling left out you will see the angels doing everything to give them courage and confidence to get up and join the other children and play. The angels try to get them to forget that they were feeling a little disappointed or shy.

A couple of months ago, my daughter Megan had to sit her driving test. On that particular morning, I gave out to God and all of the angels because when I went out to check the car to see if everything was working perfectly I discovered one of the bulbs was gone. We headed straight down to the local garage that does repairs and as we drove down I didn't let my daughter know that I was praying that they would have a bulb and it would be easily fixed, as she was stressed enough. I didn't want to stress her any more.

The angels just kept whispering in my ear, 'Don't worry. Everything will be fine.'

Every time the angels say something like that to me I always say back to them, 'It's all right for you to say that, but you are not the ones that have to go and get it fixed.'

I always hear a little laughter when I say that to the angels. They don't laugh loudly. It is always kept low-key. I always smile to myself because I believe that if all the angels that were in the car laughed loudly like thunder the vibrations would make the car rock.

Megan turned to me and said, 'Mam, what are you smiling about? This is serious.'

I said to her, 'Don't worry. I know the garage man will have a bulb and it will be easily fixed.'

As we drove in I saw the owner and one of the mechanics. I told him that Megan was doing her test at eleven that morning and that the bulb was gone in one of the front lights. He had it fixed in a jiffy. It was a great relief.

When the owner said, 'All fixed,' my daughter said, 'Thanks!' with a big smile on her face.

He wished her luck and we headed off to the driving test centre.

She parked the car and said, 'Mum, I'm very nervous. Do you think I will pass?'

I said, 'Of course, you will pretend you are listening to the satnav and that the examiner is not in the car with you.'

I walked into the centre with her and we sat down and waited. There were others ahead of us and they all left one by one with the examiner. I said a prayer for each one of them, and then Megan was called. She disappeared into one of the offices. A few minutes later, she walked out with the examiner through the doors and I watched them head for the car. A few moments later they drove away.

I decided to walk down around the business centre, praying that Megan would pass the driving test. I saw two young men going off to do their test and I prayed that they would pass too. I walked around, from the centre up to the main gate and back again to the driving centre, praying that Megan wouldn't make any mistakes. Sadly on one of my walks towards the centre I saw a young girl and her mother walk out through the doors. The young girl was in tears. She had failed the test. Her guardian angel had its arms wrapped around her. The mother was trying to comfort her daughter.

The angels allowed me to hear some of the things the young girl said to her mother: 'I forgot everything. I made one mistake after another. I was hopeless.'

Her mother gave her a big hug and held her in her arms for a moment. At the same moment the mother's guardian angel and her daughter's guardian angel embraced. Both of them embraced at the same time with love but what was more beautiful than that was seeing the love coming from the mother and spiralling around the daughter. A mother's love comforting her child. That love coming from the mother's soul and touching her daughter allowed her daughter to feel that pure love. Then I saw the love coming from the young girl's soul and touching the love of her mother.

I wish I could see that more often than I do but I don't see it always. I try to remind people how important it is to let those that you love know that you love them. It is important to say the words or to show it with a hug to give comfort. Each and every one of us has this beautiful gift inside of us; our soul that is pure love. What a wonderful gift that spark of the light, that tiny speck of God, is. It is your soul and it fills every part of you. It is pure love. You are pure love and because of this God has given each and every one of us a unique and powerful gift: the ability to love with the pure love that is your soul. As I got closer, the mother and the young girl headed towards where their car was parked. The mother got into the driver's seat and the young girl into the passenger seat. As they passed me by I said a little prayer that the young girl would pass the driving test and become a safe driver. Hopefully, at her next driving test she would.

It must've been ten minutes later when my daughter drove past me. I saw her park the car and the driving examiner got out of the car and walked towards the entrance of the testing centre. My daughter hurried after him. He had a quick walk.

I said to the angels, 'I don't know if that looks good. Did she pass?'

They never said a word to me. I must've asked about five times but they never answered my question. A few minutes later, my daughter came out through those doors.

She had a smile on her face and jumped with joy and said, 'I passed.'

It was only at that moment that all the angels around us jumped for joy as well. Let me tell you, the angels always keep me in suspense. I wish they had let me know beforehand. That would have saved me all that anxiety, but as I walked towards the car with my daughter I understood why they kept me in the dark. It wasn't for the angels to tell me that my daughter had passed her driving test. It was for Megan to share that joy and excitement with me, her family and friends that now she has a full driving licence.

When we reached the car I automatically walked to the driver's side and Megan said, 'Mam, who has the keys?' as she shook them.

The two of us burst out laughing.

I said to her, 'I'll have to get out of the habit that I have to drive the car. I'm so happy now and I thank God and the angels. Well done, Megan.'

We sat in the car for a few minutes just talking. 'Megan, I saw you when you were walking behind the driving tester. I didn't know what to think.'

Megan replied that when she got within earshot of him she said to him that the most nerve-wracking part of the driving test is this part, walking back into the driving centre to find out whether she passed or not. He laughed. I never saw a driving examiner like him. All of the other men had short hair but he had long hair and he looked cool. He reminded me of an artist or a musician, not the examiner for your driving licence. It made me feel relaxed. Megan having her full licence now gives her a lot more freedom. I don't have to drive her here, there and everywhere. In fact, she is driving me. I ask her guardian angel and all the angels to keep her safe and of course, I ask the soul of her dad to watch over her. I ask for Joe not to take his eyes off all my children and grandchildren. I know he is watching over them all.

CHAPTER 21

Butterflies

IT WAS A WARM, SUNNY DAY AND EVERY TIME I LOOKED
out the window I was fighting not to go outside.

My guardian angel whispered in my ear saying, 'Lorna,
don't be thinking about it. You do deserve a break.'

Angel Hosus said, 'Yes, Lorna, your guardian angel is
correct. Off you go now.'

Within a few minutes I had left the house and had gone
for a drive. I ended up at one of the big houses open to the
public on the outskirts of Kilkenny. It had a beautiful wood
as well, but first I decided I would go in and have something
to eat. I was dying to have something a little different. Instead
of just plain food, something with a nice taste. I found a
lovely table beside a window. I had decided not to sit outside.

When the young waitress came along and asked me what
would I like I said to her, 'I need to give your chef a special
request.'

She gave me a smile and said, 'Okay.'

I asked her, 'Could you ask the chef if he would be able

to make up a vegetable and noodle stir-fry and to make it as tasty as possible, but I do not want it spicy. It is very important that you let the chef know that I am allergic to fish and shellfish.'

The young waitress said, 'Oh I'm sure the stir-fry will be fine.'

I said to her, 'You really do need to say to him.'

She said, 'Okay,' and off she went. I saw three unemployed angels running after her.

Her guardian angel was whispering in her ear. I smiled at her guardian angel. It gave a female appearance and was dressed in a beautiful white and silver gown. What made me smile was that her guardian angel had a black tie hung loosely around its neck. Then the young girl walked through some doors and I could not see them any more.

On my way in I had picked up a newspaper off the counter just inside the door. I started to turn the pages and look at all the pictures. They were mainly all of Trump, Clinton and our own Taoiseach and the new prime minister in England, Theresa May.

As I was turning the pages an angel said, 'There is no good news in that paper, Lorna.'

I said without looking, 'I know. We are at war.'

'Yes, Lorna.'

I recognised the voice. It wasn't just any of the angels that was there close by me. I looked out the window and in the distance, not too far away, just where the trees were I saw Archangel Michael standing.

I spoke to him silently saying, 'How can I help to end this war of terror?'

He didn't answer me. He just gave a wave and disappeared.

The next moment the young waitress came to my table

and said, 'The chef said he will make you up a vegetable stir-fry with noodles but he can't use the sauce that he uses every day. So he'll make up something different and do his best to make your meal as tasty as possible.'

I said to her, 'Please thank him for me.'

A few minutes later she brought me back some coffee and hot water. When the meal came I really enjoyed it.

Afterwards, I headed off on my walk. I was just enjoying the sunshine. I wasn't taking any notice of the angels that were around me. I was just listening to the birds. I came to a pond and some of the lilies were just starting to blossom. So I started to take some pictures. I think I took some nice photos but I'm never too sure. Just as I was walking away from the little pond a white butterfly flew around me as if it was dancing through the air. You know those cabbage butterflies? They are white with little black spots on their wings. When I was a child there were always loads of butterflies around in the summertime. Some of them were different, and beautiful colours, but when growing vegetables in the garden of the little cottage in Maynooth we would most often have the cabbage butterfly around. They would lay their eggs under the leaf and in no time at all, there would be lots of caterpillars. Green ones, that is. They would wiggle all over the cabbage eating the edges of the leaves. We would pick them off and carry them over to where we put the old cabbage leaves and other bits of vegetables.

Sometimes, there would be so many of them on one cabbage plant that we would pull it up and put it over at the bank that surrounded the garden. As well as loads of cabbage butterflies there were lots and lots of other kinds, especially the red admiral butterfly. They were, then, in abundance, but nowadays they are not.

When this cabbage butterfly flew around me as I walked away from the pond, I turned around and said to all of the unemployed angels that were with me, 'Where are all the butterflies?'

They said, 'Lorna, there are not many any more. Their numbers have dropped considerably.'

'Surely, we will find more,' I said to the unemployed angels.

Then the butterfly headed towards the little gate. I followed this butterfly all over the place trying to get a photograph but it was really hard.

The angels were helping me when another one, an unemployed angel, called out, 'Lorna, this one over here.'

Then I turned and saw another two unemployed angels whooshing the butterflies in one direction. I stood there for a moment, just watching the three unemployed angels with the three cabbage butterflies trying to keep them flying in a particular direction over to one of the gardens. I just stood there watching for a moment and then I walked as fast as I could after the unemployed angels and the three cabbage butterflies, hoping to get a photograph.

Eventually, after about twenty minutes, I managed to get a photograph. When this book is published I think I will put that photograph on Facebook and let you know that this was one of the three butterflies I'm talking about here. The butterfly in the photograph I managed to take was actually on a plant that in one way looked similar in some ways to a cabbage but with bigger leaves and stalks.

I said to the unemployed angels, 'Do you think that there would be any chance that I could find a red admiral butterfly?'

They said, 'Lorna, we think that will be very hard.' But I said to them, 'Let's go in search anyway.'

I smiled at times because the angels still had three cabbage butterflies flying with us. Sometimes, they flew around my head in a circle. I must've walked around for about an hour through wild flowers, along bushes and through the grass looking for a red admiral butterfly but we never came across one. Even as I walked back to the car park I was still looking for that particular butterfly that I used to see in abundance even in my own garden and here in the countryside. This year I have not even seen one.

'Where are they all gone to?' I said to the angels.

They never said anything to me. I turned and walked into the forest. After walking a little distance I saw a tree trunk lying on the ground and I sat there for a few minutes. There wasn't much light in among the trees but that is something I don't mind once my eyes adjust and I can see where I'm going. I spoke out loud to the unemployed angels. One of them stood at the end of the tree trunk and another under one of the big old trees. The other unemployed angel stood in among all the underbrush.

I said, 'There should be lots of butterflies but we have hardly seen any. That is really sad and disappointing.'

The angel that was standing at the end of the tree trunk said, 'Lorna, what else has crossed your mind?'

'I remember God showing me one of the possible futures.'

Just as I said those words, a beam of light shone through the trees to my right and out from among the trees walked Archangel Michael. As he walked towards me the beam of light disappeared from behind him but all the time remained shining in front of him.

I smiled and said, 'Hello, that is something, Archangel Michael. I wish I could do that when it is dark. To have a beam of light in front of me so I can find my way in the dark would be really helpful.'

Archangel Michael told me that he didn't need the beam of light. He had done that just for me.

'Lorna, you are remembering one of the futures that God showed to you a long time ago.'

'Yes, I am, Archangel Michael, and it's really worrying me today. I am realising, and I know it's not the first time, but it always feels as if mankind, the human race, is not listening at all. Man seems to have his ears closed. Only thinking of himself here and now, and not thinking of the future as well.'

Archangel Michael said, 'Lorna, tell me about that future.'

I looked at him surprised. 'What do you mean, Archangel Michael? You must know.'

He said, 'Yes, I do but tell me the part that touched you most.'

So I said to Archangel Michael, 'Where should I start?'

He replied, 'Anywhere. Just start talking and let the memories flow through your mind as God shows you.'

Mankind must think of the future. When God showed me one of the futures of mankind it was heart-rending. There were so few children and the few children there were lived in what looked like bubbles. Their clothing was like a sealed suit and their teacher was showing them what our wonderful world looked like in the past, all the life on the planet. The teacher was pointing to a picture of butterflies with a little girl running through long grass full of wild flowers. In the picture she had in her hand a long, light stick with a net like a cup at the top that blew in the wind.

The teacher said, 'She is trying to catch the butterfly so she can have a closer look at it.'

One of the boys, aged about eleven, said to his teacher, 'It is not fair. Why did the people of the past destroy everything? Look at how we have to live today.'

A young girl stood up and said, 'Were they stupid or something?'

The teacher showed them many photographs of trees, as well as birds, horses, elephants, cats, dogs, and lots of other wild and domestic animals. The children were mostly interested in the picture of the little girl running through the long grass trying to catch a butterfly. I could feel the sadness as I stood there, Angel Michael. It hurt that they could not run and play out in the fresh air because there was none. The children of that future didn't know what it was like to touch a tree or to run through the grass.

Another younger child aged about six said, 'It's obvious they had no brains and that they never listened to God or their guardian angel.'

That was the part that surprised me. God ruffled my hair at that instant and told me that I had to go now.

I was back in Maynooth in the little cottage. I stood up and walked with Archangel Michael out of the little forest to the footpath. He was dressed in clothes that looked like working clothes; they seemed at first a little tattered but as I looked at him closely I saw that they were actually perfect.

I said to Archangel Michael, 'What if someone comes along and sees you walking with me?'

Archangel Michael said, 'Lorna, don't worry. They definitely will but just think a workman on the grounds talking to you isn't strange. God would not let them recognise you. It's very quiet here today and no one is around.'

Archangel Michael stopped and took both of my hands, saying, 'Lorna. I know your heart is heavy.'

'Yes, it is,' I said thinking of that particular future. 'It wasn't a very good future. It's frightening actually. Really quite horrible to think that those children have never seen a real butterfly. They only have pictures.'

'I know,' said Archangel Michael.

There are still butterflies in the world but I know here in Ireland the numbers must be dropping. Before we started to walk again I asked Archangel Michael, 'Could you hold one of my hands, because it helps me to feel a little better?'

He took my right hand in his and we walked around the grounds where all the wild flowers were, through the gardens, in among the trees and along the riverbank.

'Look, Lorna,' said Michael, 'the butterflies are coming to join us.'

The three white cabbage butterflies flew around Archangel Michael and myself. They were flying the way butterflies do, never in a straight line, but up and down. I would often say they are dancing through the air. They flew around us as we walked.

'I have not seen one red admiral butterfly since we talked about them, Archangel Michael. I have only seen the odd moth.'

Moth numbers are probably dropping too. I know the world has been conscious about bees and how scarce they have become and how precious they are, but all insect life is very precious. We are forgetting that we need them. What a shame it would be if the butterfly disappeared and the only time anyone would see a butterfly would be at a butterfly farm.

'Archangel Michael, I feel really cross. I don't like feeling like this.'

He stopped, reached out and took my other hand. His love flowed through me, helping me to feel at ease and, of course, those three cabbage butterflies flew between us and around us. That made me laugh and Archangel Michael laughed as well. Not too loudly, though, and I was glad for he knows his laugh can be like thunder.

We started to walk again.

I said to Archangel Michael, 'I know we have a butterfly farm here in Ireland. Maybe some day I will get a chance to go and visit it but I would rather see the butterflies flying across the fields and in our gardens.'

When my little grandson Billy Bob was only a year old – this is going back about four years now – I was out in the garden with him. I was showing him butterflies landing on flowers. They weren't just cabbage butterflies or red admirals but other ones as well. I don't know their names. I said to Archangel Michael, 'This is August. There should be lots of butterflies around. Has mankind killed them off with insecticides, weedkillers and other chemicals?'

'Lots of things have disappeared in nature, Lorna. The sad thing is you can never get them back. Keep helping people to grow spiritually and help them to become conscious of the beautiful planet and of the nature that God has given them. Help them to stop destroying it.'

We walked further along the path. I stopped after a while and I just looked around at all the beautiful trees, the birds and the wild flowers in the grass.

I turned to Archangel Michael. 'How sad it is to think that we might lose all of this.'

He didn't answer me but we were getting close to the car park and he simply said, 'Lorna, I have to go.'

He walked back towards the trees. Just before he disappeared, he turned and waved to me. That is something Archangel Michael doesn't do very often. He suddenly became radiant and very bright. He was no longer dressed in workman's clothes. I cannot describe the clothing he had on now or how beautiful he looked or how incredible. He was so radiant. I could see the flickering of his sword and shield. I knew he was going straight to the throne of God, and then he was gone.

Within a few minutes, I was in the car and I drove slowly home. When I got to the gate I stopped the car, got out and opened it. I got back in and parked the car. I don't know how I can describe what happened next. I had just stepped out of the car and as I was doing so I was saying to myself how sad I didn't get to see the red admiral butterfly. It would have been lovely to have got a photograph of one.

As I turned to close the car door a beautiful and magnificent red admiral flew into my face. It was as if it flew out from the walls of my house and touched my nose, hovering there for a moment in mid-air at the tip of my nose. It completely startled me. What a surprise! It was incredible. It flew past me and I turned around instantly, but it was gone. I gave out to the angels and they just laughed at me.

Angel Hosus was standing by the gate. 'Lorna, God wanted to surprise you. He sent that butterfly just for a moment. He has it in the palm of His hand now.'

'Couldn't God have allowed it to linger just a little bit longer? Allowed it to land on the flower so I could take a photograph?'

Angel Hosus replied, 'No, Lorna, not that butterfly. It's from heaven.'

Angel Hosus said he had to go and disappeared. I didn't get a chance to ask any other questions over the next few days. I don't think I missed noticing any butterfly that flew past me. So far they have only been the cabbage butterfly, for butterflies are too short in supply. I didn't see any red admiral butterflies. Hopefully, I will before the summer is out.

CHAPTER 22

The Church

ST PAUL'S CHURCH IS A BEAUTIFUL, SMALL PROTESTANT church in Ardmore, County Waterford. I was invited to a festival to give a talk there. It's a small town on the coast with a beautiful beach. My daughter Ruth and the children had come to visit for the weekend before we left for the festival.

Ruth was in the barn setting the table for dinner.

She turned to me and said, 'Mum, you need a few days break and this is an opportunity for you to go down a few days before you give your talk.'

I was a bit hesitant. I had been playing on the couch with Billy Bob with his toy Transformers.

I said to my grandchild, 'I need to talk to your mum for a minute.'

I got up off the couch and I said to her, 'I don't think I can really take the time off. You know I have three books to write and at the moment, I am working on the main book.'

'Mum, I'm sure God doesn't want you to burn yourself out. You need a break.'

Just as Ruth said those words my attention was drawn to the curtains at the barn door. The one on my left became a little brighter and a the corner of a cape appeared. Straight away I knew who it was.

'Hello, Angel Hosus,' I said just as he stepped out from behind the curtain.

'Good evening, Lorna. You must listen to Ruth and suggest to her that maybe it would be a good idea to take the children as well. Spend some time on the beach. The children would love that and so will you. God does not want you to burn yourself out.'

'I know,' I said to him.

When Ruth said, 'Mum, are you listening to me? Please pay attention! What do you think?' I said to her, 'I'm thinking.'

Little did she know that Angel Hosus was standing by the barn door. I would have loved to have told her but Angel Hosus said that I must not.

I turned to her, giving her my full attention, and helped her to pull out the table, saying, 'Okay, Ruth, let's all go. Billy Bob and Jessica would have a great time. It is a festival and I know there will be plenty of things for the children to experience as well.'

'Mum, I have looked it up to see what's available for the children. There's something with robots and Billy Bob will love that. There's music, storytelling, Lego building and lots more too.'

So Ruth went ahead and found a hotel about half an hour's drive from Ardmore. Then she laughed and said to me, 'Mum, you better get back to work seeing as you're going to have a few days off.'

I smiled at her and said, 'It will be great. I'm looking forward to it already.'

Billy Bob ran into the barn and said, 'Granny, come out and play!'

I went out the barn door.

Angel Hosus was standing now by the swing as Billy Bob ran over and sat on the swing, saying, 'Gran, push me!'

As I reached the swing, Angel Hosus said he had to go and disappeared.

It was a few weeks later and I had just got out of bed when two unemployed angels standing by the door said to me, 'Lorna, nine days to go.'

I looked at them surprised, saying, 'What do you mean nine days to go? To what?'

Simultaneously, they said, 'Ardmore Festival. Your talk in St Paul's Church. Your grandchildren are really looking forward to their holiday.'

I occasionally use an expression Oh my God when the angels show me something extraordinary or simply, as here, to try to attract God's attention, and I did that morning as I got out of the bed. But every time I say, 'Oh my God' the angels always go silent and their heads bow. I know they are in prayer for that moment. I don't say those words very often but that morning I couldn't help it.

I sat at the side of my bed to say a few prayers and I thanked God for another day. I know each day is precious for us all. I prayed for you too. You, the reader, are always in my prayers. I ask for all the blessings you need in your life and I know there are many of them. You don't recognise those blessings that happen every day for you, like being able to get up in the morning and do the things you do. All the things you take for granted are blessings. I thank God for the blessings I have each day and that morning, I thanked

Him for the blessing of being able to get out of bed, being able to walk downstairs, look after Holly and enjoy the fresh air.

I had just walked back through the barn doors when my phone rang. It was Ruth. She didn't know I had a big smile on my face as she spoke to me because she said the same thing as the angels did when I got out of bed.

'Mum, nine days to go.'

I didn't tell her that the angels had only said that to me that morning. As the days passed, an unemployed angel would often tease me and make me smile as they would pretend to have a bucket and spade in their hand. Sometimes, an unemployed angel would thrust a bucket into the air. The bucket would have been full of water and as the water went across the air it would turn into a rainbow. The water would never fall to the ground. It would remain a rainbow, full of beautiful colours, for a few seconds and then disappear.

One day I said to the unemployed angel, 'I hope it is not going to rain every day when we are down at the festival.'

The unemployed angel said, 'No, the sun will shine. There will be a little rain but not too much, Lorna.'

Those nine days passed very quickly.

On Thursday evening, Ruth arrived with the children and on Friday morning, we headed off for the Ardmore Festival. The children were very excited. They thought they would never get there. I'm going to share with you some of the things that happened during those few days.

When we arrived at our hotel, we unpacked and went out to have something to eat. The children were very excited.

They wanted to go to the beach. Ruth calmed them by saying, 'Let's go to Ardmore town. We can see where St Paul's Church is and then we can go to the beach.'

The children were all for it. So, after a while, we headed off.

When we drove into Ardmore, there were cars parked everywhere and lots of people about. The place was crowded. We drove slowly and when we reached the crossroads in the centre of the town we turned left, up the hill. There on the right-hand side, about a quarter of the way up, was a tiny little church. We couldn't stop so Ruth drove by slowly.

I said to her, 'That's it. That's the church.'

There was no doubt about it. There was a beautiful, golden angel standing outside the gates of the church. It didn't give a male or female appearance. It was tall and elegant. It was dressed all in gold and its clothing was pleated. As I glanced in through the gateway I saw two other angels standing close to the church. They were dressed all in white.

Ruth continued to drive on up the hill.

I glanced back to look at the beautiful angel. Ruth said, 'Mum, you're right. That is the church.'

I said, 'I know.'

I didn't tell her why I was looking back.

I just said to her, 'I was just checking.'

Of course I knew it was the church. Weren't the angels there to show me that? Every now and then as Ruth drove she had to stop to let a car pass. Further on up the hill there was a tower and a graveyard where lots of people were sightseeing. We didn't get out of the car as the children wanted to get to the beach. Ruth found a spot to turn the car and we headed back down. We drove back in the direction we had come and parked at the school. Then we walked down to the town, heading towards the beach, but when we came to the centre where the crossroads was I looked to my right and up the hill to where St Paul's Church is. That beautiful, golden angel was still standing there.

I spoke to the angel without words, just for a brief moment, saying, 'Hello. I'm hoping you're there for everyone that goes into the church.'

The golden angel answered me, saying, 'Yes.'

Ruth said, 'Everyone hold hands to cross the road.'

There was lots going on. It was crowded with families, teenagers and holidaymakers. Never mind the angels. There were so many of them there too. I always find it very hard to put into words all that I see. There was a young band playing at the pier and there were angels playing music with them. I could hear the music of the band but I could hear the music of the angels too. They were playing musical instruments.

One angel was playing a musical instrument that I have never seen before. It was enormous inside and it was directly behind the young musicians. Part of it gave the appearance of an Irish harp but on each side of it there were two enormous trumpets. The bottom of the trumpets spiralled upwards to the big horn. They were golden in colour. The angel didn't blow on it but when the angel touched it the instrument made a beautiful sound. At the same time, the angel would run its fingertips across the strings of the harp. The harp was silver in colour. When the beautiful angel played music from this instrument the other angels stopped even though the band continued playing. I really cannot describe to you the beautiful tune that was being played on this instrument. All I can say to you is that it was incredible just to see that light of the angels lighting up the stage. I really can't put into words the music of the angels. Especially when it mixed with the band that was playing.

When an angel sings with the singer it is as if the angel carries the voice of the singer and the music across the air in waves. As the band played in the company of angels I wanted to stand there just listening but I couldn't, so I walked by as slowly as I could.

I had a fantastic few days at the beach with my grandchildren. When it came time for me to give my talk in St Paul's Church the beautiful, golden angel was still outside waiting on me.

The church, which was shaped like a cross, was crowded and I said to the angels, 'I'm nervous.'

They just replied, 'Lorna, look at all of the people and all of us angels here with you.'

I just smiled at them. When it was time to go out and stand in front of everyone all the angels waved. I could see the guardian angel of every single person in the church that day. I stood there a moment just watching the angels as they continued pouring into the church.

I even asked the angels silently, 'Any more? If more of you come in there will be no room for all the people here. You will only push them out.'

An unemployed angel said to me, 'Lorna, don't worry. There's plenty of room.'

That morning before I went to give the talk my daughter Megan, who had joined us the morning before, wrote down on a piece of paper some of the things I might talk about but would you believe that in the event the angels told me to talk about other things and I never mentioned one of them.

I usually tell people about angels I can see in the audience when I give a talk but what I don't tell them is if Archangel Michael or Angel Elijah or Angel Hosus are on the stage with me, telling me what to say. On this occasion, Archangel Michael stood to my left and Angel Hosus about four feet away on my right. Every now and then Angel Hosus went down among the crowd and Archangel Michael stood directly beside me so I would pass on what the people needed to hear.

When this talk was over I welcomed everyone to come up for a blessing. One woman said to me she didn't want the blessing for herself but would love the blessing for her son who was having a hard time. Many asked for a blessing for someone they loved and cared for. God granted the blessing for them as well as for those they loved.

I left the little church with my daughters and my grand-children. We went for something to eat but all the children wanted to do was get back to the beach. On our way, we met a group of women with their children.

They stopped us and said, 'Thank you! You have given us a lot to think about.'

One of the young women was about eighteen years of age. Her boyfriend was with her.

She said, 'You have changed our lives. You gave us back hope.'

We were close to the beach when Ruth said to me, 'Mum, one of the young families gave you a donation for your Children's Foundation but I can't remember the mother's name.'

I said to her, 'It's okay. Maybe if you see this family you can point them out to me?'

Before we headed back to our hotel Ruth said she wanted to drive up the hill past the church to look at a hotel on the cliff front that faced out on to the sea.

I said to her, 'Are you sure?'

She said, 'It would be nice to see it. I've heard so much about this hotel and how beautiful the scenery is around it.'

I smiled as we passed St Paul's again. The beautiful, golden angel was still standing there. The hill was like a rollercoaster with all of the cars, never mind the pedestrians, so it took a while to get up the hill. Eventually, we got up there but we only looked at the hotel in the distance. We did not go down the road to it because we thought we may not find room to turn. But we could see it was beautiful and situated in a nice spot.

I said to Ruth, 'It looks nice but I think the hotel we're staying in is much nicer. If we get a chance to come back another time I think I would stay in the hotel we are in now.'

We turned the car around and started to head back down the road. Ruth stopped every few feet because of the crowds spilling on to the roads. She was only inching along. It was chaos going back down the hill. Then the angels in the distance attracted my attention. Further on down some unemployed angels were waving. There was a black car parked with a mother and children inside. We inched our way down towards them. I was watching the angels with the children. They were doing their best to keep them safe.

I remember the little girl's guardian angel opening its enormous, snow-white wings. It was dressed in a dazzling yellow. Guardian angels don't always allow me to see their wings. The little girl's guardian angel cupped its wings around her and as she got out of the car whispered to her to keep close because it was very dangerous. I smiled because the little girl did exactly as her guardian angel said. She was listening.

The unemployed angels that had attracted my attention were standing in a row. There were at least six of them doing their best to keep the mother and the children safe. It was a family of three or four.

One boy's guardian angel gave a male appearance. It held its two golden hands, full of light, on the young boy's shoulders as he moved around the car. His guardian angel was dressed in different shades of red and towered over him. I could see clearly the guardian angels of these children doing their best to keep them safe with the help of their mother.

As we got closer I said to the young boy's guardian angel, 'Does he know you're there?'

His guardian angel said, 'Yes. This family know they have guardian angels. They are great listeners.'

As we approached the family Ruth said, 'Mum, that's the family that gave the money for the charity.'

We gave them lots of waves as we passed by. They waved back to us but we could not stop. Slowly, we continued down the hill.

I said to Ruth, 'That was very good of that mother to give that fifteen euro.'

My heart was moved by her kindness to think of others, especially children. Being a parent is the hardest job in the world and the most important. I could see this mother was doing her best. Her guardian angel told me as we drove past that she is a mother full of compassion and love. She only wants the best for her children. I asked all the guardian angels of the family to take care of them as I glanced back at them. They were still waving.

CHAPTER 23

Mother Earth

IT WAS A SATURDAY SO I DECIDED TO TAKE A LITTLE TIME off. Well, just the morning. I went for a drive to Mount Juliet to treat myself to tea and poached eggs. I really enjoyed just sitting there and watching life go by. It wasn't very busy in Hunter's Yard, the restaurant at Mount Juliet. As I gazed out through the windows on to the golf course and across to the mountains I noticed a lot of clouds in the sky. At times, it looked like it might rain. I could still feel the warmth in the air though so I decided to go for a walk.

I walked up along the river, taking in the fresh air and enjoying every aspect of all those simple things of life that surrounded me as I walked along the riverbank. The only angel that was with me was my guardian angel.

I came across a man-made lake. I stopped for a moment to see if I could see any swans or ducks on the water but there were none.

I said to my guardian angel, 'That's disappointing.'

I looked in between the reeds and along the bank of the river for any movement.

My guardian angel said to me, 'There are some further on up the river. You may not see them today.'

I continued my walk until the trail started to become overgrown. I stopped and was thinking maybe I should go back when I saw an unemployed angel standing in among the overgrowth a little further up on my left, in a place that led to the river.

The unemployed angel waved to me, calling out, 'Come this way.'

As soon as I entered this overgrown path the unemployed angel said, 'Follow me.'

Many times the unemployed angel disappeared out of sight as the overgrowth was so thick. The trail was very narrow. Many times I had to turn sideways to get through.

I called out to the unemployed angel, 'This is really difficult. I may have to turn back.'

But the unemployed angel said, 'No, keep coming, Lorna.'

The stingers, as I call them – a lot of people call them nettles, I know – were as tall as myself with brambles and branches twisted in among them. As I followed the narrow little path, one step at a time, I thought to myself that it looked like a path a fisherman would follow to get to the river. I was being very careful as I got closer to the river. I could hear the sound of water rushing.

I said out loud, 'Is there a waterfall here?' I expected the unemployed angel to answer me but I got no reply.

When I reached the water I saw that it was going fast over big rocks in the centre of the river. That was what made the sound like a waterfall. I climbed down off the riverbank to where there were lots of smaller stones. I crossed them to sit on what looked like the remains of an old pier. I sat there looking out across the riverbed, just listening to all of the sounds of the river. There was nothing else but silence.

I must've sat there for ten minutes, then I heard my name being called. I turned around and there was Archangel Michael walking across the stones towards me. He was dressed like a fisherman with those big, long boots right up to his hips and he carried a fishing rod.

'Hello,' I said, 'I wasn't expecting you. This is a surprise.'

Archangel Michael didn't answer me. He just came over and sat to my right on part of the old pier wall. What was left of it anyway.

He smiled at me, putting down the fishing rod, and said, 'Good morning, Lorna. I hope you are enjoying yourself.'

I said, 'Yes, I am. It's lovely just sitting here.'

Archangel Michael reached out and took my hand as we sat there.

He said to me, 'God knows how hard it's going to be for you to write about the Crucifixion. God has changed his mind because He knows that writing about any of it, even a small part, will hurt and how afraid you are. God will only allow you to write a small part of what you had seen and experienced when your soul was taken back to the past to witness the Crucifixion. God knows how much it takes out of your human body and how every Easter when you are shown more of what happened at the Crucifixion it makes you weaker.'

There were tears running down my cheeks as Archangel Michael spoke.

I looked up at him, confused, and said, 'I thought God wanted me to write about the Crucifixion.'

He answered, 'Yes, he does, Lorna, eventually, but when you do, he's going to have a lot of his archangels surrounding you.'

Archangel Michael reached up and wiped my tears with the snow-white handkerchief that he always uses.

'Will you be there too, Archangel Michael? Will you be with me when I start to write about the Crucifixion?'

'Yes, I will, Lorna, and in a week or so you will be ready to write what God wants you to about the Crucifixion. Lorna, maybe I will do some fishing?'

That made me laugh. Archangel Michael didn't laugh though. He just gave me a big smile and said, 'Look, there is a swan coming down the river.'

A few moments later he said he had to go. He got up and walked in the direction of where he'd appeared first. He crossed back over the stones, still dressed like a fisherman with those long boots, and disappeared.

I sat there on the old pier for a few minutes thinking of what Archangel Michael said and about God's message. I decided to put it to the back of my mind, for now anyway. The same unemployed angel appeared to my left, standing in among some trees. I got up and walked towards it.

The unemployed angel said to me, 'Lorna, you would enjoy an adventurous walk in among this overgrowth along the riverbed. When it is fully flooded it becomes part of the river.'

I followed the unemployed angel. I don't know how far I walked but I was walking on the dry riverbed looking at all the plants that live beneath the water when the river rises. I could see the marks on trees of how high the river rises in places. It definitely would have covered me. Then again, I'm five foot nothing.

The unemployed angel said, 'Lorna, it's time to turn back.'

I turned around and headed back towards the old, broken pier. Some small birds came in among the trees and perched along the branches around me. As I walked I knew I could have reached out and touched them.

When I reached the old pier I just said thank you to the birds for keeping me company. I said thank you as well to the unemployed angel and, of course, to my guardian angel.

I stopped for a moment at the river's edge. The water was almost touching my sandals. I was just looking out across the river when – all of a sudden – I felt the earth vibrate beneath my feet. I knew Angel Jimazen was about to appear.

My feet were glued where I stood, not moving. The ripples on the river became still. The water stopped flowing. Everything became frozen in time. The first thing I saw was his staff. It appeared just above the rocks in the centre of the river and then the next moment, Angel Jimazen appeared too, about four feet above the rocks.

I said, 'Hello, Angel Jimazen.'

He looked down at me and smiled. He is enormous in every way, like a giant. He dresses in red and gold armour with a tint of black running through it. No matter how many times I see Angel Jimazen I am always a little scared because he makes the earth tremble beneath my feet. He is so important to all of us. He is important to our Planet Earth. As I have already explained, he is the gatekeeper of the earth. God made Angel Jimazen the guardian angel of our whole planet. He is one of those rare angels that can never leave our planet, not even for one second, just like your guardian angel can never leave you.

It was Angel Jimazen who had explained to me when I was a child that our planet is alive. It was this powerful angel who helped me to understand why at times he looks so cross or angry but yet, shows so much compassion and love upon his face as he tries to keep Mother Earth at peace. Mother Earth is that life force inside our planet, that beautiful angel. Angel Jimazen tries to stop her from twisting and turning too much but she has to do this to heal our earth. He has to calm Mother Earth.

I have written more about this in *Stairways to Heaven*. I talk about one occasion when Angel Jimazen opened up the earth so I could see into the core of our planet. In the centre I saw Mother Earth curled up like a baby. She is so beautiful. She gave such a feminine appearance. There was no doubt about that. She was long, sleek and smooth like silk with beautiful, indescribable colours. They were amber colours of blue and green, if you can imagine that, which ran into each other like veins of gold. She was absolutely gorgeous. No matter how I describe her it will not do her justice. This beautiful, incredible angel in the core of the earth is called Mother Earth. She has many arms and they flow out from her like sails. She moves ever so gently, stretching out those sail-like arms to every part of our planet that needs healing. She is like a mother feeding her young, doing her best to take care of our planet and all the life upon it and within it.

We must help Angel Jimazen to keep her calm. We have to stop killing our planet because we are killing Mother Earth. She is doing her best to save all life and that includes mankind. Do you know our planet has slowed down? Mother Earth can do nothing about it because we keep taking from her, the oil, the gas and many other minerals, which she needs to keep this beautiful planet alive. Our earth was given to us as a gift and we treat it so badly. We don't seem to care.

Angel Jimazen has an incredible relationship with Mother

Earth. He fights with her to stop her convulsing too much but knows that she has to do it to heal our planet. He uses his staff to tap the earth to quell her. He does all of this out of love for Mother Earth. He gets so frustrated and angry with mankind because we continue killing the earth and killing the beautiful angel, Mother Earth.

Every time we, as human beings, take something from the earth through pollution or drilling holes, by taking too much oil, gas and other minerals, Mother Earth, that beautiful angel, has to strive to keep our planet as healthy as possible through it all. She needs to twist and turn for the sake of all the life on Planet Earth.

Angel Jimazen can never leave the earth, not for one second, because he is its guardian angel, but he always needs our help. Every time he appears I am always fearful but today, he just smiled at me.

He said, 'Hello, Lorna, you must keep on reminding people how precious our planet is and how precious is Mother Earth, that beautiful angel, whose arms are like sails as she twists and turns in the centre of the earth healing the damage we do to this beautiful planet. God has given this planet to all of us as a gift.'

In the next instant he disappeared.

I headed back up the riverbank. I took every step carefully so I would not get stung or have too many scratches on my legs from the brambles. Unfortunately, I was not wearing trousers that day, only a skirt. As I walked back to the car, I prayed that the people of the world would listen to Angel Jimazen so that he can keep Mother Earth as calm as possible. Every time I see Angel Jimazen I am so afraid that it's a sign that Mother Earth has to twist and turn in such a tortured way because we have given her no choice in order to heal the damage we have done. It can cause earthquakes, a volcano to erupt, a huge natural disaster that kills an enormous amount of life upon our beautiful planet. And when this happens and many people suffer, it is part of my role to help absorb their pain.

I know that Mother Earth never wants to twist and turn so fiercely, as all life on the surface of the earth is precious and she knows that. She knows that human beings are God's children and each and every one of us has a soul, but God has also given her the job of keeping our planet alive in every single way. God has created the life that is inside the planet and on the surface. Mother Earth does her best but we must play our part and listen to Angel Jimazen. All of the time, he is giving us messages not to pollute and destroy our beautiful planet. Sometimes I see him frustrated with us because we do not listen, but his frustration is love. He is trying to protect her and us but he cannot overstep our free will. We have the choice to keep our air, rivers, lakes, oceans, forests and mountains free from pollution. We have the choice to care for all the beautiful places and all the beautiful life that surround us and which we see every day. All of nature, the magnificent trees, the animals and the birds, are a gift to each and every one of us. Please play your part and help Angel Jimazen to keep Mother Earth calm so that she will only have to twist and turn in a gentle way.

Mother Earth has reacted aggressively many times because we take this beautiful planet for granted. When she does twist and turn destructively we always blame God.

We ask, 'Why did He allow it to happen?'

The reality is that we human beings are the cause, so I prayed as I made my way back to Hunter's Yard.

A few hours later, I was back home. I was going through a bundle of letters that came in the post. In among them was a letter from a mother who lived in Italy.

She wrote

Lorna, you may not remember, I sent you a letter before asking you if it was possible for you to visit and pray over my son who was in the Intensive Care Unit in an Italian hospital. I gave you my phone number. You called me and said you were in Italy for the next couple of days and if it was any way possible you would go and visit my son. You did. I just want to tell you the wonderful news! My son woke up the next day and he is at home now. I thank God for answering our prayers and giving our son back to us.

I thanked God straight away and I asked for the young man to continue healing. When I had visited the hospital, his mother had taken me to the ICU unit. As we walked, she had told me that every bone in her son's body was broken, from head to toe. He was in a critical condition and the doctors didn't know whether he would make it or not. The mother said she had already lost one son only a couple of months ago and was begging God not to take this son from her too.

Just as we reached the door of the ICU unit, I held the mother's hand and said, 'Remember, I can only ask on your son's behalf for God to allow him to live. It is all in God's hands. I can only ask.'

She replied, 'I know, Lorna, but I need you to ask. I want my son to live. I know it will be whatever God decides.'

The mother rang a bell and a few moments later, the doors opened. I walked into the ICU unit and saw the young man with tubes coming out of him everywhere. I was totally shocked to see him in such a state. His guardian angel was holding him in his arms and the angel's wings were cocooned around him. I walked to his side to pray over him. The doctors waved me in and one said, 'Come in, there's nothing more we can do for him.'

His guardian angel spoke to me without words. 'Lorna, this young man was grieving so hard. His pain was so unbearable over the loss of his brother that he lost the will to live himself.' His angel was telling me something his mother did not know.

I understood what his guardian angel was saying. I knew this young man did not really mean to harm himself. His grief was just unbearable for him.

His guardian angel spoke to me again. 'Lorna, give him the will to live. He will hear you.'

When I reached the young man's bed I felt devastated seeing him lying there. I was filled with compassion for the young man. As I started to pray the Healing Angels surrounded him. They held their hands over him. I could see their glowing, radiant light touching his human body as I whispered in his ear saying the words that I was told to say to give him the will to live.

As I stood by his bed praying, I asked God for the young man to get well again. His mother and his family needed him. He was a good young man. I told God all of this. I loved this young man even though I did not know him.

I asked God, 'Please allow this young man to recover completely.'

It was wonderful news to hear that he had woken up. His mother said that she'd meant to let me know well before now that the very next morning after I had prayed over him he woke up and now he was at home.

It makes me feel very happy to hear great things like that happening. Sometimes it's years later at a book signing, or when I'm giving a blessing after a talk, that someone says to me that God healed them. Thank you, God. It is always in God's hands as to whether someone survives. It is something we don't always understand. We ask so many questions. Why does God allow someone to live and another to die? Why does He take some souls home to heaven and not others?

I gave the mother a call and I told her I was really happy to hear the good news that God had given her son a second chance at life.

CHAPTER 24

Jesus and the Tree of Life

ON FRIDAY EVENING, I WAS SITTING ON THE COUCH WITH my daughter, Megan. She was getting frustrated and giving out about the Wi-Fi.

'You would think that the angels would help! Especially when I'm trying to put up your post on Facebook, Mum. Do the angels think I have all this time to waste?'

I was smiling at her, just watching her guardian angel.

I said to her, 'I don't think angels can do much about the Wi-Fi.'

I burst out laughing. I just couldn't hold back.

Megan looked at me and said, 'Mum, what are you laughing at? It's not funny!'

'Sorry but I couldn't stop myself from laughing this time.'

'Mum, I have so much to do. This stupid Wi-Fi is holding me up. What's so funny, Mum?'

I said to Megan, 'You are and so is your guardian angel.'

'Tell me what my guardian angel is doing, so,' Megan said.

'Do you really want me to tell you?'

'Yes, Mum.'

'I am watching your guardian angel acting out your frustration. It is just so funny and making me laugh.'

'What is she doing?' said Megan.

I said to her, 'Every time you get frustrated and blow your top I always have to leave the room. Have you never noticed? Because your guardian angel mimics your frustration.'

Megan looked at me with a surprised look on her face and said, 'Tell me what my guardian angel has been doing.'

'Your beautiful guardian angel right now is miming pulling her hair out in your frustration.'

I mimicked Megan's guardian angel as if I was pulling my hair out. The hair was left standing up straight.

My daughter laughed and said, 'Well, that's what I feel like doing.'

The two of us burst out laughing. Megan's guardian angel is always whispering in her ear when she is upset and telling her to calm down.

'Mum, does my guardian angel still give the same appearance as it did years ago when I was little? The same appearance you saw when I was holding my dad's hand and Ruth held my other hand as we walked towards you on the edge of the Dublin mountain? I love that story and that photograph you took as well even though my guardian angel didn't appear in it. It helps to keep the memory there of that day. I know I must have only been about two years of age.'

I said to Megan, 'Don't be sad. Remember, your dad is always with you when you need him. I will get that photograph. I know where it is. Would you like it?'

Megan said, 'Yes, please.'

'It's in the box up in the attic. I will go up the ladder tomorrow and I will dig it out for you. There is more than one of those photographs of your dad, your sister and you in the middle and yes, Megan, your guardian angel always gives the same appearance as it did that day.'

'Can you describe her again to me, Mum?'

I looked at Megan's guardian angel and she nodded her head, giving me a big smile.

'Megan, your guardian angel always gives a female appearance, never changing as far as gender goes,' I said. 'You know her name.'

Megan said, 'Yes, I do.'

She said her guardian angel's name but I cannot give to you that name as my daughter asked me to keep it a secret.

'Now you are a young woman so your guardian angel is no longer giving the appearance of a young child, but I do have to smile because your guardian angel is giving the appearance of being about the same age as yourself.'

I told Megan that all angels were created at the same time so there is no such thing as age to them. They do not grow old.

I said, 'She still has her hair in the same way, braided in two plaits with an orange, red and green band and with a beautiful, red feather that she has stuck in her hair. I don't see anything else attached to it. It is as if your guardian angel just put it there and her hair is holding it in place. It is at the back of her head but to the left. Of course, she has that beautiful smile. Your guardian angel's face is radiant. She has beautiful, brown eyes as big as saucers, full of glittering, radiant light. Guardian angels don't usually give a particular colour for their eyes. Most angels' eyes are like stars that we see in the sky. They are of no particular colour, just full of light, reflecting like the stars in the night sky. In the centre of your guardian angel's forehead, there is a light shaped like a star. It shimmers brightly like a star all the time. Your guardian angel is still dressed in that beautiful tunic of light gold. Your guardian angel, Megan, has just put her hands upon your head.'

Megan said thank you to her guardian angel and then she gave me a big hug and said, 'Thanks, Mum. I needed to hear that.'

A few minutes later the Wi-Fi started to work. I got up and made a cup of tea. The two of us watched one of our favourite TV programmes, *Nashville*.

A few days later, when Megan had gone off to college, I decided to go up into the attic to look for that photograph. I knew it was in one of the boxes.

As I was about to pull the ladder down, my guardian angel said, 'When you find the photograph put it away somewhere safe in the attic. Don't give it to Megan just now. Wait until Christmas time, take it down then and give it to her as a surprise.'

I just said to my guardian angel, 'Don't forget to remind me when it gets closer to Christmas.'

I was sitting in front of the computer and everything went silent. Not a sound to be heard. It was as if time stood still. I turned and looked in the direction of the door. Archangel Michael appeared with Angel Amen.

I said, 'Hello, I was not expecting you.'

Archangel Michael said, 'Angel Amen is going to take your soul to heaven.'

I felt fear as Angel Amen knelt in front of me on one knee. She raised her hand in a slow motion. I started to feel weightless, like a feather floating in the air. I felt that peace and tranquillity that always comes over me before my soul is taken.

Angel Amen smiled and spoke to me softly: 'Don't be afraid.'

I spoke to her silently for I knew she could hear me: 'I'm not afraid. It is just when my breath is taken away for that moment it is a little frightening. I don't think I will ever get used to it.'

As her hand got closer to my chest she reached in, saying, 'Lorna, God wants you. There is no need to be afraid.'

At the same time as Angel Amen reached into my soul angels surrounded me. They were putting that special blanket around me to keep my body safe.

The next moment I was in heaven. Angel Amen was standing beside me. Angel Amen took my hand and we started to walk. I knew where I was going. God had shown me this place before many times. I could feel the sand beneath my feet. It was like silk. Everything was so white. The light seemed to glimmer all around but it was not blinding as I walked with Angel Amen hand in hand across the hills. I know the journey only took us a few minutes if I was to describe it in human terms, but it wasn't really as there is no such thing as time in heaven.

When we stopped, Angel Amen pointed across to one of the hills and said, 'Lorna, you are to go there. God will be with you in a moment.'

I saw an enormous tree on top of the hill. There were no other trees anywhere to be seen. The hills were all covered in glowing, white sand. There wasn't even a rock or any other plants. I recognised that it was the Tree of Life. It's gigantic. I have been there many times before.

A moment later, I stood at the bottom of the hill. I scrambled up as quickly as I could on my hands and knees. When I reached the tree I sat on the roots. They were as big as the branches of the tree and twisted and turned above the surface. Then some of them would disappear below the sandy hill.

I was no longer an adult. I was only a child of about ten years of age. I was dressed in a snow-white tunic. I am always a child when God takes my soul to heaven, for we are all God's children. I know that's hard for adults to understand but to God we are only children.

I heard my name being called and I turned around. There was a young boy about my age standing close to the tree trunk, holding on to keep his balance as he stood on one of the big roots. He was dressed like me, in a white tunic with trousers, as he always is.

He said, 'Hello, Lorna.'

'Hello, Jesus,' I said.

I stood up and started to step across the roots of the tree. Sometimes, I had to jump down between them. We sat together looking across the hills and letting the sand run between our fingers.

Jesus said to me, 'Father said we are to play together. You know who my father is?'

I looked at him surprised and said, 'Yes, of course I do. Your father is my father, our heavenly Father God.'

The young boy said, 'Do you know who I am?'

I said again, 'Yes, of course I do. You are Jesus – God's son.'

He laughed and said, 'Lorna, I am only testing you.'

The two of us jumped up and we started to play, running and jumping around this gigantic tree. We were chasing each other, laughing and talking like two children. Jesus was forever catching me but I could never catch him.

We rolled down the hill, tumbling together. Sometimes head over heels but we never hurt ourselves. Our game was to see who could reach the bottom of the hill first and then we would race back up as fast as we could. We laughed the whole time. We had such fun.

Afterwards, we sat between two of the big roots of the tree.

It was like a little house and we were letting the sand flow between our fingers when Jesus said, 'Lorna, let's climb the tree.'

I looked at him.

'The tree is so tall, Jesus. I cannot even see the top of it. How on earth could we climb it?'

Jesus said, 'No problem,' – he put his hand on the tree – 'let's start here.'

He started to climb and I followed him. I didn't see any way to climb up the tree when I looked at it but when Jesus put his hands upon it, it changed just a little. We went from branch to branch with no effort.

We didn't go all the way to the top because at one point Jesus said, 'I think this is far enough.'

We sat on one of the big branches and we looked out across heaven. Heaven looked like a radiant light that didn't seem to have a beginning or an end. I saw millions of angels and millions of souls: men, women and children who had died and were in heaven.

Now, I could see and feel the love coming from everywhere, from all the souls and from all the angels. I knew that love was God.

Jesus reached out and put his arm around me and said, 'Lorna, it's time to go.'

I said to Jesus, 'I don't want to go. I want to stay here with you.'

He said, 'No, Lorna, my father won't allow it. It's not your time yet. You must let Angel Amen take your soul back to your human body.'

We climbed back down the tree. We had a race.

Jesus said, 'Let's see who can reach the bottom of the tree first!'

This time Jesus allowed me to win the race. Angel Amen was standing at the bottom and she reached out to take my hand. I turned to look back at Jesus but he was already gone.

In the blink of an eye, I was back sitting at my computer. Angel Amen was standing in front of me.

She said, 'Lorna, go and make yourself some tea.'

She had to go. She walked towards the door of the little room where I work and vanished.

CHAPTER 25

Angel Amen, Everyday Life and My Friend Catherine

ANGEL AMEN HAS BEEN IN MY LIFE SINCE I WAS A SMALL child. She taught me how to pray. It was when I lived in the house in Old Kilmainham that I first met her. She used to sit on my bed. She taught me how to bless myself and how to say the Our Father and Hail Mary prayers. She taught me how to pray with every part of my being, every particle of my body and soul. My soul comes forward to be one with God in prayer.

Angel Amen always gives a female appearance and she is always wearing a beautiful dress that almost reaches her ankles. The waist and top of her dress is like something you would have seen long ago. She is elegant, tall and very beautiful. Her hands are slender. When she was teaching me to bless myself at about four years of age she would touch my hand with hers. It made me laugh because her hands would light up. Her fingertips would be the most radiant part. They would turn gold and a beautiful light would flow from them to my hand as I blessed myself. To this day, Angel Amen comes in and out of my life and, often, still prays with me.

I was praying when Angel Hosus knocked on the door.

He called out, 'Lorna, you're late. You'd better get a move on.'

I swivelled around in my chair and said to him, 'What am I late for?'

He said, 'The hairdressers!'

I looked at the time and saw that it was ten past three. I jumped up, grabbed my bag and ran down the stairs. I put my boots on and grabbed my coat off the chair. It was lashing with rain outside. There was a very strong breeze also, so I had to tie the gate so that it would remain open and not slam open and shut in the wind.

When I got into the car Angel Hosus was sitting in the passenger seat.

I said to him, 'Thank you. I completely forgot about the hairdressers. What would I do without you, Angel Hosus? I had also forgotten the charity tea on Saturday in Kerry. Let's pray the laneway won't be blocked so I won't have to stop and reverse back.'

Angel Hosus said, 'Take your time. The girl, Eimear, is waiting on you.'

There was an awful lot of traffic for such a little town. Cars were parked everywhere. I had to go to the car park on the far side of town. Angel Hosus told me he had to go when we reached the car park.

He said, 'Don't forget to lock the car, Lorna.'

Then he disappeared.

I walked as fast as I could through the little streets to the hairdressers but it was half three when I got in the door.

I said to Eimear, 'I'm sorry for being late!'

She said, 'Don't worry. I actually gave you a call.'

'I never heard it on my phone so I must have been in the car when you called. Traffic was chaos.'

Eimear said, 'It has been like that in the town for the last few weeks for some reason.'

I spent about an hour and a half getting my hair done.

Afterwards, I went to the chemist to collect a prescription. When I got back to the car Angel Hosus was sitting in the passenger seat again.

He said, 'Lorna, you should go and get some food for Mimsy: carrots, lettuce and broccoli. You won't have time in the morning as you have to get to Maynooth.'

Just as I pulled out of the car park, Angel Hosus said he had to go and disappeared.

I headed to the supermarket to get those few things but I automatically turned right at the roundabout.

I said out loud, 'Oh dear, will I take a chance and go this way through the lane to my house?'

My guardian angel said, 'Yes.'

I replied, 'But what if I meet some other car or van or truck?'

My guardian angel said, 'You won't.'

So I was home in a few minutes and drove in the gate. It was still lashing rain. I decided I would take a break and cook something as I was feeling very tired. I had been writing all day and I was feeling a little burnt out but I knew that later on, in a couple of hours, I would have to go upstairs and write some more.

It's starting to get dark as I write. Looking out the window into the field next to me, I can see all the cattle and young calves running up and down. They are a bit frisky. I don't know what startled them. Maybe the farmer is meant to arrive soon. He usually does an evening check on them and I think they are waiting anxiously for him.

I was in the kitchen making myself something to eat. I was chopping up vegetables and I had just turned on the oven when I noticed, out of the corner of my eye, a light in the barn.

I called out, without turning around, 'Is that you, Michael?'

I was chopping onions and my eyes were all watery, starting to sting.

'Lorna, you called me,' said Archangel Michael.

I replied to him as I walked over to the sink, 'I didn't realise I had called you.' I put some water on my hands and rubbed my eyes. I reached out for the dishcloth to dry them. Archangel Michael entered the kitchen and touched my shoulder to turn me around.

'Lorna, have you forgotten?' Michael replied, 'you don't need to actually call any angel by name when you want us. All of God's angels are with you all of the time.'

I asked, 'How did you know then that it was you who I wanted to speak to?'

'Lorna, you have definitely forgotten what I told you long ago. Your mind and soul are connected and know ahead of your consciousness who you feel you need to talk to.'

I smiled and said to Archangel Michael, 'Yes, you are right. I always forget that my human self, my mind and my soul are connected as one. I know that you know even before my human self is aware of it that it is you I need to talk to.' I smiled at Archangel Michael. 'It does sound crazy that my soul knows ahead of my mind that I need to talk to you. I am feeling heartbroken, Archangel Michael.'

Archangel Michael reached out and held my hand in his, filling me with love.

Catherine and her mum were the first friends Joe and I

made in Johnstown. We used to go down to them at Christmas time and they would come and visit us in Maynooth.

I said to him as I stood there in the kitchen by the sink, 'I never thought my friend would die. She has always been so close to my heart.'

'Lorna, don't you remember what I told you two years ago?'

'I know,' I said, 'I remember that day when I saw Catherine in the distance and I saw her guardian angel taking hold of her soul and preparing to carry it up to heaven. When I got home, you were standing here just where you are, in my kitchen. I was praying to God from that time on. As she got sick, I implored him to allow her to recover. When it got closer to her death she was asking for prayers just to relieve some of the pain and when she spoke to me from her hospital bed on the mobile I felt so devastated because her voice sounded so bad, so weak. Even then I prayed and prayed. I was still hoping that she would get well. Yet, in my heart, I knew she was going home to heaven. But, Archangel Michael, it has just been such a shock to me. I thought Catherine would be going to my funeral. Instead, it turned out the opposite way around. I went to her funeral – it's so hard to believe. I pray for her children and her grandchildren. I know they are grieving and my heart goes out to them.'

'Lorna, you are grieving too,' replied Archangel Michael, 'finish cooking your dinner and I will join you.'

Archangel Michael disappeared. I said to myself I thought he said he was going to join me but he's gone. I finished cooking my dinner. Just as I was lifting up the plate, Archangel Michael appeared again in the barn by the table.

I said to him, 'I didn't realise you were coming back.'

'I told you I would join you, Lorna.'

I put my dinner on the table in the barn and pulled out a chair.

Laughing, I said to Archangel Michael, 'Would you like to sit at the end of the table?'

He said, 'Yes. Lorna, you are almost finished the book.'

'Yes, I am. Can I ask you a question, Michael?'

He replied, 'Yes, you can ask me any question you wish.'

'I know all of you angels have taught me so many things and I would like to put something else into this book to help people to connect with their guardian angel and with all of you angels, but it's difficult to pick what would suit. Do you have any suggestions, Archangel Michael?'

'I thought you would never ask, Lorna. God told me one of the lessons you can teach people. I know you remember doing it when you were a child. We taught you all of these things so that you can teach people how to connect to the spiritual side of themselves: their soul, and the guardian angel with each one of them.'

'Archangel Michael, what were you going to suggest?'

Archangel Michael said to me, 'You must suggest a few but first eat some of your dinner.'

I said to Archangel Michael, 'I can talk at the same time.'

He laughed at me and said, 'Of course.'

You know what Archangel Michael's laughter is like – thunder – but he only laughed for a couple of seconds.

I said to him, 'If you had laughed any longer I think my dinner would have ended up on the floor.'

He just gave me a big smile. I smiled back. I had some more dinner. Then, I gave three suggestions from among the games the angels had taught me: blowing gently, closing my eyes and counting to ten, and the one to do with the flowers and smell.

'Which one do you suggest, Archangel Michael?'

'None of them. Lorna, do you remember the one I taught you?'

I looked at Archangel Michael and I said, 'Yes, I do. You used to do it with me.'

Archangel Michael said, 'I still do but I do not allow you to see me. When you were out the other day in the orchard, Lorna, you were practising it yourself.'

'Yes, I was standing in the middle of the orchard. The grass was almost to my knees and the sun was shining through the trees. I remembered practising it with you last year too. I had my arms slightly out from my body and my hands pointing straight down to the ground with my fingers close together. I turned slowly, allowing all human sound and all nature to disappear so I could only hear the angels. I tell the angels at the time that I only want to hear them sing but, Archangel Michael, I don't think that everyone would be able to do that.'

'Lorna, people don't need to stand and turn slowly in the one spot with their arms down by their sides and their fingers pointed towards the ground. They could be sitting on a chair or lying on a bed. They could close their eyes and ask all of the angels to surround them and let themselves relax so all the other sounds will disappear.'

I said to Archangel Michael, 'Wouldn't it be wonderful if people would practise no matter what age they are? It would help them feel the presence of their guardian angel. I know what could happen as well. In the moment they open their eyes, that fleeting quarter of a second, they may catch a glimpse of an angel for a moment. They could almost miss it but wouldn't that be wonderful!'

I had just finished my dinner. I got up from the table to walk into the kitchen. Archangel Michael followed me and just before he disappeared, he reached out and took both of my hands and held them in his, filling me with love and comfort.

He said, 'I hope you're not so sad now.'

I said, 'No, I'm not. I know my friend is in heaven. She is happy and at peace with all those she loves who have gone before her. She is there for her children and grandchildren as well.'

'I must go now,' Archangel Michael said.

He walked back out into the barn and disappeared.

The angels are here for each and every one of us. We all have a guardian angel that never leaves us for one second. Your guardian angel loves you. You are perfect and unique. Allow yourself to see yourself as your guardian angel sees you.

CHAPTER 26

The Scroll

EVERY TIME I HAVE TO GO ON A TRIP ABROAD TO GIVE A talk I make appointments to get my hair done and so on. I travel up to Maynooth at least a day or two beforehand to get everything ready. I stay in my son's house. It's the old cottage where Joe and I raised our first three children through their whole childhood and adolescence. Our fourth child, Megan, lived there for five years in the cottage until shortly after Joe's death, when I moved to Kilkenny with her. We have always kept the cottage in our family. My son, Christopher, has done a great job on the cottage and the garden. He is a great gardener. He just seems to touch the flowers and they grow vigorously.

Every time I go back to Maynooth it brings back a lot of memories. Sometimes, when I am just sitting on the couch in the front room I will remember Joe sitting in the chair, reading a book or watching the news. I also remember him sitting at the kitchen table playing cards. When I returned home from the shops and passed by the kitchen window I would see him washing the dishes at the sink. When he spotted me coming in he would give me a big smile and wave from the kitchen window as I passed by. A few moments later, he would open the hall door with the dishcloth in his hands as he dried them. I guess I mostly remember his smile.

I have to go back about four years in time and I'd love you to come on this journey with me. Actually, I hope you have been doing so all the way through the book, walking in my footsteps, seeing and hearing all the different things that go on in my life. I'm trying to help you to connect to the spiritual side of yourself.

I went to the post office in the industrial estate beside the roundabout in Maynooth to see if there were any letters for me. There was a large bundle and I remember carrying them out to the car and just plonking them all on the back seat. I didn't give them much thought at the time because I was about to head back down to Kilkenny.

It was about two days later, in the evening, when I was sitting on the couch that one of the unemployed angels said to me, 'Lorna, why don't you open some of those letters?'

I looked back at the table and I saw the big plastic bag full of envelopes. There was another bundle of maybe thirty letters also scattered on the table.

I said to the angel, 'Don't bother me. You know I am quite tired. I planned to go to bed early.'

But this particular unemployed angel just stood in front of me, giving such a human appearance, with his hands upon his hips. He reminded me of the way my little grandson would sometimes stand when he insists on me going outside to play with him. It made me smile.

The angel said, 'Lorna. Come on. Open a few letters.'

I gave in and said, 'Okay.'

I wrapped the blankets from the couch around me and got up. I took the big, white bag full of letters and dropped them over the back of the couch. Then, I gathered up the remaining letters on the table and did the same with them. There were angels in a line, standing between the couch and the dining room table, which was about four feet away from them. My couch is L-shaped and divides the room in two so it is both my sitting room and my dining room.

I said out loud, 'First of all, I'm going to make myself a cup of tea. I hope you angels are going to help me with the reading of these letters. I know some of them will be in English but even when they are they are very hard for me to read.'

It's only because of the angels that I can read them. Without them I would not be able to manage it at all because of my dyslexia.

A few minutes later, I brought my cup of tea and a biscuit in and put them on the little table beside the couch. I got comfortable and rewrapped myself in the blankets. The unemployed angel that had his hands on his hips earlier was still standing in front of me, a little bit to the left of the little table. Now this angel did not have his hands on his hips but was holding a pen and paper.

He said, 'Lorna, drink some tea and taste that lovely biscuit.'

He gave me a big smile and I smiled back as I picked up my cup and sipped my tea. The biscuit really was tasty. I said thank you to all the angels, picked up the first letter and opened it.

The angels behind the couch began bending over and whispering in my ear what each letter was about. I would try to read a little bit of it as well. My reading is improving over the years.

I don't know how many letters I went through. Over an

hour must have passed. I was getting very tired at that point. Each time I read a letter with the angels, I prayed that the request in it would be answered. I asked the angels to put it on the prayer scroll, which they did. Every prayer, every request that anyone ever makes to an angel is put on this scroll. Then the angels give me this scroll to take to God.

Sometimes the letters were very sad. They might be about someone who was very sick, the loss of a loved one or a mother or a father trying to cope with difficult situations within their family. I suppose most of the letters are usually from mothers and fathers who are worried about their children, wanting them to pass their exams, find employment, get married, have children or simply be happy.

Some parents just ask, 'Lorna, please put our name on the prayer scroll that you hand to God. I know He will listen to your prayer for our child.'

They could be asking God to help their child to give up drugs or alcohol or for their child not to end up back in prison. Often, they ask for their child to make friends. Sometimes, a parent will say their child has no friends, no one to talk to. This is something that always hurts me when I read a letter because I know there are so many people, young and old, who feel so lonely. They have no one to talk to. Making friendships is very important and holding on to those friendships is equally important.

I say to parents all across the world, 'Encourage your child, no matter what age they are, to join a club, go dancing, hill walking, or cycling, play football, go swimming, do horse riding, join something to learn about nature. Encourage your children to partake. Remind them to try not to be too shy. Tell them to help others they meet because it will help them to make friends.'

I was just about to finish reading the letters and praying when that same unemployed angel who had been standing in front of me at the little table said, 'Lorna, just one more letter.'

As I unwrapped the blankets from around me I said, 'I'm really tired. I'll do the rest of them tomorrow night. I know you will be here to help me.'

I pushed the little table to the right, being careful of the empty cup and saucer. The unemployed angel said, 'Lorna, just one more letter and then you can go to bed.'

I gave a sigh and said, 'Okay. Just one more letter. No more.'

I sat back down on the edge of the couch. As I went to pick up one of the letters I stopped and looked up at the unemployed angel as the thought that I am always employing unemployed angels went across my mind.

I said to the angel, 'You are employed now because you are helping me with these letters.'

The unemployed angel replied, 'Lorna, you employed me a long time ago.'

I laughed and looked more closely at the unemployed angel. 'Yes, you're right. I'm such a feather head.'

I recognised this particular angel. He is always with me when I am opening letters.

He said, 'Lorna, back to work.'

I fumbled through the letters that were scattered on the couch, trying to decide which one I would pick up.

Just as I was about to choose one of the letters the angel said, 'Lorna, not that one.' He pointed to the pile of letters.

'Which one?' I said. 'It's hard to guess.'

The angel leaned over and let the light from his fingertip highlight the corner of a letter that was sticking out among the others. I picked it up and opened the envelope. It was a short letter. It turned out to be from a young boy of fourteen years. One of the angels standing behind the couch leaned over and started to help me to read the letter. This boy apologised for his broken English but spoke about his mother who was terminally ill with cancer and how scared he was that she would die. He said there was only his mother and himself. No one else and if his mum died he would be put into a children's home. That terrified him. He asked me to please pray for his mum to get well. He asked that I pray to God to grant that miracle. He wrote that he loves her so much.

This young teenager didn't give an address or a phone number. I had no idea where he was from. When I asked the angels they would not tell me, but on one of my tours during that year to some Scandinavian countries I met this young man.

I was there to give a talk from God and the angels about love, peace, the environment, saving our world and healing. I can't remember exactly which country it was. The one thing I do remember is that the hall was crowded, including a huge number of young people. I remember being very taken aback by that – all these young teenagers wanting to know about God, their guardian angel, love and peace. The angels told me that the young people have great faith. They believe in miracles.

I bless everybody individually at my events and ask for healing, whatever way the person needs it. I don't know how long it took me to bless everyone that evening. When I blessed people they often told me that they didn't want the blessing for themselves but that they would love God to pass the blessing on to those they loved, to their family and their friends.

I moved along the line of all the young people, blessing them as I went.

Just as I was about to step forward and bless a young boy, the angels around me whispered, 'This is the young boy of fourteen who sent you a letter about his mother having cancer.'

The angels, at that very moment, allowed me to see myself on the couch reading the letter the young boy had sent. The young boy stepped forward. As I reached up to bless him he whispered in my ear, 'Lorna, I don't want this blessing for me. I want it for my mother. I sent you a letter. She has cancer. I want God to make her well so we can be together.'

'I remember the letter you sent me,' I whispered back, 'I have been asking God every day since I received your letter. Don't worry, I'm going to bless you and at the same time, I'll ask God to send a blessing to your mother that she will be healed.'

I blessed him and then the angels told me to move on to the next person.

As I did, I said to God, 'He is so young, only fourteen years of age. He is so desperate that his mum will get well. God, please grant a miracle for this young boy.'

I continued on, blessing one person after another. I know many miracles happen during the blessings, and some later on. That young boy had great faith. He believed in asking that God would grant a miracle for his mum.

The other part to this story is that two years passed and I returned to do another book tour and to give talks in the same country. I remember the angels telling me that at one of the talks there would be a little surprise for me. During those two years, this young boy and his mother, even though I had never met her, would often cross my mind. The angels never told me if God had granted the miracle for his mum or not. I never asked Archangel Michael or God Himself if He granted that miracle. It is something I never do. I just pray that God will grant as many miracles as possible for people in their lives. I simply always prayed that God did grant the miracle for this boy's mum to be healed and to live so he would not end up an orphan.

During the blessing at one of my events the young man, now sixteen, stood in front of me and said, 'Thank you, Lorna. God granted the miracle. My mum is alive and well. She's right here behind me.'

Just as he told me this the young man was suddenly surrounded by angels and so too was the woman, his mother, standing behind him. His mother stepped forward to stand beside her son. My heart jumped for joy. I was so happy to hear this good news.

The young boy, now a young man, said, 'Lorna, this is my mum.'

I smiled at her and said, 'Hello. I'm so happy to meet you.'

I know she didn't understand how overjoyed I was. I could see her son's guardian angel with its hands upon his shoulders. It was showing the young man so much love. Her own guardian angel was embracing her with such gentleness and love.

I proceeded to bless them, asking for the miracle to continue for his mum so that she could continue to be a great, loving mother to her son. I asked God to allow the mum to grow old so that her son could have her in his life. I asked too that the young man will find employment when he leaves school, that he will be happy and that he too will have a family. I know he would make a great father. I know in my heart that I will meet them again.

The young man said to me, 'I believe in God. Thank you for letting me know that I have a guardian angel.'

When I finished blessing them, both mother and son said goodbye.

Before they left the young man gave me white rosary beads and said, 'Lorna, I want you to have these. These are the beads I used to pray every night to Our Lady so that she would ask her son to allow the miracle to happen for my mum. Lorna, I want you to have them. I know I don't need them now any more.'

'No, they are yours,' I said. 'We always need to pray.'

The young man replied, 'I can get another set but I want you to have these rosary beads. They are the ones I prayed with every night for my mum because you gave me faith. You made me believe in God.'

I didn't want to take them but my guardian angel leaned down and whispered in my ear, 'You must.'

I said, 'Thank you.'

I held them in my hand but then I had to pass them on to someone else to mind so I could continue on with the blessing. I don't know how long it took to do the blessing. Sometimes it takes two hours, sometimes more, but I always pray that God will grant healing for everyone, no matter what kind of healing it may be.

When I got back to my room in the hotel I put them safely into my bag to bring home. Now, in my own house in Ireland, I have those white rosary beads under my pillow. I use them myself. I have never seen white rosary beads like them. They are different than the traditional ones we use here in Ireland. I will always keep them close to my heart and I will never forget that young boy and his mother. They will always be in my prayers, for ever.

CHAPTER 27

Olivia, Aged Thirteen

I DON'T KNOW HOW MANY TIMES I HAVE UPROOTED myself and Megan. It has happened four times already. I seem to live between Maynooth and Kilkenny. This is something I give out to God about all the time. I would rather have a home in one place and not have to keep on moving.

The second time I had to move, I cried and I don't mind saying it. I found it very upsetting and I know it was upsetting for Megan too. I was up in my bedroom, sitting on the bed, saying to myself, 'This is just so unfair! I don't want to have to move again. God, please give me roots so I can stay in one place.'

Just as I said these things to God, Archangel Michael came into the room.

I looked up at him and said, 'Hello.'

He reached out and put his hand on my head and said, 'Lorna, it will be okay.'

I said to Archangel Michael, 'I just hate moving house. I

know I shouldn't be complaining but how many times do you think I will have to move home?'

'Lorna, you know God told you that you may have to move house on many occasions.'

'How many is many?' I said to Archangel Michael.

'Lorna, I don't know the answer to that because God hasn't told me.'

I took a deep breath and said, 'It's okay. I'm all right now.'

Archangel Michael then said, 'I must go.'

He disappeared.

You may not know this but I am a very shy person and I'm not very good at socialising. When my children were young the angels always had to encourage me an awful lot, especially when I had to go down to the school for a parent/teacher meeting or if there was something like a nativity play put on by the children. It took an awful lot of courage. It was only because of the angels, who would almost push me out the door and tell me I'd be okay, that I was brave enough to go. I guess my shyness was really because I didn't know very many people.

I remember when Megan was about five years old. She was going to the convent school for girls. The school was putting a play on and Megan was very excited about this as she was taking part. I was very nervous about going but I never allowed her to know this. We left in plenty of time for the play. All those playing a part had to be there early, so Megan and I walked from Old Greenfield down to the school.

Sometimes, I would give out to Archangel Michael, Angel Hosus or, on occasion, my own guardian angel because they would say 'Lorna, you must not look for an excuse not to go.'

I walked down to the school with Megan and as I walked I was giving out to Angel Hosus. He was walking beside us and I said to him, without using words, 'You know I want to go back home but I know I can't. I must do this for my little girl.'

Angel Hosus just said, 'Lorna, you will be okay.'

He was encouraging me not to be nervous and told me I would enjoy the play.

We were almost at the school gates when Megan stopped and said, 'Mam, don't be worried. You will enjoy it.'

I smiled at her and said, 'Of course I will.'

I glanced at her guardian angel, for it was whispering in her ear. Megan gave me a big hug and held my hand as we walked through the gates and into the school.

As we walked into the school hall, I saw there were already lots of parents and children sitting down. Of course, the teachers were milling about too. The hall was absolutely packed with angels. Some of them were sitting in the rows of seats that were still empty of people. Other angels were moving among the parents and children as if to welcome them.

Megan ran off to her friends so I found myself a seat down near the back. There were empty chairs around me. Angel Hosus sat on one of them.

I said to him, 'I feel completely out of place. What am I to do? Just twiddle my thumbs?'

Just at that moment, Megan came up to me with some of her friends. She was just checking to see if her mum was okay. I said hello to the other little girls that were with her and told them I was looking forward to watching them play their parts on stage. They just said thank you and hurried back up to the side of the stage. I nearly burst out laughing and I know I gave a big smile, because a group of angels ran after the little girls imitating every single move they made. As they giggled and talked to each other so did the angels.

The hall was full in no time. When the play started I became engrossed in watching the young children on stage and all of the angels mimicking them. When the children were singing a group of angels stood behind them singing as well, holding the songbook in their right hands and a lighted candle in their left. The children sang beautifully. In the case of the children who played musical instruments, an angel stood beside each of them playing the same musical instrument but their musical instrument would glow. I knew what the angels were doing. Singing and playing the instruments enhanced the children's performances. I feel very privileged every day of my life seeing how the angels are involved in our lives.

When the play was over, the whole audience clapped and gave big cheers. The children bowed and the angels bowed with them. At that moment, it was as if the angels had put a rainbow right across the stage of all colours. I watched my daughter jumping for joy with her friends. I watched the rainbow of light, full of colours, break up and scatter across the stage like flags and bubbles. I watched Megan coming down off the stage with all the other young girls. As she made her way through the crowd of parents she stopped every now and then to say hello and goodbye to a friend. She made her way down to the back of the hall to me. She was all excited and happy.

On the way home, all Megan did was talk about the play and her friends. It was great listening to her. Angel Hosus walked home alongside us.

I had enjoyed watching everything that was going on but I never spoke to anyone. They had not spoken to me either, because we did not know each other. I know I'm always talking about friendships but I have to admit I was never very good at that. God never allowed me to have many friends involved in my life, and that is still the same today.

I have to say, even to this day, I'm not very good at socialising but I am a good listener. I suppose when I'm in the company of others there is so much going on. I listen to everything that everyone is talking about but I also listen to the angels that are around as well.

Another social encounter that I dread is going to parent/teacher meetings. I know a lot of other parents are nervous as well because they are afraid the teacher is going to tell them negative things about their child.

My daughter Ruth is married now and has two children. Her youngest boy is going to school and she too hates the thought of going to parent/teacher meetings.

The other day she said, 'Mam, what if the teacher says Billy Bob is naughty in school or is not doing his homework properly or paying attention?'

Like all mothers, these are some of the things she fears about going to parent/teacher meetings but we should remember, the teacher has your child's best interests at heart.

I said to Ruth, 'I don't think his teacher will have much to complain about. He's a really good boy.'

Ruth replied, 'I hope so.'

I know when Ruth reads this book she's going to discover more things she didn't know about her mam and this is one of them. I had to go to a parent/teacher meeting for Megan. It was making me very nervous and one of the reasons it did was because I am dyslexic. When my children were going to national school and secondary school I wasn't able to read very well, actually very little. So when a teacher showed me the marks my children got I could not make head or tail of it. I was afraid the teacher would hand me something and expect me to read it. It was really very difficult to keep the secret that I couldn't read or write. If I had to sign my name on something I had to spell it in my head so I would write it correctly and that wasn't easy. I managed with the help of the angels teaching me all they possibly could, and they still help today.

I don't believe my mum or dad or siblings realised I could not read, but Joe did and so did my children. Even today, I still have great difficulty. My reading is improving but I do learn things off by heart as well.

When I am signing books the angels repeat the words over and over again in my ear and spell the words for me but I still do make mistakes. It has taken years of practice but it has not stopped me in life. I have gone on the journey that God sent me and I am doing what He has asked of me. Let me tell you, God is real, you have soul and a beautiful guardian angel right there with you all the time that surrounds you with its love. God has appointed your guardian angel as the gatekeeper of your soul.

A few years after I had written my book, *Angels in My Hair*, I was in Liffey Valley Shopping Centre. It is about a twenty-minute drive from Maynooth. I had a little shopping to do and when I finished I went up to the top floor of the department store to get something to eat. The restaurant was to the left when I went up the escalator, as far as I remember. I queued up and bought some roasted chicken with vegetables. Then I found a table in a quiet spot along the wall. It wasn't busy. I had started to eat my dinner when I heard my name being called. I looked up towards the entrance. There were two angels waving at me, and they were walking alongside a young girl. She was maybe about thirteen years old. She had a schoolbag with her but she wasn't wearing a school uniform. The angels were looking after her. I saw the light of her guardian angel right behind her and the two other angels were walking with her, one on her left and the other on her right.

These two angels didn't say anything to me so I carried on enjoying my meal. A few minutes later, the young girl sat down at the table across from me. Every now and then, the angels with her called me and I would look up. Every time I did I would catch the young girl looking across at me, so I gave her a big smile each time but she didn't smile back at me. The angels continued to call me. The young girl was always looking in my direction when I glanced up. I kept giving her a big smile. It must've happened about seven times.

Eventually, the young girl did smile back at me. I gave her an even bigger smile in return. At the same moment, the light of her guardian angel opened up. It's what I saw her guardian angel doing that upset me. It was holding a light in front of her and straight away, I knew exactly what it meant. This little girl sitting across from me, who was meant to be at school, was feeling very sad or depressed.

I asked her guardian angel without using words, 'What is wrong?'

Her guardian angel did not answer me but one of the angels standing beside her replied that the little girl was considering suicide because she felt useless and was being bullied at school.

I said to the angel, 'Do you want me to get up and go over to her?'

The angel said, 'No, Lorna. Just give her a big smile. Your smile is working to help give her courage.'

So every time the angels called my name I looked up and across at the young girl to smile at her. She seemed to play with the food on her plate, not really eating it. The angel who had spoken to me gave a female appearance and was dressed in a beautiful, purple robe with golden light flickering through it. The other angel gave a female appearance as well and was dressed in radiant pink.

I had just finished my food and was sipping my cup of tea when the young girl got up from her table carrying her schoolbag. She looked like she was going to leave the restaurant. I saw the angels whispering to her. I could not hear what they were saying so I didn't know what thoughts they were putting into her head, but she stopped and turned around. She walked back to my table.

She said, 'Hello. I hope you don't mind but I think I have been reading your book, *Angels in My Hair*?'

She said this very nervously. Her voice was trembling. I smiled at her and invited her to sit down beside me. She did. She gave a big sigh and I asked her what was wrong. She started to cry and in between her sobs she spoke about how she wanted to end her life. She felt that her parents didn't care that she was being bullied constantly in school. Everyone was laughing at her and telling her she was ugly, stupid and fat.

At one stage, I reached into my bag, took out a hanky and handed it to her.

The angel said, 'Get the young girl to look at you.'

I reached out and put my hand under her chin, raising her head, getting her to look at me, to make eye contact.

I said to her, 'That's much better now.'

All of a sudden, she threw her arms around me. Then a moment later, she shyly let go.

I said to her, 'I love you even though I don't know you.'

She gave the biggest smile ever. The angel standing to the right of her spoke to me. I repeated the same words to the young girl.

I said to her, 'Your parents love you and I know you love them. Why would you want to kill yourself? To satisfy those that bully you? You are much better than them. You are not ugly. You are very pretty.'

She looked at me in astonishment and said, 'But they say I'm ugly and I'm fat.'

I said to her, 'You are not. When you go home look in the mirror. You are very pretty. You have read *Angels in My Hair*. You know you have a guardian angel and I can see your guardian angel right here with you. Never mind the other two beautiful angels as well. Your guardian angel is holding that light of hope in front of you and does not want you to take your life. You are precious and you are not alone. Your guardian angel wants to help you and so do the two other angels that your guardian angel has appointed to help you through this difficult time. You are not to commit suicide because that will hurt me, your parents and all those that love you. It would tear me apart. I don't know you but I love you.'

The young girl started to cry again.

'Don't cry,' I said. 'You never told me your name?'

'Olivia,' she replied.

I reached out my hand to take hers.

She laughed at this and as we shook hands I said, 'My name is Lorna.'

'Mine is Olivia.'

At that very moment, as the young girl said her name for the second time, I watched her guardian angel bend over her and wrap its golden wings around her. Yet, it was still holding that light of hope in front of her.

Her guardian angel said, 'Lorna, she can see the light of hope now.'

'Olivia, go home and tell your mum why you didn't go to school today. Share everything with your mum. Tell her what is happening to you in school. Don't leave anything out. Your parents love you. Ask your guardian angel to help you. Your guardian angel is already helping you. You heard your guardian angel whispering in your ear. You listened to your guardian angel instead of leaving. You stopped and turned around. You recognised me. You did as your guardian angel said. As it whispered in your ear to go over to me and say hello you did exactly that. Can you read, write and spell?'

She looked at me, a little startled, and said, 'Of course I can. I love reading and I know I am a good speller.'

'Well, then, you can learn anything.'

One of the angels standing beside Olivia spoke to me without words: 'Ask her about maths.'

So I did. 'How good are you at maths?'

She said, 'Okay,' as she shrugged her shoulders.

'Olivia, you seem doubtful.'

'I guess I'm not too bad at maths. I just find it very hard.'

One of the beautiful angels that were standing beside her, the one dressed in purple with the golden light flickering through it, said, 'Lorna, tell her all she needs to do is work a little harder on the maths and it will get easier for her. She's better than she thinks.'

I did as the angel said.

'Do your studies and do them for yourself with a little extra study for your maths. I'm positive you will find it much easier in time. What age are you, Olivia?'

She answered, 'I'm going on thirteen.'

I told her, 'The angel standing there beside you is all dressed in a beautiful purple colour with a golden light coming through it. The other angel is dressed in a vibrant pink. They are telling me that you do have one friend.'

She looked at me and said, 'No, I don't.'

I said, 'But the angels are saying you do. This other girl is very shy.'

As soon as I said that she said, 'Oh yes, I know who you mean now but we're not friends.'

'When you go to school tomorrow go over to her and say hello. Just remember, she is shy so it might take a little time. You will become best friends.'

As we said goodbye, Olivia threw her arms around me and said, 'Thank you!'

I reminded her about her guardian angel and as I watched her walk away into the shopping centre the two angels that were with her gave me a smile. I sat there for another few minutes before I got up to leave. I prayed and asked for this young girl never to take her own life. I prayed for her to know that her parents love her and that she has friends. I asked just for her to be happy.

It was a few years later when I was signing books in one of Easons' bookshops that a young girl of about seventeen said to me, 'Lorna, thank you. You saved my life when I was thirteen. You had time to talk to me.'

I said to her, 'You're welcome.'

She stood to one side waiting for her friend to have her books signed as well. The angels reminded me in an instant of the time I first met her. I don't know how the angels do that. It is like in one second I remember everything. I don't even have to think about it.

When I finished signing Olivia's friend's books Olivia came

over and reached out to take my hand and said, 'Thank you again, Lorna.'

The two of them said goodbye just as someone else walked up to have their books signed. I turned and glanced at the two girls as they walked away. I saw their guardian angels, as I see everyone's guardian angel, but I smiled because I also saw the same two angels that had been with Olivia when she was almost thirteen on that day I had met her in the Liffey Valley Shopping Centre. Both the angels still gave a female appearance. Just the same as then, one was dressed in a radiant pink and the other in a beautiful purple colour with golden light running through it. The two angels waved to me simultaneously as they called out my name in farewell. I thanked them without using words for helping Olivia to get through that rough patch in her life and I went back to signing books.

CHAPTER 28

The Energy of Nature

GOD GAVE JOE ANOTHER SPIRITUAL EXPERIENCE OF seeing energy. Joe's first experience was along the canal in Maynooth, when the angels showed him energy coming from the wild reeds and flowers growing along the water. His second spiritual experience was about six months before God took him home to heaven. Sometimes I took Joe out for a short drive. He had said to me a few times that maybe we could go down to the theological college in Maynooth, to the beautiful gardens there. I was a little apprehensive because I didn't think we could get in the college gates with the car as there is always security on the gates. I had seen them turn cars away before so I can tell you I prayed for weeks. Then, one day, I met someone I knew who worked in the college.

I asked them, 'Would it ever be possible to drive the car into the college?'

They said, 'Yes, Sunday would be the best day. They are not as strict. As you go in the gates just turn left and go into the first car park. Don't say anything if there is someone on the gates. Just act as if you know where you are going.'

I said, 'Thanks. That's a great bit of news. I will tell Joe. I know it will really make him happy because he's really looking forward to coming down and going for a walk in the gardens.'

We said goodbye and when I got home I told Joe that I would be able to bring him down to the college but it had to be on a Sunday so we could drive in the gates and go to the car park on the left.

He was very happy but it was many weeks later before we went. I had to wait until Joe was well enough.

One morning, I brought a cup of tea and a sandwich in to Joe. I had just stepped through the bedroom door when I saw his bed was surrounded by angels – glowing, white angels.

I said to them, 'Is everything all right?'

They turned to look at me and said, 'Lorna, everything is okay. Joe is just sleeping.'

As I walked towards the bed I looked at Joe. I saw that he was sleeping like a baby. I knew he hadn't slept well that night so I left the room quietly and went back to the kitchen.

I said to Megan, 'Let's get ready to go down to the shops. Your dad is asleep.'

Megan was about three and a half years of age so I put her into her buggy. As I went out the hall door I saw Archangel Michael standing at the gate.

'Hello, Archangel Michael. What a surprise! I wasn't expecting to see you.'

Archangel Michael said, 'I know, Lorna. I am just passing by. God wants me to let you know that in another few weeks Joe should be well enough to go down to the college for that walk he is always dreaming about.'

I said to Archangel Michael, 'Joe never said anything to me about dreaming of walking in the college. Now, I have to make sure it happens for him.'

'You will get in the gates, Lorna.'

'That's a relief,' I said to Archangel Michael, 'because I was scared we would be turned away if one of the security guards stopped us. I have been praying. No matter where I parked in the town it would be too far for Joe to walk. He would never make it to the college.'

'Just keep on praying, Lorna,' Archangel Michael replied. 'Joe will say to you one Sunday morning that he wants to go for that walk. Just take him. You will have no problems going through the gates. Now I have to go, Lorna.'

Archangel Michael disappeared.

I opened the gate and went back to get Megan. She was sitting in her buggy in the hall. I walked down to the village in those days. I became a fast walker because I never wanted to be away too long from Joe. In no time we were back. I took Megan out of her buggy, took her coat off and left her in the kitchen playing on the floor. I walked down the hall quietly, towards the bedroom. I peeped in through the door and opened it slowly, not making a sound. Joe was still fast asleep with the angels surrounding his bed. Some were sitting on it. I closed the door gently and went back to the kitchen. Megan was still playing on the floor. It was about half an hour later when I heard Joe calling.

Megan ran down to his room with a colouring book in her hand and some crayons. When I got there she was already on the bed beside her dad. Joe had started to colour in a picture with her. The room was still full of angels.

I walked up to the side of the bed, gave Joe a kiss and asked him, 'What would you like for breakfast?'

'I would love a boiled egg and toast.'

Megan said, 'Me too, please!'

'Okay.'

I headed back to the kitchen and prepared breakfast for the three of us, even though Megan had already had her breakfast!

I was just about to put everything on to the tray when there was a little tap on the kitchen door. As I've said before, it's very unusual for angels to intervene in the world in physical ways, so I knew this was to be a special occasion. I looked up and smiled for Angel Hosus was standing there.

I said to him, 'There was no need to knock since the door was open.'

Angel Hosus gave three taps on the door again and that made me laugh.

He said, 'Hurry up with that breakfast. You've two patients in the bedroom waiting anxiously.'

So I picked up the tray and carried it down to the bedroom.

As I walked in the door I spoke to the angels without words. 'It's a bit crowded in here. Maybe some of you should leave?'

In that moment, loads of angels disappeared leaving just four. One was looking out the window. Another sat on the end of the bed. The other two moved around the room, staying in no particular place.

I smiled and spoke without words. 'Thank you, angels.'

Joe said, 'About time. I thought you would never come with breakfast. I'm starving and Megan said she is to put the tray on the little cabinet beside the bed.'

I was afraid Megan would drop the breakfast tray so I said to her, 'Let's do it together.'

I sat down on the stool beside the bed. I still have that

stool to this day. It's always being moved around the house in Kilkenny. Sometimes upstairs, downstairs, or even out in the garden during the summertime. I've had to repair it many times and I know one day I probably won't be able to repair it any more. It will simply fall asunder and will not be repairable but until then, I love that little stool.

Joe didn't mention about going out for a walk until many weeks later. He spent most of this time in bed and, on occasion, got up and sat in his favourite chair in the front room and watched TV. Then, one Sunday when I was sitting on the stool beside the bed having a cup of tea while Joe was eating a sandwich, Ruth came into the bedroom and sat at the end of her dad's bed. We talked for a little while and Joe had her laughing.

Ruth turned to me and said, 'Mum, where's Megan?'

'She is in her room having a little nap.'

'When Megan wakes up I would love to take her out for a walk and over to my friend's if that's okay.'

'Yes, that would be great but take the buggy as well. I know you will need it. Megan will get tired before you reach your friend's house. I know she will enjoy walking part of the way though. She is bound to wake up soon.'

Ruth stood up and walked towards her dad, saying, 'I'd better get everything ready before Megan wakes up.'

She gave her dad a kiss and said, 'I will see you later.'

Just as she was walking out the room I smiled because I saw three angels following her.

I said to them, 'Take care of Ruth and Megan for me today.'

They did not answer me but I knew the angels heard me clearly.

The next moment, Megan called out and Ruth went in to her. I heard the two of them laughing. By the sounds of it

Ruth was tickling Megan. A few minutes later, Megan came into the bedroom. She ran to her dad and gave him a hug and a kiss. She told him she was going out with her big sister. She was so excited. He told her to be good and she said she would be. A few minutes later, we heard them going out the hall door and then the house was silent.

Joe reached out and took my hand.

He said, 'I would love to go for that walk now down in the college?'

I smiled at him and said, 'Great.'

I helped him to get dressed and about fifteen minutes later we were ready. We got into the car and I drove down. It was only a short journey and I never stopped praying, asking that we could just drive through the gates, that no one would say a word to us. When we got to the college gates two angels were standing at each side. They were dressed in clothing that resembled the colour silver. There were no security guards in sight.

I smiled and said thank you to the angels over and over again as I drove straight through the gates and went left into the car park. One of the angels that had been at the main gates was now standing just inside the car park and was pointing to a spot where I was to park. There were quite a few cars there already but where the angel had pointed to park gave plenty of room for Joe to get out of the car without any bother. I was grateful to the angel for helping.

Slowly, Joe opened his car door and got out of the car. He stood there for a moment and took a deep breath.

He said, 'I love the clear, fresh air.'

At times he was very wobbly on his legs so I linked arms with him. He wanted to take the rough walk to the flower gardens but I wouldn't allow it.

'I think we should go the easy way.'

In the end, Joe agreed with me. We walked towards the gardens very slowly, stopping every now and then as Joe would look around, pointing out how beautiful the trees and the flowers were. He looked back towards the gates we had just driven through and said how he loved the old buildings of the college.

We were almost at the walled garden. The fragrance of the flowers was beautiful. I could see the entrance. It was just ahead of us, about twenty feet away. There was a gentle breeze blowing in our direction. Joe stood for a moment and took a deep breath, smelling the fragrant flowers.

He said, 'I'm loving this.'

I was so glad Joe had made it this far and I thanked his guardian angel and the angels that were around us, helping me to support him. In no time, we walked in through the gates of the walled garden. To the left there was a bench, so we walked over to it and Joe sat down. He must've sat there for twenty minutes or so. He told me to walk around the garden on my own. He would watch me from where he was sitting. Every now and then, when I looked back at Joe, I saw his guardian angel had its wings wrapped around him. I knew his guardian angel was helping to keep him warm. I could see Joe was really enjoying himself, just sitting there in the sunshine. The odd time when I looked back he would give me a wave. I watched as some small birds came and hopped around him. They were only about a foot away from Joe. He looked down at the birds and started to talk to them but they didn't seem to take any notice.

I walked around the whole garden, stopping many times to admire all the different flowers and shrubs. Some of the trees that grew in the walled garden were enormous. Then I went back to Joe and sat beside him chatting about different flowers that were growing in the garden. He wanted to hear every detail. I told him there were still some goldfish in the little pond at the top and there were many tiny delicate flowers growing in the different beds. I told him how the gardener was doing a good job looking after all that was growing there. There were many birds as well. I described all I saw: finches, thrushes, blackbirds, sparrows, robins, even the little blue tit.

Joe said, 'I know. Some of them came and said hello. The birds in the garden here, Lorna, they're very tame. They are used to people.'

'I know, I saw them around you,' I said. 'Will we go back to the car?'

To my surprise Joe said, 'No, I want to walk up through the aisles of the trees at the back of the college.'

I was just about to protest when Angel Hosus stood to the left of Joe at the back of the bench and said, 'Lorna, take Joe to wherever he wants to walk.'

I said to Joe, 'Okay, let's take our time.'

We walked back through the gates of the walled garden and up to the apple orchard. I was praying because I didn't know whether Joe could do it and I was concerned about making it back to the car from the avenue of trees, but Angel Hosus walked beside Joe on his left side.

He spoke to me without words and said, 'He will be able to do it. You are not to worry. Remember what Archangel Michael told you and the message that God gave him for you that Joe would have a spiritual experience of seeing more energy.'

I said, 'I forgot. I always get stressed and fearful that Joe might collapse on me.'

Angel Hosus replied, 'He won't. Lorna, trust.'

I turned to look at Joe as I linked arms with him. That's when I noticed his guardian angel had its arms around him, this time not just helping him keep warm but supporting him. His guardian angel's hands looked enormous. They were full of white and golden light. The guardian angel's fingertips radiated a brighter light of gold and I could see every detail. I knew his guardian angel was holding him firmly but gently with such love. I spoke to Joe's guardian angel silently, saying thank you.

Joe said to me, 'What did you say?'

I said, 'I was talking to myself.'

Joe laughed. We stopped and stood for a moment.

Joe said, 'That's not a good sign, talking to yourself.'

I said to Joe, 'How right you are!'

We both laughed. We continued on our walk, stopping every now and then. Eventually, we made it to the back of the college where the avenue of trees is.

Joe stood there for a moment, just looking down the avenue.

Then he turned to me and said, 'Let's walk.'

We walked slowly. At one stage he stopped and turned to me and said, 'Lorna, I feel like walking on my own. Just walk alongside me.'

I did as Joe said and he took a few steps. He stopped and then started to walk again. There were trees on both sides of us. Joe stopped and looked around.

Angel Hosus was still with us when Joe turned to me and said, 'Lorna, do you see what I am seeing?'

I said, 'Yes, I do.'

'What is happening to the grass?'

I said to Joe, 'God is allowing you to see the energy coming from the grass.'

I could see the excitement on Joe's face.

'Energy is coming from every blade of grass. I've never seen so many colours. They're like knives shooting off like fireworks from the blades of grass,' he told me, laughing.

I said to Joe, 'I think you should look up at the trees.'

Joe stood there looking from one tree to another. I could see what he was seeing but I had to smile at Angel Hosus because there was no one around. Earlier on, as we walked through the college, a few people had passed us by but now, I could see no one on any of the avenues of trees. I knew in my heart that God had kept them clear especially for Joe.

Joe reached out his hand to me. I stepped forward and linked arms with him.

He said, 'What is happening? This is incredible. I always remember the day along the canal and seeing the energy from some of the flowers growing there.'

I said to him, 'I remember.'

He said, 'Look, Lorna, it's quite different.'

I said, 'I know because God is allowing you to see a little more.'

'I know God is real, Lorna, and sometimes I feel my guardian angel holding on to me. Watching that green and purple energy flowing from trees here, it's like every now and then the energy seems to stretch out as far as it can to touch the energy of another tree. It is as if they are shaking hands.'

I said to Joe, 'That is right.'

Joe took a deep breath and the next moment, he laughed and said, 'Lorna, what do you think is happening here now as balls of energy jump from the branches across to the other trees?'

I said to Joe, 'No one knows this but the trees are talking to each other. That's what I call what you are seeing. They are communicating with each other. It is not really talking as we talk. It is helping each tree to grow strong. It is like medicine to the trees. Can you see what's happening there, Joe, as well?'

Joe looked down to where there were some little shoots of young trees. They were very tiny. Joe saw balls of colourful energy, green and purple, fall upon them from bigger trees and burst. The energy disappeared into the little saplings. That is one reason why there should always be some mature trees where young saplings are planted.

Joe tugged at my arm and I turned to see where he was looking. He was looking to the left of the trees.

He said, 'Lorna, I really think . . . I think I see angels, but not very clearly. They are like shadows but extremely bright-eyed. Are they coming for me?'

I said, 'No, not yet.'

'You know I'm ready to go.'

I said, 'I know.'

It was then, at that moment, the angels came from everywhere. They walked through that veil. I have never really described the veil to you. It is like a veil between time. It is like the air itself but smooth and clean. It's like silk, a veil of light, but with no flaws whatsoever. I'm aware of it all the time, but at different times the veil is more visible. Mostly I don't focus on it, unless like now the angels draw my attention to it.

At that very moment, when the angels stepped through this veil, a golden line appeared as if someone had drawn a straight line with a pencil and ruler in the veil. As soon as the angels stepped through it the golden line disappeared. It was as if it had never happened. The veil became whole again.

Joe just stood there as if he was in a trance. He never said a word. A few minutes passed and all of the angels and the energy coming from the grass and the trees ceased. It all went back to normal, for Joe at least.

Then he said to me, 'Let's go back to the car.'

It took us a while. Angel Hosus remained with us, helping Joe. Joe's guardian angel still had his arms around him. When we reached the car Joe got in.

I was just about to start the engine when Joe said, 'No, let's just sit here for a few minutes.'

I said to him, 'You have been very quiet.'

'I know,' he said, 'I was just remembering my dream. I never told you, Lorna, but for months, for such a long time, I have been dreaming of walking in the college and in my dream you were with me. The sun was shining like today and at the avenue of trees in my dream I saw what I saw today.' Tears ran down Joe's cheeks as he spoke. 'I even thought when I was standing there that I was in a dream. It was like I blinked my eyes and everything was gone and you were standing beside me.'

I said to Joe, 'This time you weren't dreaming but sometimes God does it that way. Like the blink of an eye.'

Joe reached over and we gave each other a hug. He kissed me on the cheek. I started the engine and headed back home, thanking God for allowing Joe to have that spiritual experience of seeing all the energy and vaguely seeing the angels.

Energy comes from everything. I believe it is something that mankind does not fully understand. Energy even comes from food. We eat food to give us energy because it is full of energy itself. I see energy coming from everything. Even when I'm in the supermarket I see energy from vegetables, fruit, tin cans, bottles, plastic bags and cardboard boxes. Maybe one thing people don't understand is that different energy comes from different things. The food that is in the tin can has a different energy than the energy that comes from the can itself. Maybe one day I'll write a book about all the energy around us, the energy that comes from plants, water, the earth, animals, people, insects, even the energy that seems to flow around a planet. Maybe I will write this book and leave it to be published after my death. I always say to God that He needs to give me time to get around to writing it, but at the moment, I'm only writing this book.

All you really need to remember is that some day in the future you will be able to see the energy coming from everything, including yourself, those you love and your children. Sometimes, I wish God would allow people to see this energy clearly because I believe that then we would not be destroying our planet as we are. I going to leave this as something of a mystery for you, for now.

CHAPTER 29

Strangers Calling at the Gate

A KIND LADY, FIONA, TALKED TO MY DAUGHTER AT ONE of my events and told her of the refurbished old mill that she and her husband rent out to holidaymakers who are looking for somewhere peaceful to stay. She invited me down to take a break or even to use the mill as a quiet place to write. I don't often have the chance to take people up on such kind invitations but this time I was able to. I travelled to their old mill in Dunshaughlin with my youngest daughter, Megan. Fiona met us in the town. We went for coffee and after we caught up we followed her in the car to the mill.

When Fiona turned the key in the door and Megan and I followed her through it was like walking back into the past. We stepped into the old-fashioned kitchen and dining area. It had a flagstone floor, something I have not seen in a long time. The rest of the house had wooden floors and the windows had shutters. As you all know, I love everything that is old and I found the wildness of the back garden beautiful too.

We were there a few days when Megan came running up the stairs and said, 'Mam, Fiona called saying that delivery truck will be here with the table and chairs for the garden in about ten minutes.' I had only just come back from a tour in Italy and was upstairs lying on the bed resting. I got up a few minutes later and walked down the stairs. Just as I stepped into the sitting room I saw two angels on the couch.

I smiled at them and said, 'Did you come to join me for my few days' rest here?'

The two angels said, 'Yes, Lorna.'

Then they disappeared.

I smiled to myself and said, 'They didn't stay long.'

As I turned into the kitchen the same two angels were standing one each side of Megan, who was sitting at the kitchen table studying for her college exam on Thursday. Just as I glanced out the kitchen window I saw a white truck pull up outside the gate.

I said, 'The delivery truck is here.'

Megan got up from the table and said she would go out and see if she could help.

'Mam, come with me!'

I held back and said, 'No, you go ahead. I'll be out in a few minutes.'

The reason I did this was because of that shyness I have. I went to put on the kettle. Then I walked across the flagstone kitchen floor to the little front door. I peeped out, making sure I was not seen. I saw Fiona talking to a young man who was delivering the garden table and chairs. Her beautiful eleven-year-old daughter, Ava, was there too.

I closed over the door as the kettle had just come to a boil.

I was going to make a cup of tea and walk out into the garden with that in my hand and see if anyone else would like a cup of tea, but the two angels that remained in the kitchen said, 'No, Lorna. They are around the back of the house now.'

As I went out the back door there were a few raindrops falling from the sky.

I said a little prayer: 'Please let the rain stop.'

I said hello to Fiona and her young daughter. We stood there talking for a few minutes before the young man appeared from around the corner of the house carrying the table.

He said, 'Hello!'

He put the table down and asked Fiona, 'Would it be okay to leave the table outside the shed?'

She said, 'Yes.'

He disappeared, walking back around the corner of the house to get the chairs. A few moments later he was back, packing the chairs into the shed.

It was at this time that my daughter turned and said to the young man, 'We forgot, we were talking so much, we were meant to help you.'

The young man said, 'No problem,' with a big smile on his face. 'All done.'

He locked the shed, said goodbye and waved as he went around the corner of the house.

Fiona's daughter Ava is very pretty. She stood there shyly, swaying from side to side. I could see how happy she was. This young girl was full of lots of love as we stood there chatting. Her guardian angel at times was swaying in rhythm with her. The angel was like a giant. She looked so tiny compared to her guardian angel who was looking down at her. It gave a female appearance, elegant in every way, dressed in a flowing gown that was light like silk and crimson-blue in colour. It radiated and reflected waves of light. The hands of her guardian angel were glowing. Those long, elegant fingers moved gently across Ava's shoulders. At times they stroked her gently upon the head.

I talked with her for those few moments as we walked back through the house to the front gate. I spoke to her guardian angel as well at the same time and said, 'You think you would make yourself more in proportion to this beautiful little girl.'

Just as I said those words her guardian angel made itself more in proportion to her height. Yet it remained very tall, about ten feet, head and shoulders over the young girl. Her guardian angel brought its arms around her and clasped its hands together delicately in a loving embrace. We all stood in the kitchen talking for another few minutes. Then Fiona and her daughter left.

I made that cup of tea for Megan and myself. Then Megan went back and continued her studies for her exam. I went for a walk up the lane. We enjoyed the few days we stayed in the mill and in between writing, I walked on fabulous routes through the forest and to the nearby castle.

CHAPTER 30

My Bird of Love

IT WAS THE MONTH OF MAY IN 2016. ON A WEDNESDAY morning back in Kilkenny, I was getting out of bed. I put my slippers on and reached out to open the shutters of my bedroom window. As I looked out the little window to see what the weather was like an angel joined me, bending down to look out with me. I turned to the angel, smiling at the sight of this extremely tall angel bending down to look out my little bedroom window just to see how the weather was. I knew the angel knew already exactly what the weather was like.

The angel gave a female appearance. She was very beautiful and elegant. All dressed in silver light with long, silver hair. I remember as she was bent down to look out the window with me that her long, silver hair touched the windowsill. As it did so, it seemed to sparkle.

I said to the angel, 'What do you think? Maybe I should go back to bed and have a few hours' extra rest?'

I was hoping the angel would say yes to me. It was that

kind of morning. I would have liked to snuggle back under the blankets.

The angel said, 'No, it's already eight o'clock in the morning. In another few minutes decide what you want to do.'

The angel stood upright, moving ever so gracefully and slowly.

It turned and said, 'Goodbye.'

The angel went to walk out of the room. I followed but the angel seemed to be a great distance away from me, hundreds of yards away, even though we were in my smallish bedroom. The angel went through the door, and when I reached it I looked out into the hallway, but of course, I knew deep inside it would not be there.

Little sparks of light jumped from the windowsill in the hallway, but she had disappeared and hadn't even given me her name. Angels do that often. There is not always a need for a name. I always say to people angels just love to be called angels.

I dressed quickly and did all the usual morning chores. I spent a little time with Holly and Mimsy, my rabbit. Holly and I went for a walk out into the orchard and up along the boreen. You know of course that we didn't go for a walk on our own. The angels followed us out through the little front gate of the garden. Holly did all the usual things: running around and sniffing through the grass. Every now and then, she would stop and look back. I knew at times she was getting glimpses of the angels with us.

It is something the angels often do, allow animals to see them. It's not exactly that they see them but rather they get a glimpse, just for a moment, so the animal knows everything is okay, just as Holly did. She continued sniffing the grass. It was a dull day, very overcast and it started to drizzle rain.

Eventually Holly and I headed back towards the house accompanied by the angels. Just as we got in the door it started to lash rain.

I made a cup of tea and some toast. Then, I went upstairs to work. It was about one o'clock when I stopped. I turned in the swivel chair and saw the weather hadn't changed that much but it was no longer raining. Every now and then, the sun would try to peek through the clouds.

Seeing the sunlight made me feel like it would be nice to go for a proper walk so I turned off the computer and walked out on to the landing. Just as I turned at the top of the landing to go down the stairs I met four unemployed angels who were standing on some of the steps.

They said, 'Lorna, don't just think of going for a walk. Why not drive?'

As I continued down the stairs I said to them, 'That's not a bad idea. The weather is quite overcast and it is raining. Maybe I could stop the car somewhere and be still in prayer for a little while.'

I love spending time in nature, for I have it all around me so I appreciate it very much. I spoke my thoughts out loud to the unemployed angels as I got ready to leave.

I drove out the gate and down the lane. I had no plans of where I might go for a drive. I always prefer it that way. I kept to the country roads, not following any road signs. I ended up in a very hilly area. I drove slowly, admiring the scenery. Maybe three cars passed me going in the opposite direction. I waved to them and they waved to me, returning my greeting. It is something that those who live in the countryside usually do here in Ireland. I'm not sure about other countries but in the countryside here it is one way to get to know your neighbours. You get to recognise them and then if you meet them in the supermarket or the petrol station you say hello.

I was well wrapped up. The sun would peep out between the clouds but only for a little while before disappearing again behind them. It did little to lessen the cold. It drizzled rain as I drove along the roads. Looking ahead, I saw the sky darkening. I thought to myself that it was going to rain really heavily.

An unemployed angel said, 'Look, Lorna!'

One of the angels pointed towards the sky. The sun slowly started to peep out from between the clouds. It seemed to shine more brightly this time. The beams of sunlight shone directly upon a small river. I know I would never have noticed the river if the sun hadn't shone on it because the day was quite dull. Then I found a spot to pull in and parked the car to go down to the river.

As I was getting out of the car I asked the unemployed angels, 'Were you the cause of the light of the sun shining more brightly on that little river?'

They never answered me. Angels have a habit of ignoring me when I ask a question. Many times it's like they aren't even listening or taking any notice of me but it doesn't bother me. It is the way of the angels.

I walked through a small forest following a little path that I knew was used, probably by foxes and badgers. Maybe even the deer. It was winding in and out through the trees. Some of the trees were quite big. Just as I came to a small clearing, the sun came out again. I walked towards the river. It wasn't a big river. Maybe one would call it a stream. There were lots of rocks and some of the water flowed over them like a waterfall. It was very beautiful and peaceful. There were more trees on the far side of this little river. I was thinking to myself that I could cross the river stepping from one stone to another.

Just as I was about to I heard my name being called. Archangel Michael came out of the trees.

He said, 'Hello, Lorna.'

'Hello, Michael,' I said. 'What are you doing here? I wasn't expecting you.'

Archangel Michael smiled at me, but did not answer my question.

He said, 'Don't cross the river. Stay here and enjoy all the natural elements around you.'

Then he disappeared without saying he had to go, which as I've been saying is quite rare. So I sat there upon one of the rocks listening to the noise of the river as it flowed over the rocks like a waterfall. Some small birds came to drink and hopped along the rocks, picking at them. I became peaceful and quiet, just listening to all of the sounds of stillness and the silence of nature.

The angels taught me as a child to separate every sound and at times, just to focus on one and only one sound, to hear that one sound, to listen to every note of it. I was to learn to listen to what it was saying. Sometimes, I listened to an insect. Other times, it was a bird or the whistling of the wind. I would follow the sound as it was carried through the air. Then, it would break into loads of splinters. The sound scattered in all directions. I would always thank God for this beautiful planet with all of its nature.

Again, this is something all of you could try. It's another lesson, something to learn. I have been learning how to do this since I was a child. Many times I jumbled it all up. I found I was listening to the wrong sound and not the one the angel wanted me to listen to.

Maybe if you are sitting on a bench you can hear all the chit-chat of the people around you. Pick one voice and listen to it. Travel with it and see where it goes. Over time, you will get better at it. It's not easy to do but if I could learn how to do it I know you can.

Maybe your children would learn it much easier than you but there's no harm in trying. Even if you are sitting with friends you could all make a game of it. Each of you could pick a sound. Tell each other which sound you picked and then give it five minutes. See how well you have done. How many times did you lose the sound? Did you hang on to it for a minute before you lost it? Have a pen and paper with you and every time you lose the sound make a mark on the paper. Every time you hear it again put another mark down. Use whatever symbols you want. It's an exercise you can do anywhere and especially when you are on your own. Ask your guardian angel to help you. I know it will probably have other angels around you to help you too.

I don't know how long I sat there for but when I felt the hand of my guardian angel upon my shoulder I looked around. I saw there were lots of angels. Some were sitting on the rocks and others were walking along the riverbank.

Most of the time when we are in nature we become peaceful within ourselves, we let go, we allow ourselves to go out into nature and then we may be carried over into the spiritual part of ourselves. This is what was happening to me.

The angels' feet were not touching the ground, not even a blade of grass. But as I watched I could see the blades of grass moving as if the cushion of light that is between the earth and the angels' feet was touching them.

One of the angels was walking along the little river pointing to the forest. I turned and looked. There again was Archangel

Michael, walking out of the beautiful forest towards me. He was dressed in a long trench coat that fell below his knees. It was blowing in the wind. His coat was beige in colour and he was wearing dark trousers. They were a deep brown like some of the trees. As he walked towards me I watched the cushion of light beneath his feet. It stopped Archangel Michael's feet from touching the ground but I know if someone else saw him they would think he was walking on the earth.

Each step he took was like thunder. His trench coat sometimes blew open more and I could see the top he was wearing beneath. It was golden in colour. He looked as handsome as ever.

I said, 'Hello, Michael. By the way, you never said you had to go before. You just disappeared!'

He ignored that and just said, 'Hello, Lorna.'

Archangel Michael came over and stood by me to my left, a few feet back.

He said, 'Have you been enjoying your time out here?'

I replied, 'Yes, very much so.'

Archangel Michael said, 'Lorna, look across the river, to your right, up into the tree.'

I looked across the river and asked, 'Which tree are you talking about?'

Archangel Michael said, 'The one there that stands out the most.'

All of a sudden, the biggest tree on the far side of the river became brighter. Some of them had more leaves on them than others, which were only starting to bud. Because of this you could see all the branches quite clearly.

I looked up into the branches and then I saw what I knew Archangel Michael wanted me to see. I saw a bird of prey. They stand upright, more so than other birds.

Without turning around to look at Archangel Michael I said, 'It looks like a falcon. It's beautiful.'

It suddenly took off, gliding among the high branches of the trees. Then, it came back and landed on the branch in the tree where I first saw it.

It always gives me great joy to see one of these beautiful birds. The bird sat there for a few minutes looking all around.

I said to Archangel Michael, 'Thank you. I always like when God allows me to see a bird of prey because it always reminds me of the gift God gave me when I was a child. The helpless, baby bird that was a little bird of prey – my Bird of Love.'

Archangel Michael stepped forward and touched my hand, filling me with peace and love. I always love when Archangel Michael takes my hand.

He said, 'This is why I have come for you, Lorna, because God wants you to see your Bird of Love again.'

I always get very emotional when I think about the Bird of Love, because it's about my mission on earth and all that is most wonderful – and most difficult – in my life, the worst of times and the best of times.

The Bird of Love is a symbol, and like all the symbols that God and the angels have given us down the ages it has many different layers of meaning that we may gradually be able to interpret and understand over time, one layer after the other.

And it is also a living symbol, because when the Bird of Love first came to me it was a living spiritual being, a perfect and radiant being that had manifested as a physical being. On the very rare and precious occasions it comes to me later in life, like the one I'm describing here, this same living being is inhabiting a creature of flesh and blood, but when it first came into my life it *was* that creature.

Usually it's very hard for spiritual beings like angels to make direct changes in the physical world. In my writings I've given a few examples of angels knocking on windows or doors or causing winds to blow. But although such things have started to happen around me more frequently now, they are still very, very rare. I've also written about Archangel Michael appearing to people as if he were an ordinary human being. But what happened when the Bird of Love first came to me was of a wholly different order to all these sorts of things, because the first time the Bird of Love came to me a spiritual being had actually materialised and made itself flesh and blood.

I don't understand this symbol completely, but I understand it's connected with what God wants from me and what He wants me to bring to the world. God needs my love and that is why the sparks of God, the souls in every single human being, need me too. Loving someone and being loved both bring great responsibility, and sometimes God's love is so overwhelming if I am in His presence, so powerful that I want to run away. That's why God sometimes says to me 'Why are you hiding?'

I think the Bird of Love, as a symbol, is saying something very important about a new way that love is working in the world, a great change that is happening. It's about a spiritual process, the way that love is changing matter, starting with our own human bodies. It begins with the intertwining of body and soul.

On rare occasions I'm privileged to see this intertwining when I see people in deep prayer. For this process to take place the soul must come forward, which is to say move partially out of the body.

Sometimes when I see the soul coming forward it is because

a soul is preparing to leave the body. When death is approaching, people are often more open spiritually. They tend to be more loving and caring and ask more questions when they know death is near.

And some of the same changes also happen to people when they are in deep prayer. A lot of the time people don't pray often enough or deeply enough. They may be mechanically repeating phrases, praying without enough belief or conviction.

But if you pray with every single particle of your being, so that you feel it even in your bones, you are giving your soul permission to come forward, and when that happens, the intertwining can begin. Spiritual experience intensifies. As you accept that your soul is pure love in a loving universe, you may encounter spiritual beings. Then the body feels lighter.

In an earlier book I wrote about one of the visions of the future I have been shown, a future in which children can be seen walking upon the water of a river. They can do this because their bodies are lighter, because they have been transformed by this intertwining of soul and body. After his death, when Jesus Christ rose again, he was transfigured, so that afterwards when his disciples met him walking along the road, they did not recognise him, because his whole being, including his physical body, had been transfigured and made perfect again. These are some of the layers of meaning, some of the mysteries that the Bird of Love has come to reveal to us.

So when Michael said God wanted me to see my Bird of Love again, my eyes started to tear up, not with sadness but with joy.

Archangel Michael said, 'I hope they are tears of joy.' He reached up to wipe them away with his fingertips.

I said, 'Yes, they are.'

'Lorna, enjoy what you see. Where is the bird?'

As we turned towards the enormous tree and looked up I said to Archangel Michael, 'There it is. Isn't it beautiful?'

The falcon perched on one of the same branches, looking so proud. I was just admiring its beauty when all of a sudden, it swooped downwards, gliding swiftly, and then it hovered over one of the rocks about ten yards away before landing upon it. It just sat there. It was so close. I was afraid to move in case it might fly away. I became aware of Archangel Michael letting go of my hand but I didn't take my eyes off the beautiful bird.

At the same time Archangel Michael spoke to me softly: 'The bird will not fly away. Just keep watching.'

We stood there watching the bird. I don't know for how long. Maybe it was only a few seconds, maybe a few minutes.

It's hard to know how to put it into words or describe to you what happened next. The water of the little river flowed over some of the rocks. Abruptly the bird flew up and away from the water, which swirled in and out between the rocks making white bubbles and froth. Every now and then, these bubbles and froth splashed as if in slow motion upon the rock where the beautiful falcon now stood. The bird turned its head gracefully, looking downwards at the rock on which it stood. It watched the bubbles splashing on the rock and sometimes touching its claws. The bird did not move when this happened. It was as if the splashing was perhaps a little bit of an annoyance to the falcon but it knew it was in no danger.

It seemed to be oblivious to Archangel Michael and myself standing there. We watched as it turned its head, slightly to the left and then to the right.

I said to Archangel Michael in a quiet voice, 'The bird of prey is looking at us now directly, isn't it? It's not taking its eyes off us.'

Archangel Michael said, 'No, Lorna, the bird of prey only has eyes for you. It has never taken its eyes off you. You are only noticing this now.'

I was about to turn and look at Archangel Michael as he said these words but he said to me, 'No more talking.'

I didn't say another word. I just stood there beside Archangel Michael watching.

Suddenly, everything became silent. The breeze that had been blowing became still. Not a sound was to be heard of a bird or an insect flying through the air. The butterfly I had seen flying over the water a moment ago had disappeared.

The bird never took its eyes off me. Neither did I take my eyes off it. It started to open its wings slowly as it stood on the rock. As it did this I noticed too that the river was still. It was not moving at all. The water had stopped flowing. It was like crystal glass and looked so delicate. Even the water that splashed over the rocks was still, paused in the air or like beads upon the rocks.

The falcon's wings stretched out as if it was going to take off from the rock. As its wings moved the tips of them started to change colour. Each feather individually started to turn to a beautiful, glittering gold. It was like I was watching this in slow motion. Gold rippled through each feather. It started from the top of the falcon's head and rippled right down to its claws. It was all gold. The bird of prey had changed completely. I was now seeing my Bird of Love.

I became so overwhelmed. I started to cry. Tears of joy flowed down my cheeks. I smiled but did not take my eyes off my Bird of Love. My Bird of Love started to hover over the rock. Its wings seemed to shimmer in the air. It seemed to have an effect on the water. The drops of water that were frozen in the air began to move as if they were getting out of the way of the falcon's wings.

Then, the falcon glided swiftly but yet smoothly along the small river as it passed us by. It was moving fast but I could still see every detail, every feather, of the bird clearly. I was sure it turned its head to look at me before it soared up into the sky, leaving a trail of golden light flowing behind it.

It started to soar higher and then descended like waves of the sea, soaring upwards and downwards with this golden light flowing from it. Every feather of my Bird of Love left a trail of sparkling gold.

Just when I thought my Bird of Love was going to disappear it turned and started to descend. It glided swiftly and then slowed down, as if it was taking its time, before it flew back in among the trees, gliding effortlessly in and out between the branches once more. It came to rest upon the branch of the tree where I had seen it first.

I was just about to say something to Archangel Michael when my Bird of Love took off again. It soared higher and higher into the sky, leaving a trail of golden light, and then it disappeared.

Everything came back to normal. I could hear the birds, the insects and the water of the little river splashing and flowing over the rocks. I felt sad and happy. I could not see my Bird of Love any more and that is why tears were coming down my cheeks, but I was happy too. Archangel Michael took my hand again and with his right hand he took his snow-white handkerchief out of the pocket of his trench coat. He reached up and wiped away the tears from my eyes.

He said in a gentle voice, 'No more crying.'

As he dabbed my cheeks with the white handkerchief, wiping away the tears, I found myself filling with joy. I was smiling now and Archangel Michael was smiling too.

'Ask your question, Lorna, before I go.'

'Why did God allow me to see my Bird of Love again?'

'Because God knows how much you miss your little Bird of Love, Lorna. God wants you to always remember all He said to you about your Bird of Love. It is very important. Lorna, recall what God said to you as a child when you asked Him why He called you His Bird of Love. Tell me the exact words God spoke to you.'

'I still don't understand, Archangel Michael. I am kind of afraid of them. I am always afraid that I will let God and the people of the world down. God said so much to me that day. One thing He said was that I carried love like my little bird did. One of the other things He said that crosses my mind a lot and I find hard to fathom is that God said He needed me. I don't understand that and God never answers that question for me.'

As Archangel Michael stood in front of me he took both of my hands in his and joined them together as if in prayer.

He said, 'Lorna, God could not come today but He sent me, His archangel. Every time God allows you to see your Bird of Love, He is reminding you of what He said that day about your Bird of Love and about you. Now I must go.'

Archangel Michael let go of my hands but I kept them joined together as I was now in prayer. Archangel Michael walked towards the forest but just before he was about to enter it he turned and smiled at me. Then he disappeared.

I don't know how long I stood there praying. When I stopped I noticed I was surrounded by angels. My hands were cold so I rubbed them together.

All of the angels spoke simultaneously to me: 'It's time to go home.'

I don't really remember walking back through the forest but I remember being in the car and realising that I was almost home. I drove up the lane, got out of the car and opened the gate. I lit the fire and made dinner. That evening, I went upstairs and sat in front of my computer and wrote some more.

CHAPTER 31

Remember You Are Loved

WHEN I RECEIVED A WEDDING INVITATION FROM MY TWO friends Don and Pascal I was blown away. I felt so privileged to be asked. It was at Ballyheigue Castle. I had been there the summer before when I spent a few days in Don's family home.

This time I spent four days in Ballyheigue. On my first day, before the three-day wedding, my son Christopher and I went for a long walk that took us three hours. It was up and across the surrounding hills. We stopped on many occasions to admire the beautiful scenery. It was a wilderness of wild grasses, heather and wild flowers. As we followed the path over the hill we came across some wild cotton. I stopped and rubbed it between my fingers. I turned to Christopher and I told him that when I was in Africa, in Ethiopia, the women gathered the cotton and spun it into thread to make clothes by hand.

I said to him, 'Why do we not do that since it grows here?'

Christopher said, 'I think it would be too expensive to

grow cotton the way they do in other countries. Our weather is not good enough.'

We stood there for a few minutes. We could see the ocean from where we were.

Christopher started to follow the path again and I followed. We walked a fair distance that day.

We stopped at Don's father's house, O'Neill's B&B. We were made to feel so welcome. We sat down and had tea and home-made apple pie and scones. We had about two and a half hours to go before Pascal's birthday party – which was being held in the middle of the three-day wedding! – so we had time to relax for a little while. There was great hustle and bustle going on as everyone was preparing for the wedding and I was so glad to be part of it.

Christopher and I left and headed back towards the hotel. We wandered down in the town for a while as we still had plenty of time before the birthday celebration. The wedding was going to be the next day.

I'm going to share with you a few things that happened spiritually when I was there. Don's mother had died a few years previously and on occasion, when Don's father was dancing on the floor I saw the soul of Don's mother dancing with him, so they moved across the dance floor together. It would only be for a couple of seconds, sometimes a little longer, but I know that if Don's father felt her presence at all it would have seemed much longer to him. I believe on occasion he did feel the presence of his wife.

God always allows our loved ones to be in our presence on special occasions, for both happy and sad ones. I guess this occasion was a happy and sad one mixed together as it was his son's wedding but his wife was not there to celebrate with them.

This wedding was full of love. I could see the love radiating from everyone. I was sitting at a table with Christopher, some of Don's family, some of Pascal's family and a couple of their very special friends. I really felt privileged to be sitting there. Don and Pascal were entertaining all of their guests and when it came to time to start dinner Pascal got up from the table, took the microphone from the stage and went out into the middle of the floor to talk about their love. He told the story of how they met twenty years ago.

To my surprise, when Pascal sat back at the table, the soul of his father as a young man stood right behind them holding an enormous red heart. He was acknowledging the joining of their love. They were surrounded by angels, about ten of them, in a half circle. When I turned and looked around the room I saw an angel standing beside everyone holding up a red heart.

This wedding, this marriage, was about love. Love has no boundaries. One thing that God has always spoken to me about is the love that He has for all of us. God loves all of His children equally. He has no boundaries. We are all God's children and on that day, this is what God showed to me. He showed me the love He has for Don and Pascal. The blessing for their marriage was of love, unity, friendship, caring, understanding, happiness and joy for their future. God blesses all marriages of love.

The angels standing beside each person at that wedding threw the hearts they were holding up into the air. They exploded, bursting into tiny little pieces. I watched many of these little pieces as they were guided into each person's heart to help them to love themselves more. This allows them to love others and to stop fearing the differences that exist between each and every one of us. We must remember, in our hearts and in our minds, that love conquers all. Love is never-ending. Love is one thing we all yearn for, so don't close the doors. Keep them open. Allow love into your life and into the lives of all of those around you.

On their wedding day that is exactly what Don and Pascal did. They allowed all of their family and their friends to share in the love that they have for each other. Their love touched everyone including me. I have kept their love in my heart.

Instead of going straight back to the hotel to pack I went for a beautiful walk along the beach. There was a downpour of rain. The wind was very strong and it sometimes made me shiver but I enjoyed every moment. On the way back, I watched fishermen fishing from the strand with their poles stuck in the sand. As I passed I said a little prayer that they would catch some fish. Further on, as I got closer to the end of my walk, I saw a young woman with a little girl and a brown, curly-haired dog. They were having great fun.

As I got closer to them an angel said to me, 'They are going to head home now.'

I don't always know why the angels sometimes state the obvious. I saw the mother go after the lead of the dog, which was trailing along the ground. They headed up from the beach in my direction but I cut through the car park. I was surprised when I got back to the hotel. I never realised the walk had taken me two hours and during that time the angels hadn't said a word to me. They knew I was enjoying myself.

My guardian angel woke me up last night by blowing on my face, moving my hair.

In my sleep I said, 'Go away. Leave me alone. I'm tired.'

But my guardian angel didn't.

'Get up out of bed,' is what I heard constantly.

It was four in the morning.

I turned over, opened my eyes and said, 'Okay.'

I threw the blankets back. My guardian angel does this sometimes, as does Angel Hosus or Archangel Michael, but last night it was just my guardian angel. I was giving out as I put on my dressing gown on and slippers.

I said, 'What is it? What do you want me to do?'

Without my guardian angel using words I knew exactly, so I went into the room where I work and turned on the computer.

My guardian angel spoke softly and gently. 'Lorna, you need to remind men, women and children that their guardian angel loves them, no matter what. Remind them that they are beautiful, unique and perfect. Their guardian angels only have eyes for them. They are not to feel alone.'

Your guardian angel wants to remind you that it is right there with you and never leaves you for one second. You are not alone and even if you think no one loves you always remember your guardian angel loves you. I do too even though I don't know you. Your guardian angel wants you to see the light of hope in your life all of the time. You are never to allow that light of hope to go out because your life is precious to your guardian angel, to your family and to your friends. Your life is precious even to me and you are probably a stranger.

I turned to my guardian angel and said, 'We are talking about when someone is in a dark place? When they are lonely and feel nobody loves them? They are in that dark pit struggling and unable to see any way out? We're talking about suicide?'

My guardian angel said, 'Yes.'

It's at these times, if we think someone is depressed or full of anxiety or nervous and feeling alone, that we must all help them to see the light that their guardian angel is holding in front of them – that light of hope.

'Do you remember, Lorna, when you were in Maynooth a few months ago?'

I thought for a minute.

Then I said, 'Yes, I do.'

I had been in the Elite cafe, my favourite place. Every time I go back to Maynooth to my son's house, even though I don't live there any more, it still feels like home and I always visit the Elite cafe. There I meet my family and sometimes my friends. Or I might just sit on my own and enjoy the company of everyone that is in the cafe. Of course, the food is just scrumptious.

Sometimes, when I am abroad on my travels, I'll say to the angels that are around me, 'I would love to just go to the Elite cafe now and have something to eat.'

Naturally, I would list off a few things: the beautiful home-baked cakes, their bread, the baked potatoes, salads and quiches. Everything is home-made. The thought of that food now is making me hungry.

I heard my name being called and turned towards the door and there was Angel Hosus.

He said, 'Good morning, Lorna.'

'Hello, Angel Hosus.'

He walked over to me and put his hand on my shoulder.

'I will help you to remember.'

I said to Angel Hosus, 'That day, I met my daughter, Ruth, and my little granddaughter, Jessica. When we left the cafe I helped my daughter to do some shopping. A couple of hours later, I gave Ruth and Jessica a hug and said goodbye.

'As I walked out of the shopping centre I decided to go for

a walk. I walked into the college grounds. It had been quite some time since I had been there last. The weather hasn't been great in Ireland this year. It's kind of very mixed with an awful lot of rain. I was wearing a jacket, jeans and my walking boots. I walked through the college orchard thinking of the times Joe had walked with me and with the children. It brought back old memories, happy ones.

'Angel Hosus, any time now when I walk through the orchard in the college I remember meeting the nuns. They would say hello to me and stop and talk for a moment. I remember one nun in particular. On occasion when I met her on her own she would be filling her bag with apples that had fallen from the trees on to the ground. I asked her if it was okay for me to take some. She said yes, that it was better than letting all of them rot away on the ground. She suggested we make some apple pies. She had another bag in her pocket and she told me to fill it for myself and to take the apples home. When I think about that it always makes me smile. The nun is no longer with us. She's gone home to heaven.'

Angel Hosus said, 'Yes, Lorna. I know you liked her.'

I said, 'Yes, she was one of the few people that I spoke to on the odd occasion when Joe was very ill but still alive. She told me of the work she did and how she and the other nuns housed and fed many young girls who were studying in the university. She had a hearty laugh as well. One time, when she bent down to pick some apples up off the ground, a jackdaw flew over and perched on the branch of the tree above her. Just as it did the apple fell from the branch and hit her on the head. She said ouch but then started to laugh. She saw the funny side of it and I laughed too.'

Angel Hosus interrupted and said, 'Go back to telling me about the day a few months ago.'

'I walked up and down the path lined with trees at the back of the college. I think I only saw one or two people that day. No one seemed to be out walking. On my way back through the college grounds I decided to go into the garden. It's a small garden but it has some beautiful trees and flower beds. Of course, there are places to sit as well. I didn't notice anyone in the garden. I didn't see any angels in there either. A robin had hopped across in front of me when I heard my name being called. It was you, Angel Hosus, you were down the far end. Standing under the large tree that twists and turns. You told me to walk in your direction. You never said there was someone sitting there but as I got closer I saw a guardian angel before I saw the man it belonged to. It's usually the opposite way around. It was holding a light in front of him. Three other angels were there as well, all holding lights, trying to get him to see the light of hope in this life.

'The man was hunched over when I saw him. He appeared to be about forty years old. I stopped and said hello. I didn't know whether I would get a response or not but the man looked up and said hello back. I asked him if he was okay. He told me he wasn't really. I could see he was in a dark place with his mind. He didn't believe in himself any more. He didn't think he was capable of anything. I noticed a wedding ring on his finger. I asked him if he had a wife and children. It was then that he broke down. He told me he was of no use to his wife and children. He thought he would be better off dead.

'You told me, Angel Hosus, to ask him why he felt that way. He didn't know. He told me he just felt that way. He couldn't feel anything. He said he felt empty as if he was in a dark room with no door or windows, just blackness surrounding him with no way out. I asked him if he realised he was depressed. I told him he needed help. He knew he had depression. He had even seen a doctor but it wasn't doing much good. I reminded him of his wife and children. I asked him if he loved them but he didn't know. You spoke to me without words, Angel Hosus, and I repeated it to this man. You said to tell him his wife loved him but that she was very scared. She knew he was depressed. She knew something was very wrong and she was trying to help him. She didn't want to lose him. You told me to remind him that his children loved him. He was their father and they loved him. He was to try and feel their love. As his wife and children reached out in love to him he had to reach out in love to them as well. You said to say their arms were outstretched in that darkness but their hands were full of light and of love reaching out to him. I told him that I knew his love could reach back and let them lift him out of the darkness.

'He looked up at me with tears in his eyes. He asked who I was but I only replied that I was no one. I made him promise not to take his own life. I told him how I wanted to pass him by one day on the street or in the supermarket or maybe there in the college with his wife and children. I told him he wouldn't recognise me but I would recognise him. I told him he wouldn't want his children to keep on asking their mother, "Why did Dad leave us? Why did he abandon us?" I told him again that they loved him and that he was to start putting windows in that dark room and a door. Then he was to open them up wide and let the light of hope, the light of love that his wife and children carry for him, in. When I left he smiled. I could see he was letting the light of love back into his life. His guardian angel had his arms around him, embracing him with love.'

Every day, I pray and ask for that young man. Sometimes, I ask Angel Hosus how he is doing. Angel Hosus has said he's getting there. He has reached out to his wife and children, allowing their love to touch him. He no longer feels unloved.

Love has to seek out that pit of darkness that dwells inside a person who at that time sees no point in living and considers taking their own life. Family, friends and loved ones always try their best if they know that someone they love is in that pit of darkness. They help them to strive towards the love that is inside of them and help them to see the love that is around them. It is important to encourage them, let them know that they are loved, help them to get back their confidence and belief in themselves.

Your guardian angel, at different times in your life, whispers to you, especially when things are bad or scary and when you have lost the energy for life. You may feel as if you are in that pit of darkness but your guardian angel is telling you that you are loved. You are perfect. You are unique and you are needed in this world. You have a part to play. Everyone in this world needs you. I need you, so I always ask people not to take their own lives. Remember, you are loved. You can make it through any dark patch of your life no matter how disastrous you may feel it is. You may feel you are not able to climb out of that dark pit but I know you can.

There is help out there. Don't be afraid – ask your family and friends to help you. Seek out the help you need. I will not give up on you. God and your guardian angel don't want you to give up on yourself either. Remember, God loves you.

I met a mother on one of my tours and she told me that she lost her young daughter to suicide. She said that she knows she is in heaven and at times, feels the presence of her daughter around. Every time I hear of someone taking their own life, no matter what their age, I am shattered, absolutely broken-hearted. I give out to God. I ask why but there is no why.

There is nothing any of us can do sometimes. No matter what help and love a person is given, their pain and hurt can be too much for them and they never climb out of that dark pit.

Those who are left behind really find it hard. They struggle with the thought that their loved one killed themselves and that tears many families apart. It takes, for some, a lifetime to accept. Many families find it impossible. It's a struggle that they have to live through every day. Their loved one is in heaven. God wrapped them in that blanket of love and took them to heaven.

During the time when I was living in Maynooth, before Joe died, when he was in reasonably good health and working for the county council, a woman called at the house. She was about sixty years of age. She was visiting the area, just driving around. Her husband was in the car. She said that she saw my hall door open. She asked me if she could use the loo.

I said, 'Yes, but it is around the back.'

I brought her around and I took some washing off the line while she was in the toilet.

When she came out of the loo she said, 'Thank you.'

Angel Elijah was standing at the corner of our cottage and told me to invite her in for a cup of tea.

I called her back and said, 'Would you and your husband like a cup of tea?'

She was surprised and hesitated for a moment.

Then she said, 'That is so kind of you. We would love a cup of tea.'

She walked to the gate and called her husband. He got out of the car and followed us into the cottage to the little back-room that Joe had turned into the kitchen with a sink, cooker, a couple of presses, a kitchen table and a big, old fridge.

'Sit down,' I said.

I put the kettle on and I took out a couple of cups.

I said, 'I have no biscuits but I do have some bread and jam.'

The husband said, 'Thank you. I do feel a little peckish.'

The woman said, 'By the way, my name is Josie.'

Her husband said, 'I'm John. It's nice to meet you. I see you have children.'

I said, 'Yes, two little boys, Christopher and Owen. Christopher's at school and Owen is having a little nap.'

John started to talk about his grown-up children, his two sons and his daughter.

'They're all married now,' he said. 'We were married very young, Josie and myself. We have six grandchildren already.'

Josie never said a word when John was talking. I looked over at her and she seemed sad. Her guardian angel had its arms wrapped around her and told me she was in great pain, but it never said what the pain was. I thought maybe it was physical pain.

The next moment, water was steaming from the kettle so I made some tea. I poured out three cups of tea. John buttered his own bread and jam.

He said, 'This jam is good.'

I said, 'I hope so. I made it myself. It's last year's jam made with blackcurrants from some old bushes in the garden.'

Josie said her mother used to make home-made jam too. She started to talk about her mum and dad and how she came from a small family. Just herself, a sister and brother. Then she burst out into tears. She said her brother had committed suicide when he was only twenty. She was thirteen at the time and her sister was eighteen.

'It was horrible. We were not allowed to talk about him and it was hidden because of the shame.'

It was as if her brother had never existed. It wasn't her mum or dad's fault. They loved their son, but they were victims of society's attitudes at the time.

'His name was John. I guess that's partly why I fell in love with my husband because of his name being John too. My parents are dead a long time now but I always remember my mum and dad praying so hard for my brother.'

They believed he had gone to hell because that is what they were told, and so was she. As she grew up and even to this day, with her own children all grown and married now, she cries thinking of her brother, that he is burning in those horrible flames of hell.

When she said this her guardian angel shook its head, saying, 'No. She is wrong.'

At the same moment, Angel Elijah appeared beside her and spoke to me without words, telling me to let her know that her brother was in heaven with God and their parents and others who have died since. They are all together.

When I said those words she reached out and grabbed my hands.

She said, with tears of joy and happiness running down her cheeks, 'Do you really think so, Lorna?'

I said, 'Yes, God loved your brother. He is God's child.'

'That's all I wanted to hear. Now, I can have peace in my heart for the rest of my life.'

As soon as Josie said these words her guardian angel unwrapped its wings from around her. The soul of her brother stood at the kitchen door with a smile on his face. He looked like such a handsome young man.

The next moment he was standing next to Josie. He was looking down upon his sister with love. Josie took a deep breath.

I said to her, 'I know you often feel the presence of your brother.'

She looked up at me. 'Yes, Lorna. I feel him right now. I feel so happy.'

I reached out and took her hand.

Her husband put his arms around her and said, 'I told you that your brother is in heaven.'

The two of them hugged each other through smiles and tears.

'Thank God, thank God,' Josie repeated a couple of times.

I could see the stress and worry lift from her. Josie was a completely different person now.

A minute or two later, they got up to leave. The soul of Josie's brother remained with her as I walked to the gate with them. They said thank you for the tea and bread and jam. Then they got into the car and drove away. I don't even know where they were from. I never asked. I never saw them again.

That's the way things always seemed to happen when I lived in Maynooth before anyone ever knew anything about me. When I think of it now it makes me smile. Sometimes, it was a truck driver who turned up or someone who had got lost, or a tourist. Not that we had many of them. I always remember two men and two women from China. They had been visiting the college and had gone for a walk around Maynooth.

At this time, there were no housing estates around us, mainly just fields. We were in the last cottage on the road of Old Greenfield. This afternoon the children were playing in the garden and the chickens were out. Our dog, Heidi, was a gentle Alsatian so she never chased them. She just stood at the gate.

Christopher came running up to me and said, 'Mummy, there are strangers outside!'

When I went out the door I saw them standing at the gate. I saw they were surrounded by angels.

I said, 'Hello. Can I help you?'

One of the men started to talk about what a big garden we had. He could see the vegetables. He started to ask questions so I invited them in and showed them around our vegetable patch of potatoes, cabbage, cauliflower and Brussels sprouts. Heidi was very friendly towards them. She just sat on the grass most of the time. There was a tent in the little front garden and a blanket on the grass. Two of the visitors sat on the doorstep and the other two on the blanket. The children sat down beside them. I made them a cup of tea and we all had it out in the garden as it was a lovely sunny day.

They talked mostly about how beautiful Maynooth was and the college and that everyone was saying hello to them as they walked around all the different parts of Maynooth.

The older of the two men said, 'This was the only house we felt we could stop and say hello.'

A few minutes later they left, feeling very happy. This often happened. There was nothing wrong whatsoever. The angels would just say to me the visitors needed to feel the warmth, the love and the friendliness of family.

CHAPTER 32

Passing Judgement

A QUESTION I HAVE OFTEN ASKED ANGEL HOSUS, AND the other angels that are with me at different times, is why do people judge those who have died and decide they didn't get to heaven for this, that or the other. I even remember one day asking God. It was a time when I lived in Edenmore. I was a young teenager of about fourteen. A neighbour around the corner from us had died. I didn't know him but I had seen this man on different occasions when he'd walked down to the shops. I had seen him maybe twice shortly before he died. Once when he was coming out of the grocery shop and another time, as he walked down the road smoking a cigarette. At that time, we did not know that smoking cigarettes was bad for your health, that they are life-threatening.

At that time, when someone died nearly the whole neighbourhood would go to the funeral. Everybody seemed to know who was who in the community. I didn't go myself but I stood by the road and saw the funeral car leaving the church. Everyone followed. I knew the man had gone to heaven because on the last few occasions when I'd seen him his guardian angel was holding on to his soul.

I never really took much notice as a child when I saw a guardian angel holding on to a soul. I knew the person was going to die soon but that never concerned me in any way because I knew they were going to heaven.

One thing that used to upset me an awful lot when I was younger was hearing adults talking among themselves, passing judgement, wondering whether that person was good enough to go to heaven. I used to feel very sad when I heard people say, as they were now, that someone hadn't got a hope or a chance of getting through those gates of heaven. St Peter wouldn't allow them. They will be sent to hell. I would give out to my guardian angel and the angels around me. I would get very annoyed. Even a little bit cross. Maybe more than a little bit. I often would kick a stone. I would run as fast as I could until I was out of earshot.

I would give out, saying, 'Don't those silly adults know that God loves us? I just want to scream at them.'

The angels would say, 'There's no point, Lorna. They will not listen to you. They think you are just a silly child. They know no better.'

After the funeral, I brought my neighbour's dog, Shane, for a walk out through the estate and up into another one. I walked along a country road. Only one car passed us by.

I was still giving out to God and the angels about how adults could say such cruel things about someone who has just died when I heard my name being called. I looked up the road and there I saw an angel standing at the side of the road. Just as I approached the angel to say hello it disappeared.

There was a farm gate open so I went into the field and

let Shane off his lead. I went to the far end of the field as I wanted to keep Shane away from the open gate. He always stayed close by, just running around and sniffing the grass. I sat on the bank. I was praying for the family of the man who had just died.

As I sat there, I spoke out loud to God. 'How horrible it is for adults to think that someone has gone to hell. Please, God, don't let that ever happen to anyone who dies in the world.'

I heard, 'Lorna, don't upset yourself.'

I stood up immediately for I recognised the voice. It filled me with such love. It was overwhelming.

I looked around and said, 'Where are you? I cannot see you.'

'There is no need for you to see me, Lorna. You know I'm right here with you.'

I was a little disappointed and sat back down again.

Maybe it was a minute later when I said, 'Are you still there?'

God answered me, 'Yes, Lorna.'

God spoke with such love and compassion.

'It's not for man to judge when someone dies, Lorna. You know at that moment of death when the human body dies the soul is leaving the body at the same time. They know then that I am God. In that instant, they see their guardian angel and all the souls of their loved ones standing before them. Nobody knows whether any man, woman or child at that moment of death asked me for forgiveness.'

I said to God, 'I know you love every single man, woman and child in the world. No matter what.'

'Go home now, Lorna.'

I didn't say another word to God. I called Shane over and put him on his lead. The two of us walked across the centre of the field and stopped at the gate that was still open. I looked left and right to make sure no cars were coming, and then I headed home.

I know it's very hard for many people to even contemplate that when someone has done something very evil, they have the chance when they die of going to heaven, but we have to remember that none of us know whether that person asked for forgiveness at that moment of death. I know God loves us all and wants all of His children back home, and have never been shown God sending someone to hell. Remember, our souls are that speck of light of God. Your soul is part of God, so He wants us all to come home to heaven when it is our time, but no sooner.

I know the hurt must be horrific when a parent has a child who has been murdered. There have been many leaders in the world who have committed huge atrocities that are so horrific: genocide, slaughtering of men, women and children. I could name a few of those leaders, some of the past and some of today. It's so hard for us to forgive them because we feel so much pain. Our hearts are torn apart. I know many people try hard to forgive and some succeed.

Then again we should never forget these crimes, so that we don't repeat the same horrors again and again.

Sadly, today, we are still not learning the lessons of the past. Atrocities are still happening in the world today. There is still genocide, war and terrorism. This is one of the reasons we have to connect to the spiritual side of ourselves – our souls. We must listen to our guardian angel to hear the messages that God is giving each and every one of us.

God said, 'Love one another as I love you.'

CHAPTER 33

Meeting Brian

BRIAN WAS A VERY SPECIAL PERSON WHO CAME INTO MY life and my young daughter, Megan's life. I mentioned earlier that on many occasions that towards the end of his life Joe had often said to me that when he wasn't here any more I should allow someone else into my life.

I used to ignore his words and say, 'One man in a lifetime is enough. Why would I want someone else in my life? I love you. Your love will last me through my lifetime.'

Then one day I was washing dishes in the sink and Joe got up from the table and put his arms around me and said, 'Lorna, I'm dying. I know my time is not too far away. I want you to know that I want you to let someone else into your life. Then, you won't feel so lonely. I will be so happy for you.'

Before I wrote what follows about Joe and about Brian I spoke to Archangel Michael about finding it really hard to write about some of these things. I told him I really need lots of help and encouragement.

Michael put his hand on my shoulder. 'God knows this,

· 305 ·

Lorna, but He still wants you to write about those personal things.'

'You know, Michael, this is going to be really hard – to talk about Joe, about my family.'

'Lorna, every time you need help, God will send it.'

I was just about to ask a question when Archangel Michael said he had to go and disappeared. I was disappointed because I had lots of questions to ask.

I decided I'd go for a walk. I put my coat on and opened the door. Then as I stepped outside I saw Archangel Michael standing in front of me again. I laughed for a moment.

I said, 'I almost walked into you.'

Archangel Michael replied, 'That is impossible.'

I said to him, 'That's what makes it so funny.'

He stood there in front of me dressed in workman's clothing. I always love the way Archangel Michael dresses appropriately for where he appears. I knew if someone was passing they might see him. It's a question I have never asked Archangel Michael. I don't know why God allows this to happen on occasion. I do know that sometimes people have passed me when Archangel Michael was with me and said hello.

Now I said, 'Archangel Michael, you were only here a few minutes ago.'

'Let's go for a walk down to the orchard at the back of your house.'

'Okay,' I said to Archangel Michael, 'I better go back into the house for the keys so I can open the gate.'

I did so and when I came out I could not see Archangel Michael any more. Then, I heard my name being called. He was already around at the back.

When I got there I said to him, 'You don't need keys to open the gate but I do.'

As we entered the orchard Archangel Michael stopped and turned to me.

He said, 'Lorna, God has asked me to let you know that He has heard your prayers and that He will be sending Joe's soul to visit you.'

I just stood there looking at Archangel Michael. I was becoming very emotional.

I asked in a quiet voice, 'When?'

Archangel Michael said, 'I don't know. I have to go now.' He disappeared again.

I stood there in the orchard, feeling overwhelmed by the prospect of seeing Joe. It had been many years since God had sent his soul to me. I prayed, thanking God for whenever this would happen. I walked around the orchard and our little dog Holly ran around my feet. I bent down and patted her and said hello. I had forgotten about her. She must've followed me through the gate, so I brought her for a little walk through the fields.

A number of weeks passed. I'm not very good at keeping track of time. I was upstairs writing and Angel Hosus was with me that day. Angel Elijah had been there earlier in the morning but had left. There were some other angels in the room too.

'Lorna, you are going to have a visitor today'

'I hope not. I really don't want any visitors today, Hosus, I want to get as much writing done as possible. Anyway, who could be calling?'

Angel Hosus didn't reply to my question, so I carried on working. It must've been about an hour later, maybe more, when my name was called. I recognised the voice. I turned slowly to look, nearly losing my breath. I was full of excitement.

There was Joe standing in the doorway. He looked so handsome, so young. He was dressed in clothes I recognised from the past: black trousers and a pale blue shirt. He looked perfect in every way. He had such a beautiful smile.

He said, 'Hello, Lorna.'

He took another step forward into the room.

I went to stand up but Joe said, 'No, stay where you are.'

I must have been crying at this point because he said, 'Lorna, don't cry. God has allowed me to be here with you for a little while.'

As Joe came into the room he spoke to Angel Hosus, thanking him for being my friend.

Angel Hosus replied, 'It is an honour.'

Joe and Hosus spoke then in a language I did not understand. Many times, angels speak to me in another language and I would understand but this time I didn't.

Joe stood beside me as I sat in front of my desk. He put his arm around my shoulders. I love his touch. His arm felt weightless. It filled me with love.

Joe said to me, 'Lorna, do you remember your friend, Sylvia?'

'Yes,' I said. 'She became a widow a few years before . . .' I hesitated, looking at Joe and finding the words hard to say.

Joe said, 'It's okay.'

So I took a deep breath and then said with tears in my eyes, 'One evening, I was sitting in Sylvia's kitchen with Sylvia. It was a cold winter's evening. We were having tea. She had the newspaper on the table and I remember a pen and paper. I loved visiting and we would just chat about everything. One particular evening—'

Joe interrupted me, saying, 'Yes, I was there with you, Lorna, but God did not allow you to feel my presence. When you were sitting at that table having tea Sylvia's guardian angel allowed you to hear the words that she was whispering to her.'

'Yes,' I said, 'I was shocked.'

I remembered that I had spoken to Sylvia's guardian angel, saying, 'No, no!' Because her guardian angel was prompting her to encourage me to put an advertisement in the paper.

A few moments later, Sylvia reached out for the paper and started to tell me about a friend of hers who had put an advertisement in the paper to meet a man and that she herself had done so a month ago and had met someone. She started telling me all about the man she met and how wonderful it was to have someone to go out with every now and then.

She said, 'You're going to do the same, Lorna.'

I burst out laughing and I said, 'No way.'

The room was full of angels at this point who all said, 'Yes, Lorna.'

Sylvia kept talking. She wasn't giving up.

Now Joe said, 'You were feeling lonely and you admitted that to her. She was right that at times you did feel very lonely and you said to her that sometimes you felt you would love a man in your life but you still keep saying no. Eventually she got you to.'

Joe was laughing.

I said, 'Yes, I remember her guardian angel never stopped whispering to her. So Sylvia just would not give up on the matter even though I kept saying to her that I didn't need another man in my life. I had enough love from you, Joe, to last me a lifetime.'

'Do you remember your exact words to Sylvia, Lorna?'

'Yes,' I said to her, 'I could never love anyone the way I loved Joe.'

At that moment, Joe took my hand and he said, 'Lorna, it's okay to love someone else. Now start to write what we have spoken about here and now. Don't be afraid. If you don't share your life how can you share about God and the angels because they are part of your life too, not just your family. It's okay to talk about this part of your life.'

Joe bent down and whispered in my ear, 'I love you.'

Then, he said he had to go, let go of my hand and disappeared.

I said to Angel Hosus, 'I wish Joe didn't have to go. I wish he could have stayed while I write this part.'

Days later, Sylvia carried on trying to persuade me. She got me laughing with all the things she was saying about how she imagined me going out and meeting a man, as she would say, sitting at a table and having lunch with them or going for a walk. We laughed so much that I knew in my heart and soul that she was right. I was lonely at times and sometimes I would have loved someone in my life, but I could never figure out how a man could fit into my life. To this day, I can't figure that out but on that evening, I eventually gave in to Sylvia. She started to write out what to say over the phone. She set the whole thing up for me and the following weekend the ad was in the paper.

Two weeks had passed. Sylvia was calling me every few days to encourage me to ring the number to see if there were any messages. The angels were constantly reminding me to do what Sylvia said. I would say no, but eventually I gave in.

One evening at about ten o'clock I dialled the number and there were a few messages. My hand was shaking when I listened to them. I rang Sylvia straight away and told her four men had left messages for me and their numbers.

She said, 'I look forward to hearing those messages you have on your mobile phone when you're passing on Saturday. Drop in on your way home. This is so exciting!'

On Saturday, I arrived at Sylvia's house about seven. Before I even got to the hall door it was open. Sylvia was standing there with a big smile on her face.

She said, 'Come in, girl! Get out that mobile of yours.'

She already had tea made. She listened to the four messages and picked one.

She said, 'I like this one. He's nice and he's a widower. Lorna, you're not leaving this house until you make that phone call.'

So eventually I picked up my phone. My hands were shaking while I dialled the number. To my relief, I got no answer.

Sylvia said, 'No answer? Try again. I'm not letting you give up that easily. Give him a call again. Leave a message if he doesn't answer. You have to be honest with yourself. You are still young. You are way younger than I am. I get lonely and long for the company of a man. There's no harm in it. Come on, make that call. You are entitled to have some fun, to be taken out for dinner, to go to the pictures or for a walk.'

Sylvia made me laugh a few times so I picked up the phone and called. There was no answer again so I left a message giving my name and number.

It was a few months later when I was out walking with Megan that I got a call. I didn't recognise the number.

I said to the angels, 'I'm not answering it,' even though they said I was to. They didn't say why and I didn't ask but then a few weeks later, I got another call. I remember holding the phone in my hand and looking at it. My guardian angel whispered in my ear to answer it.

Then Angel Hosus appeared in front of me for just a brief moment and said, 'Answer it!'

I did and it was a man's voice that I did not recognise. He said his name was Brian and that I had left him a message some months ago and that he himself had answered the ad in the paper. I was shocked and I didn't know really how to respond.

So I said to him, 'It is nice that you called.'

I told him I was a widow and that I had four children, one of whom was still living with me as she was a little girl. He said he was a widower and he spoke most of the time about the loss of his beautiful wife and how hard he was finding it to cope.

We said our goodbyes and he asked, 'Would it be all right to call you again another day?'

I said, 'Yes.'

We spoke over the phone many times during the next six months.

I was out in the yard one day washing the car. I had a bucket of suddy water and a sponge. I had just finished and turned on the hose to wash the car down when Angel Elijah appeared. At the same time, a rainbow went across the car.

I said to Angel Elijah, 'Did you do that?'

'No,' he said, 'that's just the reflection of the sunlight going through the sprays of water.'

It was very beautiful.

I said, 'It's even reflecting some of the beautiful amber colours you are dressed in.'

I turned the hose off and said to him, 'Have you come to help me?'

Angel Elijah said, 'No, I don't wash cars, Lorna, but I have come to talk to you.'

So we walked around to the back of the house.

'Lorna, when Brian calls you again and asks you to meet say yes.'

'Elijah, Brian is never going to ask me to. He just likes talking on the phone and so do I. We just share things together.'

Angel Elijah said, 'No, Lorna. He's going to ask you to meet and to go out for dinner.'

I looked at Angel Elijah. I was a bit taken aback.

I said, 'I'm going to find that really strange going out with another man when it's not Joe.'

'It will be a while yet. I have to go now.'

He disappeared and I went back to finish washing the car.

Soon after, Brian called and asked if we could meet and maybe go out for dinner. I did what Angel Elijah said. We made a date for Saturday but I gave Brian a call on the Friday and said I had to cancel because Megan was unwell. Over a period of months, we planned to meet numerous times but it never happened. I was beginning to understand what Angel Elijah had meant about meeting Brian and how he'd said it would be a while yet.

Eventually, we decided if we were ever going to meet, Brian would come to my house so he could meet my little girl Megan. We decided that it was to be on Sunday. I told Megan that a friend of mine was coming to visit and his name was Brian and that maybe the three of us would all go for a walk together. She was very excited.

Brian was to arrive about two o'clock but at twelve o'clock he called. He was sitting in his car and he was crying. He was finding it really, really hard. He was missing his wife very much. He apologised and said he just didn't understand. This had never happened to him before. He told me that he had been out with other women before and he had no problems going out to meet them but that this time, it felt like he was actually letting his wife go. He said, 'I am grieving so hard. I just can't make it, Lorna.'

I said to him, 'It is okay. It doesn't matter.'

Once he was okay I said goodbye. He said he would call but I told him there was no need to. 'I don't want you to be hurting like that.'

I just said goodbye. Megan and I went for an adventure in the woods that day instead.

About six weeks later, I got a call. When I saw Brian's name on my phone I hesitated for a moment before I answered it, but it was nice to hear his voice. He said he was coming to bring Megan and me out for lunch. He was about half an hour away from the house and was looking for directions.

I asked Brian, 'What made you call me?'

He just said, 'I like talking to you and I want to meet.'

He arrived at the gate. He was a handsome, friendly man with a lovely smile and Megan took to him straight away. Half an hour later we went out for lunch.

I was all the time talking to the angels, saying, 'This is very easy. I feel as if I've known this man all my life.'

Our relationship started that day. Brian was funny and good-humoured. He was always telling Megan and me jokes that would make us laugh. He was easy to be with.

Over the years, Megan and I had happy times with Brian. We did many things together, just having fun. It was always the three of us. Brian had become like a father to Megan. They would sing the same old Irish traditional songs that Joe used to sing together with her every opportunity they got. Megan loved this. She loved when Brian took her to do the shopping because all as the two of them would do on the way would be singing. Lots of times Megan would call

Brian when she needed help with her homework, so even when we were unable to see each other Megan always had conversations over the phone with him.

The angels told me that I was to just say to Brian that I was going to write. I didn't understand why I was to say it that way. A week after I mentioned writing, he knocked on the door. I let him in and he put a laptop on the table.

That evening he gave me a call and asked if I liked the surprise. He said to me, 'Lorna, I know you cannot read or write but now you will be able to because you can just speak into the computer.' He had bought voice recognition software and a headset for me as well.

One evening, I was sitting at the fire with Brian.

I said to him, 'You seem very quiet this evening?'

He got up from the couch and put some turf and a wooden log on the fire and sat back down beside me. The fire started to blaze. It was lovely, just sitting there with someone I cared for very much. Megan was upstairs sleeping in bed.

Brian said, 'Lorna, I want to share with you the last moments I shared with my wife before she died.'

As soon as Brian said these words the light from the fire seemed to flicker all around the room. Then, the angels came into the room from every direction. A great calm and stillness filled the room with peace and love. Brian started to talk about his beautiful wife and that she had had cancer. He had never known how long they would have together.

The soul of a beautiful, elegant young woman appeared standing by the fire. Her guardian angel was standing right there with her. This is not something I would see every day. I am not always allowed to see the guardian angel of a soul that has come from heaven. Now I saw the angel was standing beside her soul, rather than behind her, and with their hands gently touching. I was extremely moved. She moved forward and stood beside Brian. The moment he started to speak she reached out her hand as if to touch his shoulder as she smiled down at him. The soul of his wife stood there all of the time while Brian spoke and when he finished telling me about the passing of his wife she disappeared.

Brian spoke about how his wife had gone to the bathroom and a few moments later, he heard her call. He jumped up in desperation. He knew something was wrong. There she was on the landing, just outside the bathroom door. He held her in his arms, telling her he loved her and to hold on. She wasn't to let go. She was to fight to live. But yet, in his heart he knew she was dying.

He told her, 'The ambulance will be here soon.'

She said she loved him but that she couldn't hold on: 'I have to go.'

He said she passed away in his arms. He was in tears as he told me. It was like he was going through it all over again.

He said, 'I never told anyone that before. Everyone believes she was alive when she left in the ambulance but she wasn't. She was already gone.'

I said to Brian, 'I understand what that's like.'

We held each other in our arms for a while.

My relationship with Brian was always up and down. Sometimes, I broke it off with him. One of the reasons for this was that Brian found it very hard to share me with the world. He would ask me to allow him into my life a little bit more but I told him I couldn't. It wasn't allowed.

I am very happy that God allowed this relationship between the two of us and I thank Joe but I could never love anyone else the same way as I loved Joe. Joe was my first love, that love that Angel Elijah told me about, that love that God had chosen for me.

I thank God for allowing Brian into my life, for allowing me to love him and he to love me the way we did. I could not allow him into my life fully but I have to say I do miss him. It was wonderful to hear him sing those songs Joe used to sing. I guess Brian is the only man who ever got a little close to me after Joe's death. I thank Joe for giving me the courage to allow Brian into my life the amount I did. It was full of love and joy and many happy times. I know it is the same for Megan for Brian was like a father to her.

God took Brian home to heaven too. He is there now with his beautiful wife, his mum and dad and all his loved ones who went before him. I am happy for him, knowing where he is. I know he is happy for me and now, he understands everything – all those questions he would ask me that I could never answer.

CHAPTER 34

A Glass of Milk

JUST AFTER CHRISTMAS, I WENT TO MEET A FRIEND IN A hotel lobby. He told me this incredible story. It happened many, many years ago to a young boy in Ethiopia. I hope I don't get any part of the story wrong. I know the main parts of it are about an incredible young boy of about twelve or thirteen. He had no parents and he was living on the streets. He was doing all kinds of jobs to make a living to stay alive. You name it, he was doing it. He saw ways that he could make a little money and he did them but it was very hard.

A lot of the time he was very hungry and thirsty. He was a good boy but he was shy. One day, he was so hungry as he had not eaten for days. He decided, if he could get up the courage, to go to a house and ask for a drink of milk. This was on his mind all day but he was very afraid that maybe he would get screamed at or even beaten. By the end of the day he was really desperate so he walked up to a house and knocked on the door.

He said to himself, 'No, I'd better not ask for a glass of milk. I will just ask for a glass of water.'

The door opened and a woman stood there.

The young boy said, 'Could I have a glass of water, please?'

The woman said to him, 'You look hungry.'

She left for a moment and went back into the house.

When she came back out to the young boy she said, 'Here is a glass of milk.'

The miracle that transpired after that day transpired in a way that cannot be told fully. I myself have never met this young man but somehow things must've changed for him after he drank that glass of milk. That act of kindness gave this young boy the will to survive. Somehow this young boy, through the kindness of strangers, became educated. The boy's guardian angel and the woman's guardian angel were working together. Both were listening. God's hand was in everything that was happening.

Many years later, it must've been at least twenty, the woman with the glass of milk was in hospital. She was very sick. She had cancer. The specialist and the surgeon in the hospital told her the only hope she had was to have an operation. She prayed day and night and so did her family that the operation would be a success.

Some time after her surgery, when she was still in hospital recovering, the surgeon who did the operation came to her bedside to tell her that it was a success and that she would be okay. He told her not to worry about the cancer any more, that he got it all.

He said to her, 'Here's the bill.'

As he handed it to her she said, 'Thank you for everything. Thank God I'm okay.'

The surgeon walked away with the nurse to another bed.

The woman lay in the bed holding the bill for the hospital to her chest, praying that it wouldn't be too expensive and that she and her family would have enough money to pay the bill. She opened it nervously and at the top of the bill it read 'For a glass of milk. No charge.'

The woman never recognised the young surgeon. How could she? He was only a boy at the time, ragged, dirty and hungry, but her gesture of kindness, a glass of milk, was the beginning of the changes in that young boy's life. He became the surgeon who would save her life and many others'.

Every time we do an act of kindness for someone else, no matter how small it is, we do not know what the outcome of that may be. That woman's little act of kindness turned out to be a very big act of kindness. I think this should fill everyone with hope, love and joy. I hope it touches your heart.

CHAPTER 35

The Crucifixion

Tonight, I sat on the couch watching the news. My daughter, Megan, sat on the other couch with her back to me, wrapped in the blankets and a couple of pillows behind her.

She said, 'A cup of tea would go down a treat.'

I laughed at her. 'You mean you want me to get up and make you a cup of tea?'

Megan laughed, not taking her eyes off her laptop. 'Yes, please. I'm working pretty hard, Mam.' She turned around to me. 'Please, Mam, a cup of tea would be a treat.'

I replied, 'Okay. I suppose I should get up.'

Megan laughed and said, 'I knew you would.'

I got up off the couch and walked into the kitchen. I had just taken the milk out of the fridge as the kettle started to boil. As I walked back towards the kitchen sink I stopped and looked through the little door that opens from the kitchen on to the barn. I stood there for a moment, looking in to the barn, watching the angels around Megan.

My daughter was busy editing my book on her laptop. There were three, beautiful teacher angels around her. Every now and then, the teacher angel standing to the right of the couch would step forward and look down at Megan, checking the work she was doing.

I said to myself, forgetting that the teacher angel would hear me, 'I suppose they are checking that Megan is doing the editing correctly.'

The teacher angel turned and looked at me but did not say a word. It just gave me a big smile, bowing its head in a yes gesture.

I said to the three beautiful teacher angels helping my daughter, 'Thank you for being there.'

The teacher angel held a book in its hand. It turned to another teacher angel standing by the fire at the end of the couch with a clipboard, paper and pen in its hand.

I heard the words that the teacher angel who was holding the book in their hand, the one that gave me a big smile, used as it spoke to the other beautiful teacher angel standing by the fire: 'You can cross that off now. Megan has done that perfectly.'

As I looked at the angel with the clipboard and pen in its hand it ticked off whatever was written on the paper. Teacher angels always show the movements that we associate with human teachers.

The other teacher angel in the room had its arms full of books of all sizes. It was standing by the leather chair at the window.

It turned to me and said, 'Lorna, the kettle.'

It was only then that I noticed the kettle was boiling furiously and there was a cloud of steam all over the kitchen. I rushed over to the kettle, turning it off, and I opened the kitchen window to let some of the steam out. I hit the fan switch at the cooker too. Some of the angels in the kitchen waved their hands like a fan, helping to clear the room of the steam. In no time at all, it was all gone.

I took the lid off the kettle to see how much water was left. There wasn't very much, because it had nearly all boiled away. I filled it again. I made the cup of tea and brought it in to Megan, placing it on the little table beside her.

This little table is very precious to me because my mum bought it for me many years ago in a shop she loved to visit in Mullingar. She just bought it for me out of the blue, saying, 'I never buy you anything, Lorna, and I want to buy you this table.'

I said to my mum, 'No, don't waste your money. Buy something for yourself.'

But my mum insisted and she bought it. Now that she's gone to heaven, I think of her every day, especially when I put my cup of tea on this little table. The top of it is shaped like a three-leaf shamrock and it's all made of wood. I love it.

I always say, 'Hello, Mum.'

Sometimes, I hear her say back to me, 'Hello, Lorna.'

Her voice is so gentle and soft. She's always just behind me. I never turn around because the angels tell me I must not, but it is lovely just to hear her voice.

Our loved ones are always beside us, especially when we are thinking of them or when something reminds us of when they were here with us, before they died. They are in heaven now and yet, they are with us at the same time. I always thank God for allowing the souls of our loved ones to be with us when we need them.

Even if you think you do not feel their presence, just because you have thought of them the soul of your loved one is speaking to you. That is why you are aware of their presence in the first place. Many people say to me that they have not felt the presence of their loved one or received a sign from them.

I would ask them, 'How often do you think of them?'

Sometimes, they would say, 'Every day.'

Others would just say they find themselves thinking of their loved ones out of the blue for no reason at all. Maybe it is something they would see or someone would say something to them that would remind them of their loved one. Or it might be an expression or maybe finding a photograph in a drawer or one falling from a book. One day you might be helping someone do some gardening; it is something you really had no interest in but you ended up helping a friend or neighbour anyway. Maybe it's while you're doing the flower bed that it suddenly dawns on you and starts to bring back memories of seeing your loved one doing gardening or buying roses or a tree for you. You, all of a sudden, know how much they really loved going to the garden centre or buying flowers for you.

If those things are happening to you then, you are aware of the soul of your loved one being with you. At those moments, just say hello to your loved one, call their name, talk to them, give out to them if you like. Share with them all your worries and all the good things that have happened, all the happiness and joy. Don't forget to ask them to give you a helping hand and thank your guardian angel as well for allowing the soul of your loved one to be with you when you need them. Remember, it is God who has given permission for the soul of your loved one to be around you and your guardian angel always does what God wants.

I put Megan's cup of tea down on the little table that Mum had bought for me.

I asked Megan, 'How are you doing?'

She said, 'Fine.' She stopped for a moment, looked up at me and said, 'Thanks, Mam.'

As Megan reached out to take her cup of tea off the little table I said, 'You're welcome.'

I sat back down on the couch. I didn't say a word to the teacher angels. I just sipped my tea.

A few minutes later, I got up from the couch. As I walked back towards the kitchen I said to Megan, 'I hope you're enjoying your cup of tea.'

'Yes, I am,' she said, 'Thanks again, Mam.'

I said to her, 'I'm going to go upstairs now, and I'll be back down later.'

I said thank you to the three teacher angels for working with Megan as I walked through the wooden door. I knew Megan was working very hard on the editing.

The three teacher angels replied simultaneously in one voice: 'It is our pleasure, Lorna. Your daughter asked for one teacher angel but her guardian angel sent three of us.'

That made me smile as I walked across the kitchen and up the stairs. The stairs are in the kitchen, you don't have to go out into a hallway. When I was halfway up the stairs I ducked down and looked through the banisters into the kitchen, through the doors into the barn, just to have another glance at the teacher angels helping Megan. Again I thanked them, and then continued on up the stairs.

I came down a couple of hours later and Megan was still working away. I said to her, 'I hope you have asked for a teacher angel to help you with the editing.'

She turned around and looked at me with a surprised look

on her face as if that was a silly question for me to ask. 'Mam, of course I did. You told me many times to call on teacher angels because they are there to help me and never to be afraid to call on them at any time. You told me my guardian angel would have teacher angels with me. I only asked for one teacher angel, Mam, but I have the feeling that there is more than one with me. Mam, every time you have that grin on your face I know there is something you're not telling me! What is it?' Megan's eyes got really big as she said to me, 'Do you see the teacher angel working with me?'

I shrugged my shoulders and started to laugh. I couldn't keep the laughter in at seeing her excitement as she demanded I tell her.

I said, 'Yes, Megan, you have three teacher angels with you. They are right here right now.'

Megan asked so many questions: where were they standing? What were they doing? What were the symbols they were holding in their hands or wearing?

We must've talked for about half an hour and then I said, 'That's enough. I'll get up and do something for us to eat.'

On different occasions, when Megan has been working hard at editing for me I've seen the teacher angels doing different things. One time, both of us were sitting on the couch in the evening. One of the teacher angels tapped her on the shoulder and whispered in her ear, and I heard the words the teacher angel was saying, 'Concentrate, Megan. Don't mind your mobile phone. You will have plenty of time later to talk to your friend.'

At the same time, Megan put her mobile phone to one side. It is always lovely to see someone listening to their guardian angel or to another angel that their guardian angel has invited in.

On another occasion, when Megan was doing the editing, again she was sitting on the couch beside me. She was a bit irritated. Seemingly, some of the sentences that she was editing were the wrong way around and really jumbled up. She was giving out. She said to me, 'Mam, this drives me crazy. When you were speaking into your computer you must have said every sentence in this paragraph backwards. In all of this chapter, Mam, you've done that an awful lot.'

I could see Megan's annoyance on her face. I really felt for her. I knew I couldn't change what was written in that chapter. I was giving out silently to the angels saying, 'Why did you not make me notice that I was saying things backwards?'

My guardian angel just said, 'You do that sometimes, Lorna.'

I could see how frustrated Megan was getting and she gave out to me for laughing at her. She was almost crying. There were tears in her eyes. I reached out to give her a hug. It didn't seem to help much. I said to her, 'You need to have a break. Maybe you have done enough for the night?'

She said, still with tears in her eyes, 'No, I want to get this finished. Mam, what are you finding so funny? It really isn't!'

I looked at her guardian angel. Her guardian angel said, 'Yes, Lorna. Tell Megan.'

At that moment, her guardian angel wasn't mimicking her but instead, his hair was standing on end, imitating Megan's stressed state. I tried not to laugh as I said to her, 'I'm so sorry. I can't help when that happens. When I was speaking into the computer I never even noticed that I was saying the sentences backwards.'

I gave her another big hug. Megan said to me, 'You've had that grin on your face, Mam, for the last few minutes. Please, tell me what's so funny.'

'Okay,' I said. 'What was really making me laugh was watching your guardian angel demonstrating your frustration to me, Megan.'

She said, 'Well, let me tell you, you can tell my guardian angel that it's not funny! I have so much work to do.'

'Tell your guardian angel yourself,' I replied.

'It's not funny, Mam.'

I said to her, 'Well, it really is.'

Megan glared at me. 'What's so funny then?'

I said to her, 'Well, I'm just watching your guardian angel.'

I told Megan what her guardian angel was doing and she burst out laughing.

I said, 'That's what I feel like doing right now.'

Megan's guardian angel was imitating how she was feeling by pulling at the hair on its head and having some of it standing up like spikes. It was throwing its arms in all directions too. As Megan's guardian angel was doing this there were so many flashes of light of different colours coming from each of the spikes of hair, flying in all directions, bursting like blobs of paint in the air and floating around the room. Her guardian angel's hair was standing on end as if it was full of electricity. Megan's guardian angel was demonstrating Megan's frustration. It made me laugh so much.

I said to my guardian angel, 'How is that going to cheer her up?'

I said to Megan, 'I could imagine you doing that.'

As I described more of her guardian angel's imitations Megan only laughed more. In no time at all, her irritation disappeared. Laughter was working and she got through the amount of editing she wanted to do that night. Now I know every time she edits my books she thinks about her guardian angel mimicking her frustration. I know it puts a smile on her face.

The angels are always there to help us, but they cannot do the work for us. Teacher angels help to give you confidence in all the abilities you have. They help you to focus on what you need to accomplish, whether you are writing a letter or doing an exam or learning something new. Don't be afraid to ask your guardian angel to have a teacher angel come into your life to help you to give you confidence and focus, to believe in yourself, to know that you have the ability to learn and to accomplish. Celebrate your abilities and accomplishments with joy when you have done them and say to yourself, 'Well done.'

It was early morning and I was sitting up in my bed, praying. The room was full of angels praying with me. I prayed for all of those on the prayer scroll and all the letters that I am sent. I was praying and asking on their behalf and, of course, I was praying for the people who have just crossed into my life and for the strangers who I do not know who are out there. I was praying for everyone in the world and for nature as well.

When I finished praying, as I was about to get out of the bed to put my feet into my slippers, I hesitated and stopped for a moment. I said, 'God, you do know that I'm getting out of the bed now, but before I do, I need to talk to you. I know my prayer will sound like I am giving out to you. My God, please forgive me before I start.'

I continued to speak out loud: 'You know I have been struggling, fighting, even running away. God, I really don't want to do it – to write about the Crucifixion. It is going to tear me apart. I go through it once a year, every year, and now you're asking me to write about that time when Archangel Michael took my soul and brought me back to the past. You allowed me to see what happened to Jesus when you were crucified. Do I have to write about every single horrifying incident? Do I have to, God? You know I am crying as I am sitting here on my bed talking to you. Why don't you answer me? . . . Okay, that's all right, but it's not fair. You could send one of your archangels to talk to me . . .'

I put the slippers on my feet and wrapped myself in my dressing gown. I walked into my little office and sat on the chair.

All of a sudden, the room lit up with a radiant, golden light. I put my hands to my face as tears ran down my cheeks. How silly of me. I was thinking God did not hear me but of course He did. My room was enveloped in the beautiful light, even the chair I was sitting on changed to a golden colour. It was no longer like my old, black office chair that is slightly broken. That made me smile and at the same moment, I heard my name being called. Archangels came from every-where. I recognised them straight away.

Archangel Michael walked out from between all of the archangels as they stepped to one side for him. He walked over to me and said, 'Lorna, God heard your prayer. You don't have to write everything that God allowed you to see when you were present at the Crucifixion of Jesus.'

All of the archangels surrounded me. Archangel Michael reached out and took my hand in his. Archangel Raphael unclipped his cloak and put it around my shoulders. Archangel Michael, Archangel Gabriel, Archangel Raphael and Archangel Uriel stood around me. All the other archangels stood behind them, filling the room. Somehow, my little office seemed to be enormous.

Archangel Michael reached out with his left hand to where my computer screen was and it became clear; I could see through it. Golden light moved away from the screen like a vapour in all directions. As I looked down, I could see my hand in Archangel Michael's hand. I looked to my shoulders, I could see the beautiful red cloak of Archangel Raphael that he had put around my shoulders. It didn't feel heavy, just like a feather.

Archangel Michael said, 'Lorna.'

I turned and looked at him. He reached out with his left hand and put his fingers under my chin. He raised my head just a little so that I looked directly into his eyes. They filled me with peace and love and a great calmness.

He said, 'Lorna, you can do this.'

'I know I can,' I replied to Archangel Michael, 'I have to do what God has asked me to do. It's just that it tears my heart apart, all of my being. My soul never stops weeping. So much so that I know I will start to cry even as I talk into the computer.'

I took a deep breath and faced the computer.

Archangel Michael said, 'We will be here with you all of the time.'

'Thank you,' I replied to the archangels that surrounded me.

On the first few occasions that I saw anything of the Crucifixion God did not allow me to see too much. At that time, I was too young. I think I may have been just about six years of age. I saw the whole Crucifixion before my first Holy Communion but again, I was only twelve years old. When the Catholic Church marks that time it tears my heart apart over and over because God allows me to relive certain parts of it.

When Archangel Michael takes my soul and brings me back to the past to be present at the Crucifixion, I always seem to be a child or a young girl. I have a physical body but I don't look like myself.

I could feel the hot air and the breeze. It was late morning. I was standing there barefoot and I could feel every pebble and grain of dust under my feet. My hair was long and loose, blowing in the wind. Archangel Michael was by my side. I was aware of his presence all of the time; though, every now and then, I would glance up at him just to make sure.

I was in an area that was quite crowded. It reminded me of a courtyard in a farm or a schoolyard. I was in a corner where standing against the wall was a pillar made out of roughly hewn stones. I hid behind it. I did not want anyone to see me. There were soldiers and some of them were fighting. I realised they were only practising. I was so afraid they might see me.

I tried to keep in the shadows and move along the wall. There was a cart full of what I think was hay. I made my way over to it.

A man shouted at me to get working and follow him. He was small and stocky.

Archangel Michael assured me, 'Don't be afraid. They will take no notice of you; only when God wants them to.'

There were sacks on the ground. They were already filled with hay. I chose the sack that looked the lightest, picked it up straight away and followed the man. He wasn't very friendly. He seemed to be agitated and this frightened me a little, but I knew Archangel Michael was right there with me.

We walked in through a heavy door. It was very dark in there. I could not see much but I followed the man, hurrying after him as fast as I could. But I was never quite able to keep up with him. I caught up with him when he stopped to talk to a man who was twice his size in every way. He was dressing himself in armour.

The two men were busy talking when Archangel Michael said to me, 'Lorna, put down the sack and look ahead of you.'

As I did I saw a light further inside the building. It seemed to be very far away. I headed towards the light. I just kept on walking in that direction as Archangel Michael instructed me to. There were fires burning. They were very small and they didn't seem to smoke. I don't know how many times I nearly fell over a stool or some of the soldiers' clothing, but most of the time, I was able to avoid the obstacles that seemed to be scattered everywhere. Most of these things were meant to be up against a wall, but some soldiers must have been in a hurry and just dropped their things on the ground.

Every now and then, Archangel Michael would say to me, 'Be careful there, Lorna.' I was there, present at these events. It was more than just a vision. I was there in a physical body.

When I got closer, I realised it was daylight that I saw, through a door that was partially open. I could hear voices. I walked more cautiously now, listening, trying to figure out what I could hear. Was it just a crowded street?

When I reached the door and peeped out, I was horrified. I jumped back and stood with my back to the door. I whispered, 'This is part of the Crucifixion, isn't it?'

Archangel Michael said, 'Yes, Lorna.'

I took a deep breath. I was trembling. 'That is Jesus I see there?'

'Yes, Lorna. It is.'

I asked Archangel Michael, 'Do I have to go out? Can I not just stay here?'

My whole body was trembling.

'No, Lorna.'

He took my hand in his, filling me with love, giving me the strength I needed.

Archangel Michael said in a gentle voice, 'Lorna, turn around.'

As I turned around slowly I reluctantly put all my weight against the door. Opening it a little bit more, I squeezed myself in through it. I checked, every now and then, that Archangel Michael was with me. I needed his encouragement.

I squeezed fully through the gap of the open door. I stood there motionless for a moment. I went to run and shout at the soldiers manhandling him and ask, 'What are you doing? Stop!' But Archangel Michael got a hold of me.

He grasped my shoulder and said, 'No, Lorna. You cannot interfere. You are only here to observe and pray. I want you to go to the pillar on the right. Just stand behind it.'

'Okay,' I said as I looked around. 'What if someone sees me?'

'They won't,' said Archangel Michael.

I hurried over to the pillar. When I reached it I could not move my feet. They were stuck to the ground. It is something the angels often do. I'm not allowed to step forward. I was partially hidden behind the pillar. The stone felt cold on my hands.

I was so close. I could see Jesus was stripped and chained half-naked to a small pillar; it was made of stone and wood. It was jagged in places and I knew if Jesus weakened physically his body would be then partly lying across this pillar of stone. He was chained in an awkward position, half standing. A soldier dressed in armour walked over to Jesus and pushed him more against the pillar of stone, causing him to lie against it.

There were hundreds of angels there encircling Jesus. Seven archangels made up the inner circle. They were the closest to him. There were hundreds of other angels. They seemed to be never-ending. They just stood there in prayer for they could do nothing. They were like me – they could not move. I knew they wanted to help Jesus, just as I did, and I felt for them.

I said to Archangel Michael, 'This must really hurt all of you angels to see this happening.'

As I looked up at Archangel Michael he said, 'Lorna, we don't feel hurt, only love. All of the angels here and all of the archangels are pouring love out on to Jesus to give him strength, even though he thinks God has abandoned him. His father has all of the archangels and angels here to remind him of who he is and that he can do this for mankind. Every angel that God has ever created has already begged God for them to take Jesus's place. I have even done so myself but God will not allow it.'

'Can Jesus see the angels?' I asked Archangel Michael.

'No, Lorna, he cannot.'

I felt panic inside of me when Archangel Michael said this. How on earth did God expect Jesus to be able to do this for us?

Archangel Michael heard my thoughts and said, 'Jesus came from God and is part of God. Like the soul of every man, woman and child. God wants every soul to come back to Him because every soul is part of God; that spark of light.' I understood that what I was seeing – and what I am able as a result to tell you – is helping us all to allow our souls to come forward. All our souls understand this. Jesus was giving his life so we would be able to allow our souls to come forward and allow that intertwining of soul and body to proceed. At the point of death, the intertwining of Jesus's soul and body produced an explosion of power and an immense flow of love that is still touching us today.

Archangel Michael reached out and touched my hand that was on the pillar and said, 'Pray.'

I said, 'I am praying.'

Archangel Michael took that beautiful, snow-white handkerchief from inside his clothing and wiped away my tears for a moment.

At that point, he said, 'It's time you had a break. Go downstairs and make yourself a cup of tea.'

As he wiped away my tears with that beautiful handkerchief I felt for a moment like I was in two places, but I knew I wasn't.

I said, 'Thank you.'

I got up out of the chair and went downstairs and made myself some tea. I don't remember very much, just going out into the garden with my cup of tea in my hand. I don't know how much later it was when I decided I'd go back upstairs.

Of course, when I reached the landing, I could see that beautiful, brilliant golden light. I knew all the archangels were already in the room waiting on me. When I reached the door Archangel Michael reached out his hand. Taking mine, he led me over to the chair to sit in front of the computer.

At the same time, I said to Archangel Michael and all the other archangels that were in the room with me, 'I can't do this. It just hurts too much. Even that little bit which I have just written does not tell every single aspect of what I saw that day.'

Archangel Michael said, 'Lorna, look at me.'

I spun my chair around.

As he was wiping away my tears again he said, 'Lorna, this is what God wants you to do.'

I took a deep breath and said, 'Okay.'

I faced the computer again, put my headset on and I started to talk, to tell more of the story.

There was a soldier standing a few feet away from Jesus. The soldier was dressed in armour and very heavy clothing. He wore a mask. I could see his eyes though. He had brown eyes and the whites of them were very clear.

I said to Archangel Michael, 'The soldier doesn't look evil. I cannot see it in his eyes.'

Archangel Michael said, 'He is not. He has no choice. There were six other soldiers and he was the one that was chosen to whip Jesus.'

'Could he not have refused?'

'No, Lorna, a soldier cannot refuse. He has a family and if he did refuse his family would have been thrown into prison or sold as slaves. The soldier himself could be made to fight to the death.'

I felt sad for the soldier as I stood there watching Jesus, who I knew was about to be whipped.

Archangel Michael whispered in my ear, 'Pray.'

I closed my eyes and asked God to help His son, Jesus.

Archangel Michael said, 'Lorna, open your eyes now.'

I did. I could see that to the right of the soldier there was a heavy-looking table. It had handles on one side. It was covered in tools. Archangel Michael didn't have to tell me what these tools were going to be used for. I already knew. They were tools of torture. They were all sizes and shapes.

All of a sudden, there was a big roar. It made me jump. I was afraid, knowing what the soldier might do next. The soldier walked over to the bench and picked up a whip that had sharp pieces at the end of each strand. They looked razor-sharp; some were like triangles, others round and some were just straight.

Then the soldier walked back to where he'd been standing and stood there for a moment without moving. There was another roar. He stepped forward and stood a couple of feet away from Jesus. He stood there for a moment and a crowd that was gathering of important-looking people, those in authority who had come to make sure the deed was carried out, went silent. There were other soldiers standing around and they did not move.

The soldier raised his arm and he lashed the whip towards Jesus. He did this twice. I was horrified. I was screaming inside as I held my hand across my mouth to stop myself from screaming out. I was sobbing and shaking. I fell to my knees. Archangel Michael had his arms around me.

I could see flesh flying in the air and blood spouting in all directions from Jesus's body, from those two lashes. Jesus's back was covered in blood. The whip did not just pull flesh from Jesus's back but went too around the sides of his body, hitting his chest, his ribcage. When the soldier lashed forward with the whip, just before it would hit Jesus's body all the strands went in different directions before digging into his flesh and ripping out lumps.

At one point, I was so sure I could see one of Jesus's ribs on the left-hand side as a strip of flesh came away. The two strokes that caused this were like twelve strokes of the whip. I could see blood running down his legs and on to the ground around him. There was a lake of blood. I could see the blood streaming down the pillar and running between stones on the ground and forming pools.

The soldier stood there, not moving. Then I heard someone shout, 'More!'

The soldier walked over to the bench and picked up another whip, but there were shouts from the crowd that that whip was not good enough so he had to pick up another one. Every time he went to pick up one of the whips there was a roar and he had to move his hand along to the next one until there was a cheer of delight from the crowd. It was only a small group of people but there were lots of soldiers there too. But the angels outnumbered the soldiers a million to one.

It was the last whip on the bench that the crowd chose. I could see the soldier was hesitant. He did not want to pick this one up but he had no choice. Everything about this whip was bigger. It seemed to have more strings coming from it and more sharp instruments at the end of each strip. Some were even higher up along the strands.

The soldier picked up the whip and walked towards Jesus, and stood in the very same spot in front of him. I could see the soldier's eyes. They looked like they were full of water and all of a sudden, I could feel his pain and hurt. I felt his emotions over doing something he did not want to do. He was praying to God and asking for forgiveness.

I asked Archangel Michael, 'Will God forgive him?'

Archangel Michael said, 'Yes, he is forgiven already.'

As the soldier raised his arm again everything went silent. He lashed out at Jesus with the whip, sending lumps of flesh in all directions. The soldier did not want to whip Jesus again but he was told to. He even protested that it could kill him but he was again told to give more lashes. He did so again and Jesus's flesh flew in every direction, tearing from his body. I saw one piece of flesh fly through the air and hit the soldier's right eye. The soldier stopped and said he could not see. He was unable to finish. At last, all the other soldiers stood back and because they did this Jesus was saved.

Some soldiers hurried over to Jesus to undo the chains. One of the soldiers, who seemed to be in charge, took his cloak off and threw it over Jesus. The soldiers picked Jesus up and proceeded to drag him across the yard and in through the door I had just come out.

God kept me invisible all the time. The soldiers never noticed me as they dragged Jesus's body in through that door. I remained at the pillar. I was sitting on my hunkers. I don't know how long I sat there. I didn't realise time was passing until the sun started to go down.

I heard footsteps so I peeped out from behind the pillar. I saw five women walk across to where Jesus had been whipped. They had cloths and buckets of water. I saw some of the water splash from the buckets and bowls in their hands.

I said, 'What are they doing?'

Archangel Michael said, 'They have come to wash down the stone, to mop up the blood of Jesus from the ground.'

I watched one of the women carefully pick up every piece of the flesh of Jesus and put it ever so gently and carefully into a bowl. The angels were helping them as well. I could hear the women. They were sobbing.

Archangel Michael said, 'The women are friends of Jesus. Lorna, look closely. Do you not recognise the woman who is lifting up the pieces of flesh from the ground? It is Jesus's mother.'

I looked closely and put my hand to my mouth. 'Yes, it is Mary! Let me go and help!'

But Archangel Michael said, 'No, Lorna. You must stay where you are.'

Mary's hands were trembling. Her whole body was. I saw her take another wooden bowl and lay down a clean cloth upon a pool of blood on the ground to allow it to soak into the cloth. Then she wrung it out into the bowl. The other women were doing this too.

My heart went out to Mary. A mother having to do this, lift their child's pieces of flesh from the ground and put them into a bowl. Filling a bowl with your child's blood soaked up from the ground is an unimaginable horror.

The women were making sure they did not miss anything. They were so careful as to where they put their feet so as not to step into any blood or on to a piece of flesh that belonged to Jesus. It took them a long time because it was dark.

When they were finished, the other four women came over to Mary and put their arms around her. Then, they picked up the bowls from the ground and the cloths and they walked away.

I will tell you one more thing about the Crucifixion. I was kneeling at the head of the cross as it lay on the ground. A hammer was lying beside the cross with some nails. The hammer looked so heavy and the nails looked so big and chunky, not like the smooth nails we have now. These nails were thick and dark in colour.

I was looking straight down into Jesus's face. I saw the terror in his eyes as two soldiers grabbed his arm. One held his arm as if he thought Jesus could resist, as if he had strength for that. I could see how weak he was. He was so pale. There was no colour in his face. The other soldier grabbed his wrist and stretched out his hand.

The two soldiers looked at each other and then in a whisper they spoke to Jesus with so much compassion. Even though they weren't speaking English I understood the words. They moved me. They both said, 'Forgive me. We will try and do this in two strokes so it will be less painful.'

Jesus looked at the soldier who was holding his arm down and then he looked at the soldier who had his hand on his wrist. I saw the love coming from Jesus and touching the soldiers for there was no need for words. Calmness and relief came over the soldiers. Then the soldier raised the hammer as he held the nail in his other hand and with two strokes, it went through Jesus's flesh.

Archangel Michael was holding on to me as I looked down into Jesus's face as he lay stretched out upon the cross. I could see the pain and hurt of not understanding what was happening – why was his father in heaven allowing this? I could see the anguish of not understanding why his father didn't do something.

'I can't write any more about the Crucifixion,' I said to Archangel Michael and all the archangels in the room.

Archangel Michael said, 'That's okay. Remember, God said you can write just what you want.'

Archangel Raphael said to me, 'Every time you sit down to write a little about the Crucifixion I will put my cloak around your shoulders.'

All the other archangels said they would be there as well. I said thank you to them all as they walked from the room. As they did the light slowly dimmed, until it disappeared altogether except for the light from Archangel Michael, who was standing right beside me.

I said to Archangel Michael, 'I will write the full story of the Crucifixion, a little bit at a time. I don't know how long it will take me but I know God wants me to do it a little bit at a time.'

Then I felt my hair being ruffled and I knew it was God's hand.

I said, 'Is that okay?'

God said, 'Yes.'

Acknowledgements

It is my greatest joy to thank my daughter, Aideen, who is known as Megan in my books, for all her help. From the time I started to write *Angels at my Fingertips* she gave me great encouragement. She was absolutely fantastic at editing the book and getting it ready for Mark Booth, my publisher. She worked night and day on the book while attending university and doing her exams so thank you a million times over, Aideen.

I want to thank my daughter, Pearl, as well who has worked behind the scenes on the cover of *Angels at my Fingertips* and in its promotion. Thank you for all of your encouragement and belief in me, Pearl, and for all of your patience. I don't know how you did it.

Thank you to the rest of my family, especially my sons, Niall and Christopher, for being here for me. You have given me enormous support and encouragement. All of your help has been invaluable. I could not do what I do without your support. It is greatly appreciated from the depths of my heart.

To all my friends all across the world, you are so appreciated and loved. I will name just a few but you all know I keep you in my heart whether you are named here or not. Thank you to all those who have helped to look after me during this time of writing. Thank you for supporting me in every way and making sure I didn't overdo it. I received enormous encouragement from Catherine and John Kerrigan, Audrey Hamilton, Don O'Neill and Pascal Guillermie, Stephen Mallaghan and his family, Peter and Rene Kastenmacher and of course, Michael and Angela Lennon.

Without the publishing team in Hodder & Stoughton this book would not exist. Thank you. Mark Booth, my publisher, has become a wonderful friend over the years. He has been there for me always and especially, during working on this new book with his belief and excitement in it. Mark gave me such encouragement as he understands me so well. Thank you Mark for having such patience.

To all those who read my books, come to my events and most importantly, spread the word of God and the angels I thank you from the depth of heart. You are my blessing.

I thank God and the angels for being with me my whole life and for enabling me to spread God's word.

To find out more about Lorna Byrne, including adding your prayers and wishes to her prayer scroll or discovering where you can meet her in person go to www.lornabyrne.com

Facebook: Angels in my Hair by Lorna Byrne

Twitter: @lornabyrne

Instagram: @lornabyrneangels